A FINE
ROMANCE

Also by Judith Sills, Ph.D.

EXCESS BAGGAGE: GETTING OUT OF YOUR OWN WAY

HOW TO STOP LOOKING FOR SOMEONE PERFECT
& FIND SOMEONE TO LOVE

A FINE ROMANCE

The Passage of Courtship from Meeting to Marriage

JUDITH SILLS, Ph.D.

BALLANTINE BOOKS • NEW YORK

Lines from *Childhood and Society* by Erik H. Erikson.
Copyright © 1963 by Norton.
Used by permission of the publisher.

Lines from *Sex Signals: The Biology of Love* by Timothy Perper.
Copyright © 1985 by ISI Press.
Used by permission of the publisher.

Lines from *Dance-Away Lover* by Daniel Goldstine et. al.
Copyright © 1977 by Ballantine.
Used by permission of the publisher.

Lines from "How to Build a Happy Marriage" by D. Sifford in
The Philadelphia Inquirer, May 11, 1986.
Copyright © 1986.
Used by permission of the publisher.

Library of Congress Catalog Card Number: 87-6501

ISBN: 0-345-38571-3

This edition published by arrangement with St. Martins Press, Inc.

Manufactured in the United States of America

First Ballantine Books Edition: November 1988
Ballantine Books Trade Edition: February 1993

10 9 8 7 6 5

Contents

Author's Note

As a psychologist, my first priority is to safeguard the confidentiality of the people with whom I work. In the interests of protecting their privacy, the case histories presented in this book are composites of individual cases. Many details have been fictionalized to obscure the identity of any one person. Unattributed quotes may be assumed to be paraphrases or typical remarks of a person in the situation under discussion.

Any similarities between these anecdotes and any actual person is purely coincidental.

Also, please note: The great risk of courtship today is the possibility of sexually transmitted disease—especially AIDS and ARC. This risk does not mean that you can no longer enjoy courtship or develop a sexual relationship. In fact, these health concerns will probably encourage all of us to work harder at our relationships and to further our courtships. However, the very real risk of disease does mean that you must approach courtship with a new attitude. You are wise to choose your sexual partners slowly and cautiously. You will need to encourage a frank discussion of sexual and health history early in courtship. And you must, male and female, use safe, protected sexual practices. It's not all bad news. The slowdown of sex will probably increase your likelihood of developing love. I think you will be trading up.

Preface

I know that you are tired of hearing that everything takes work. Success takes work and looking like a success takes even more work. Friendships take work, networking *is* work, and you've been warned that parenting is slave labor.

There's no question that maintaining your body takes work, not to mention developing your own style and managing your own money. Come to think of it, managing to get your own money to manage is nothing but work.

You've shown yourself to be more than willing to make the necessary effort. You are out there in the world—finishing your education, holding down a job, raising a child, deciphering the mysteries of Individual Retirement Accounts, and doing your dreaded sit-ups. You are willing to accept the idea that creating an adult life is a continuous act of will, calling for equal parts of courage, discipline, and the ability to laugh at yourself. Most of the time you've shown yourself to be up to the challenge.

Except? Except in the question of love.

In matters of the heart, you allow yourself to cling to the fantasy that, while everything else in life is a result of your efforts, love is a state into which you simply fall. It will hit you like a thunderbolt or sneak up from behind and plant a gentle announcement kiss on your cheek.

Love, true love, you believe, is more of a feeling than a goal. You assume that you can't *make* it happen. Worse, you assume that if you did work to make it happen, it would, by definition, miss being the real thing.

The bad news is that love, too, is work. Perhaps it's not work in the negative sense of something arduous or unpleasant. But certainly it's work in the sense that you have to put out sustained effort in order to reach a goal. The goal is the development of a deep and sustaining love that forms the basis of marriage. The work involved is the work of courtship.

My first book, *How to Stop Looking for Someone Perfect and Find Someone to Love*, was concerned with all the crazy, self-defeating ways people go about choosing a potential mate. *A Fine Romance* takes up where *Someone to Love* left off. No matter whom you choose, you will have to endure a certain amount of aggravation before you get to the point of marriage. The process by which a potential partner becomes a real partner is the process of courtship.

Contrary to popular belief, romantic relationships do not develop magically. There is a developmental flow to love and commitment, an invisible rhyme and reason. Relationships don't break up at random either. There appear to be key points at which they either progress, get stuck, or dissolve.

Becoming a couple, like so many other psychological developments, is a matter of gradual unfolding in a series of predictable stages. Each stage has its own psychological task, its own emotional issue, that must be resolved to some degree before the couple can progress to the next stage.

You are probably familiar with developmental models as a way of explaining psychological growth in many areas. Gail Sheehy and Daniel Levinson used this kind of model to describe the stages of development through adulthood, just as Freud created a model to describe the psychosexual development of the child. Piaget described the process of developing thought and Elisabeth Kübler-Ross describes the stages of development in the acceptance of death.

There is an emotional advantage to your understanding courtship as a series of stages through which you must pass on your way to becoming a couple. You may be ready for love and you are probably quite lovable, but if you don't understand how courtship works, you can't expect to make it work for you. If you have a better grasp of the courtship process, you'll be better able to understand the rules and better equipped to use them. You'll also be prepared for the built-in hurdles and therefore less likely to be defeated by them.

A Fine Romance is a road map of courtship from meeting to marriage. You can use it as a guide if your last few romances were a string of disappointments, or if you're in love but lately you're driving each other crazy. Whether you are so afraid of rejection that you can't get started or so uncomfortable with commitment that you can't close the deal, you are part of the process of becoming a couple.

The developmental model of courtship presented in this book is primarily based on my sixteen years of experience as a psychotherapist and teacher. You should read it skeptically and see if it's helpful in understanding your own experiences.

Besides my own observations, I've reviewed the social science literature on love, courtship, and romance, and it concurs generally with the scheme presented here. In fact, there's a good deal of research that supports the description of courtship in this book. The bibliography can lead you to more detail.

Initially I had hoped that *A Fine Romance* would describe the developmental process of all couples. As the book progressed, it became clear that it refers mainly to heterosexual couples. Therefore I only refer to heterosexual examples throughout the text. I do not assume that all couples are heterosexual, nor should they be. Homosexual men and women become stable, loving couples too. However, their courtships vary in significant ways from the model presented here. I did not feel I could do justice to those differences in this book.

Additionally, *A Fine Romance* refers frequently to traditional sex roles, though I'm well aware that some of these may be offensive to individual readers. I am not endorsing these roles, and I emphasize that in any courtship situation, men and women today may reverse roles. I chose, for simplicity's sake, to describe some romantic events with reference to the roles that are most typically assumed.

This is not a book about fundamentally unhappy relationships—it's about potentially happy ones. As you'll see, even the most positive courtships can have their painful moments. *A Fine Romance* discusses these difficult periods, but it does not focus on destructive relationships. It's about the normal ones.

Finally, the purpose of this book is to lay bare the hidden universal structure of courtship. From this perspective there are great similarities from one couple to the next. In another sense, each two people who come together create a dynamic and a history that are unique. It is uniqueness of the experience that makes courtship seem like a magical or a lucky chemical reaction.

No matter how much light can be shed on the structure of courtship, its spirit is still something of a mystery. Like reproduction, we benefit enormously by understanding the mechanics, but our knowledge does not make childbirth any less miraculous. That two strangers could come together, learn to love each other, and decide to share a life is equally extraordinary, no matter how clear we are about the process.

Because love and loving relationships are so central to our happiness, we often bring to the subject strong prejudices. We have powerful beliefs about the way courtship *should* be. It should be honest, ethical, sincere. It should be genuine, sensitive, direct. It should move beyond a surface concern with body parts to deeper matters of character. It should not assign men and women to rigid, sexually stereotyped roles and punish them if they dare to break out. If courtship is the road to love, it should be decently paved.

It should be, but often it is not. This book does not describe what courtship should be, but what it is. Sometimes it is the pure joy and adventure you know or hope it to be. Other times it may disappoint you or make you angry. Courtship can seem manipulative or crudely dishonest or sexist.

A Fine Romance is not about ideal courtship, but about real courtship. It describes how real, complicated, imperfect men and women go about joining together. It's about the obstacles they confront and the nice and not-so-nice strategies they use to overcome these obstacles.

The magic is that we do find each other. The magic is that despite the games, codes, and strategies, men and women still learn to develop trust. The magic is that we can feel exhilarated, anxious, disappointed, and still persevere to develop love. The magic is that even when real courtship does not resemble the ideal, it can still create a very fine romance.

Work cannot make everything wonderful occur in life. Work won't give you blue eyes, old money, or genius. But the work of courtship can give you love, marriage, and commitment, if you know how to make it work for you. That's the purpose of this book.

JUDITH SILLS, PH.D.
Philadelphia
April, 1986

xvi

Acknowledgments

Jeremy Tarcher is a singular publisher. I was lucky to get him and you would be too.

Three other professionals contributed enormously to this project: Connie Zweig, a very smart editor; Susan Schulman, my agent; and Denise Mulholland-Logan, who prepared the manuscript through dozens of revisions with unfailing cheer. Each of these women is outstanding at her job, plus each of them was nice to me the whole time we worked together. I am more than grateful.

Thank you to the following friends and colleagues for their support, both of this book and of my work in general: Donna Vogel, Pamela Diaz, Malcolm Antell, Cheryle Cotton, Brett Bender, Myrna Snider, Larry Rinehart, Joe Goldberg, Cindy Baum-Baicker, Carole Ivy, Pat Wisch, Spencer Henderson, and Jane Glassman.

Thank you to Libby and Ray Hyman, to Donna and Jim Vogel, and to Peter and Robin Reed for allowing me to use their homes as writing retreats.

Thank you to my father, Harold Sills, for his legal counsel, and to my daughter, Spencer Hoffman, for her excellent timing.

My love and gratitude to my husband, Lynn Hoffman, who is the center of my life and therefore very much a part of any project I undertake. For this book he researched and edited and proofed pages and offered opinions. All the best lines are his.

Finally, thank you to my mother, who is my foundation.

1

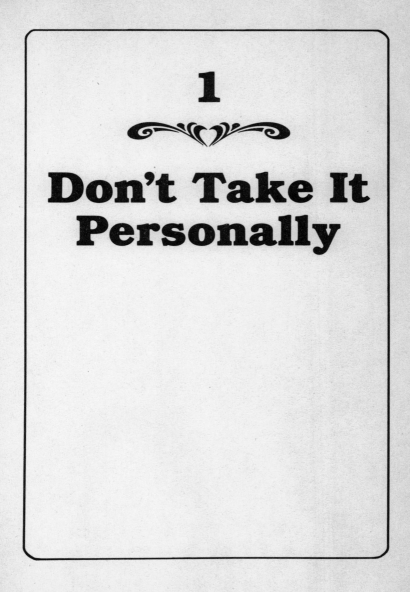

Don't Take It Personally

It starts with "Can I buy you a drink?" It can lead to "Let's buy a house." It's called courtship, and for most of us it's an emotional upheaval.

This upheaval does not resemble in the least the romance you have been anticipating, the one in which you fall magically, instantly, and mutually in love. You've been envisioning a charming, imaginative seduction, followed by an eternity of passion, all gift wrapped in the security of devotion. You've been waiting to star in your own boy-meets-girl movie, complete with clever repartee and happy ending.

What's wrong with this picture? Well, nothing, so far as fantasies go. The sweetest thing about a fantasy is its ability to re-create the world to suit our personal preference. We need the surge of hope and energy our fantasies generate. The daydream of perfect love can be a better companion than a real-life boyfriend who is more faithful to the NFL than he is to you. The fantasy is a lot more attractive than the girlfriend who weeps when you argue and is jealous of your old friends.

But there is a risk attached to the fantasy of what will occur when you fall in love. The risk is this: Reality is so different from your mental image that you might not recognize the right relationship when it comes along or make it work once you've got it.

Developing love requires mental effort. It also takes tact, timing, and the ability to tolerate anxiety. The progression from infatuation to commitment, or from best buddies to true lovers, is a delicate one. It's a long process and we see it through with very few people in our lifetime. That process is courtship.

Courtship may strike you as an antiquated phrase. It stirs images of fathers in front parlors interrogating prospective suitors. Despite the dated associations, courtship is still the

3

best word we have for describing the process between two people who are, however hesitantly, determinedly, or enthusiastically, developing a romantic relationship.

A Fine Romance is meant to offer a formal education in the principles of courtship. Each time two people meet and love, they don't invent anew the best way to develop a relationship. Every couple is influenced by the rules and requirements of the courtship process, whether they are aware of it or not. The ritual of courtship is as old as time and its stages are practically as predictable as the tides. So are its pitfalls, sore spots, and solutions.

Of Course You're Nervous

One aspect of courtship is guaranteed—anxiety. No matter where you currently stand on the desire for a mate, you are apt to find courtship an unnerving experience. Some men and women are doing nothing with their lives but looking frantically for a partner who will change everything. Others don't feel the least bit desperate, focusing instead on creating productive lives as independent adults. Oddly, no matter where we are on this continuum of neediness, when we get into a courtship we usually flounder. From the strongest of us to the most fragile, courtship tends to make us fall apart.

We are not all equally vulnerable to the anxieties of courtship, but we are all vulnerable to some extent. Finding someone to love who loves us in return is at the core of human happiness. Courtship is a primary path toward this love. When the goal is so crucial and the process seems so mysterious, how can we help but feel anxious?

Most of us would like to marry or remarry—someday, if it's right, if it all works out. Few of us have much of an idea of how to make it happen.

Often it will happen anyway. People pick their way through courtships every day without a clear understanding of what's happening to them. They get themselves off the courtship merry-go-round and into a marriage. If you ask them how they managed to work it out, they will offer a one-word explanation—love.

4

But much more often the courtship is interrupted. He never calls back, she loses sexual interest, he does something unforgivable, she becomes an insecure wretch, he meets someone new, she decides she never really fell in love. It's over.

For many of us the erratic progress of our love affairs is depressing. You want something to work out, but the development of love feels totally out of your control. You don't understand how relationships work, so you don't feel you can do anything to make them work. As a result, you may end up with a pattern of disappointing relationships that leaves you constantly stumbling over one of these spots:

- You are so afraid of rejection that you can't get started.

- You begin every romance at a peak of excitement, but it's all downhill from there.

- Love makes you more anxious than happy. As soon as you're interested, you start to worry. "I wonder how I'll mess this up. I always do." You turn into a doormat or a whiner.

- You end up finding something wrong with everybody. You can't seem to help yourself. Suddenly you become hypercritical.

- It seems as if you always get dumped, just when you get interested.

- You only want the ones who don't want you.

- Your lover won't make a commitment. You can't bring yourself to deliver an ultimatum.

- You can't make a commitment. You worry that you could wake up five years from now and feel that you made a terrible choice.

- You are longing to be married, but somehow you can't seem to meet the right person.

If you feel stuck in any of these patterns, you probably don't understand courtship. When you do, you'll see that, as with many other psychological processes, you can exercise some control over its outcome. Romance doesn't have to happen to you. You can steer it.

The first step toward understanding how courtship works is to free yourself of your fantasies of how it *should* work.

The Right Person Theory

The greatest obstacle to appreciating the hidden structure of courtship is that you've been taught that there is no such thing. Instead you've been encouraged to believe that falling in love and marrying is largely a matter of finding the right person. You believe you'll marry when the right person comes along. And, you've been assured, you will somehow "know" when it's right.

It's a seductive idea. In an increasingly technical, automated, and isolating society, it's a pleasure to trust some part of life to the magical, unknowable power of love. Love will find us, like Santa does on Christmas morning, no matter where we live or how hard we are to get to. When it does, it will be unmistakable, and it will change everything.

As delightful as the right person theory is, it is not particularly accurate. Contrary to our fantasies, love is not an event, it is a creation. A successful relationship is not the result of a fortuitous introduction. It requires the preparation, maturity, and emotional effort of two loving adults.

Most of us resist this idea with our whole hearts. We've spent our lives looking for Mr. or Ms. Right. We've worked out elaborate descriptions of what he will look like, how she will smile. We know in advance how our right person will think, dress, act. Then we move about the world trying to fit the people we meet to this mental checklist. The more detailed our mental image, the more efficient we believe we can be in finding love.

The problem is, love isn't something you find; it's something you develop. It's certainly true that love is easier to develop with some people than with others. In this loose sense, some people are more right than others, perhaps because their backgrounds are similar to ours, their looks more

6

appealing, or their personalities more comfortable for us, at least initially. It's also true that there are people with whom we have a magical instantaneous connection, the sense of having met one's soulmate, one's spiritual twin. But a soulmate is not necessarily available, or even appropriate to be your mate. And no matter how right someone appears to be on paper, if either of you is not ready or skilled enough for courtship, nothing longlasting will occur. Successful courtship is less a matter of whom you choose than of the kind of relationship you are able to create.

Contrary to the right person theory, romance can develop with a lot more someones than you've allowed yourself to believe. Still, Mr./Ms. Right is the central myth of courtship in our culture. As such, it's the cause of much of the pain of romance; it's a dead-end street that leaves you helplessly trusting to luck when you could be actively creating happiness.

If you are a subscriber to the right person theory, be prepared for two serious problems in courtship: You may have a hard time coping with the normal doubts of romance, or you may get stuck in a no-exit circle of blame.

The central tenet of the right person theory is that if your choice of partner is right, you will know. Everyone has varying mental portraits of the love of their life, but each of these portraits has one thing in common: The right person will exorcise doubt. In your heart, you'll know it's right.

Except you usually don't. Or, if she knows it's right, he doesn't. Or, if she's having doubts and backing off, he's sure, but the moment she seems confident that she wants him, he turns off.

The fact is, you usually don't know for sure that you've found the right one. You feel desperately in love, but she's treating you like something she wipes her feet on . . . He's wonderful but he's all over you and suddenly you find you'd rather read a good book . . . The two of you fight all the time or can't seem to fight at all . . . You know you're in love, but your friends think you are ill. . . .

These are some of the normal doubts with which real courtship presents you. There is no Mr. Right, there's only Mr. Maybe.

Your Elegant Circle of Blame

The second, more serious problem with the right person hypothesis is that it is potentially damaging to you. Searching for the right person inspires blame.

When a romance fails, it is perfectly reasonable to want to know why. If you believe that a successful relationship is a matter of connecting with the right person, you have only two alternatives for explaining failure: blame your partner or blame yourself.

Blame *feels* right. You are hurt or guilty, angry or regretful. Romantic failure is the ripest ground for self-loathing, man-hating, or misogyny.

Most of us start by blaming the other person. Male or female, we soothe our self-esteem by reflecting critically on his or her maturity, character, or personal style. He was too selfish, too spoiled, a Peter Pan. She was too pushy, too clinging, too greedy. She was looking for a daddy; he doesn't want a girlfriend, he wants a mother. She was a castrating bitch; he was a manipulative bastard.

If you have relatively little experience with romantic failure, you will find that placing the blame on the inadequacies of the other person will be a satisfying exercise. You will most likely heal your wounds, catalogue your errors in judgment, and continue your search.

These explanations can only work for so long. Several rocky courtships later, you will begin to have your doubts. More likely, your past lovers will blur together a bit, and you will be tempted to expand your circle of blame to include *all* men or *all* women. ("Women today are too aggressive." "Men only want mothers.")

You can firmly believe there's no one out there until your best friend gets married, your baby sister receives her engagement ring, and the office closes early for your secretary's bridal shower. While you might meet all these prospective spouses and assure yourself that none of them was someone you would want, nevertheless they plant seeds of doubt. Obviously for some people, the right one is out there. What's wrong with you?

You move right around the circle of blame and point the

8

finger at yourself. It's easy to do. Something about you was just not right. But what?

As a clinical psychologist who works with a great many single adults, I speak to a lot of people who are advanced-degree candidates in self-blame. Their underlying assumption, spiced with self-contempt and braced by anxiety, is always the same:

"My relationships don't work because I'm———."

Some of the common fill-in-the-blanks are: I'm not attractive enough; I'm not smart enough; I'm not a success; I'm not your basic blue-eyed blonde; I'm boring.

Most of us have some characteristics around which we are insecure and vulnerable to rejection. But most people have enough self-esteem to help them move past these uncertainties. Anyone can look around the world and see that love grows for short people, fat people, shy people, people who are less than brilliant, people who are less than beautiful.

So, seeking an explanation, self-blamers move on to the question of their possible neuroses. They speculate, Maybe I always pick someone who doesn't want me because I don't really want a relationship. (But it didn't seem that way in the beginning. Besides, they will puzzle, I say I want a relationship and I think I do. Still, obviously something's wrong with me or with my motivation, because I don't have anyone.)

Self-blamers give poor evidence for what they did wrong, but the feeling of being psychologically messed up in some way is perfectly sincere. They wonder:

"Maybe I don't want to be close."
"I look too desperate—I must drive people away."
"I choose the wrong people because I don't want to
   be happy."
"I have a fear of success."
"I have low self-esteem, so I can't pick the ones I
   really want."

As long as you subscribe blindly to the right person theory, you leave yourself vulnerable to its two great shortcomings. You could fail to identify a potentially wonderful relationship because you don't have the inner sense of knowing that

9

you've been taught to expect. And you could get caught up in an unending, unproductive circle of blame.

It's difficult to free yourself of the deeply ingrained notion that your romance will have a happy ending if only you'll meet your prince or princess. In order to stop blaming and start understanding, you need to turn your thinking upside down. The simplest way to do this is to appreciate the first, most basic principle of successfully developing a relationship: *Don't take it personally*.

It's Nothing Personal

You're saying, "That's crazy. There's nothing *more* personal than romance." Give the idea a chance. Your search for Mr./ Ms. Right simply reflects a way you've been taught to think about love and relationships. Seeing it as nothing personal is an alternative way of thinking about romance. You may find it eases your path considerably.

Certainly the love you feel is personal, as are the excitement, the tension, and the passion. All these and more are the emotional accompaniment of courtship, the background music that sets the tone. But the actual process of becoming a couple has less to do with two individuals responding to each other than it does with two powerful influences that are at work on those individuals. Those two forces account for much of what goes on in courtship. One is the internal world of each partner, and the other is the social world in which each of you lives.

The Internal Drama of Courtship

Generally, it feels to us as if we are reacting to the world around us. In fact, much of the time we are responding to the world inside ourselves.

In the case of courtship, the world inside ourselves refers to the complicated array of drives, feelings, expectations, and assumptions that determine our individual responses to love. Because so much of this tangle is unconscious, we pay less attention to this internal world than it merits. We assume that people are all pretty much alike when it comes to seeking a "good" relationship. On the surface this is so, but on a deeper level our individual differences are huge. They are determined partly by biology—by our temperament and genetic predispositions—and partly by our environment, especially the family environment of our early childhood.

These differences in our psychological makeup exert an enormous influence in courtship. They shape our sexual preferences, our needs for power and control, our styles of intimacy and cravings for dependence. They color the way we respond to various partners. One lover leaves us challenged but anxious; another arouses feelings of bored superiority; a third feels homey, safe, comfortable. Differences in the partners account for some of the differences in the way we respond. Our own internal dynamics account for the rest.

It's easy to blur the boundaries between reacting to our inner world and reacting to the world around us. This is a most peculiar but perfectly normal phenomenon. Quite often we experience the thoughts and feelings of our inner world as if they don't belong to us. Instead it seems as if they are occurring in another person, a friend, an acquaintance, a lover. It's called *projection*. It's a main mechanism by which we play out our internal drama during courtship.

Projection assigns to another person a motive, a belief, or a trait that is really a part of your own personality, but you don't see it that way. Instead you attribute these thoughts or feelings to other people in your world. It feels as if it is something they are directing *toward you* instead of something you are thinking, doing, or feeling *toward them*. When you are projecting you have a tendency to interpret other people's responses in terms of your own needs and interests. Here's an example:

Cindy was mortified when Jason told her off. They'd been flirting over lunch and drinks for several months. It seemed as if a romantic relationship was pending, but lately Jason had become distant. When she confronted him with his coldness, he refused to apologize. Instead Jason accused Cindy of coming on too strong sexually. He told her that she was all over him and that she really ought to learn to back off if she ever wanted a long-term relationship with a man.

Cindy was stunned. She thought they were seducing each other, and that, by age thirty-four, she was finally comfortable letting a man know of her sexual interest. Through Jason's eyes, she saw herself as aggressive and cheap. Self-blame was easy. "I've ruined another possibility."

But has she? Maybe Jason really was describing Cindy accurately. But maybe he was talking more about himself. It could be that it's Jason who is uncomfortable with sexual feelings, who can't admit to himself that he's flirting. Instead of seeing the desire to seduce inside himself, he sees it as coming from Cindy. He sees it, disowns it, and rejects it in her. It could be that Cindy came on too strongly. But it could be that Jason is projecting.

Naturally projection is a lot easier to notice in other people than it is in oneself. Have you ever heard a friend complain that someone else is pushy and domineering, all the while blind to the fact that he could be describing himself? What about the chronically jealous spouse who denies her own impulse to be unfaithful? These are examples of projection.

We all use this psychological mechanism to some extent, though clearly some people distort the world through projection more regularly than others. Also, certain situations are more likely to trigger projection than others.

Courtship is a prime example of this kind of situation. Projection is so likely to occur in courtship, especially in its early stages, that you could almost bet on it. For one thing, courtship is a situation in which people are pressured to assess each other very rapidly in order not to "waste time." The judgments we make are very firm, though the information on which they are based is scanty. Projection makes us feel as if we have more information than we actually do. Also, meeting, dating, and becoming sexually involved stir up strong, sometimes buried feelings. We are not always comfortable with the emotions we've aroused, and when we're uncomfortable we're more likely to project.

The key question is: How can you identify projection? How do you know when he is talking about you and when he's really describing himself?

The answer may be difficult to accept: You can't. You can never really know for certain if your partner is reacting strictly to you or if he or she is projecting. For one thing, we don't usually project at random. We pick a likely target. In our example, Jason may well have been projecting his own sexual impulses, but it was also true that Cindy was being overtly seductive. How could Cindy tell where the truth about her started and the truth about Jason left off?

A good rule of thumb is to assume that any personal assessment early in courtship includes some degree of projection and some degree of accuracy. Your job will be figuring out the difficult question of degree.

The more you appreciate the power of projection, the less likely you are to hunt for one right person. You will understand that it takes a long time before we sort out the boundaries between who we are and who we love. Understanding the mechanism of projection can also help you to stop being so hard on yourself and your partner.

Remind yourself of the possibility of projection when you are stuck or hurt or baffled during courtship. All you have to do is to interrupt yourself and say, "Wait a minute, maybe I don't have to take this so personally."

The Social Drama of Courtship

If courtship is not personal, then we have to realize that it is not invented anew by each two people who meet and begin to bind into a couple. In fact, the unfolding of that process has surprisingly little to do with the individuals involved. Developing a relationship, moving from the third date through the family meeting and beyond, is as codified and ritualized as a baseball game. Like baseball, regardless of who is pitching and who is batting, the rules remain the same.

Once you have chosen, however tentatively or emphatically, a partner with whom to begin a courtship, the two of you enter together a kind of social drama. You have a role and he or she has a role. Your friends and family are supporting players, and a great many of them (often unfortunately) have speaking lines.

No matter whom you choose as your partner, the play itself has a certain structure, a certain flow. There are three acts before the curtain, with some scenes so traditional, so necessary, that to omit them leaves a sense of incompleteness (e.g., the first sexual encounter, the integration into a group of friends, the first material purchase together). The play also has a set of crises (the first fight, loss of passion, or irrec-

13

oncilable differences of opinion) which every couple must resolve, no matter how right they are for each other.

This social drama, into which you slip unwittingly on every first date, is the ritual of courtship.

Courtship's stages are designed to take care of you as an individual while you develop into a couple. You need to feel close to her, but you need to feel separate and independent too. You need to trust him, but you need to tolerate the times he disappoints you. You need to admire her, but you must develop an equal sense of self-worth. You need to feel loved and accepted, but you must endure a critical appraisal. Most of all, you need to withstand the anxiety that everyone experiences to some degree while going through this process. The courtship ritual, as you will see, is designed to be elastic enough to allow these sometimes conflicting needs to be met.

The idea that courtship is not a personal reflection is very, very good news. When something is troubling or hurtful, you can come to see it as a necessary phase in a developing relationship. After all, a tough stage is a lot easier to accept than a personal rejection.

For example, Barbara, a fashion buyer in her late thirties, is depressed by her inability to work out a committed relationship with "the ones I want." The only men who stay around, she mourns, are "the ones I couldn't care less about." Barbara comes to psychotherapy to discover whether she is either neurotically attracted to immature men or has some awful trait that the "good ones" sense and reject.

A careful look at her relationships made one thing abundantly clear. Barbara was trapped by her assumption that love means closeness and distance means rejection.

In fact, as we'll discuss in chapter 7, distancing is a natural, even necessary, part of the courtship process. Barbara's lovers didn't back off because there was something wrong with Barbara or even because they were the wrong lovers. Barbara's lovers retreated simply because they were lovers and lovers must sometimes retreat. It's a stage—*it's nothing personal*.

Distancing is a special sore spot with Barbara because it awakens her fears of being rejected. Barbara needs to understand that when a man backs off, it has less to do with him or her than with a certain stage in a relationship.

14

Richard, a superbright twenty-eight-year-old engineer, had a similar misperception that left him lonely and wondering. He felt that he had a realistic mental picture of the right person. Richard's main concern was that he *feel* right about her, meaning that he feel love, admiration, respect, pleasure, sexual arousal—all emotions that one can expect to feel toward a mate.

What Richard was unprepared for was the crisis of doubt, which usually strikes for the first time between the fourth and sixth month of a love affair.

Richard interpreted his doubts as a signal that he had chosen the wrong person. In fact, a hypercritical examination of the other person, when the early infatuation fades, usually inspires doubts. These doubts are no personal reflection on you or your choice. It's a stage—*it's nothing personal.*

Both Richard and Barbara were mishandling natural, normal parts of courtship. They misunderstood the ritual element of the process.

A ritual is defined as a "regular formalized sequence of actions toward a desired end." "Regular" suggests that there are rules, as indeed there are in courtship, obscure though they may be. "Sequence of actions" in courtship means that there are predictable stages in the process of becoming a couple that are both orderly and unavoidable.

The classic "desired end" in the case of courtship is marriage, however shy you feel about this goal. You must appreciate that courtship is a *social* ritual. It is an institution set up by society, to serve the needs of society. Society needs to see you married. Marriages create families that produce babies who grow up and continue the cycle. To get this whole process going, societies set up one or another version of courtship.

The courtship ritual may have been designed to get you married, but what you have in mind may be something quite different. The ritual is goal oriented, but lots of us participate in it even through our feelings about the goal range from uncertain to appalled.

Some qualities of courtship make it different from the other rituals in our lives. For one thing, the rules of courtship are not clearly defined. You knew that the first time you fretted over whether you should call him first, or ask her out again after she said no. You longed for rules, consulted your friends in the hopes of at least arriving at a consensus.

Second, the overt rules of courtship are difficult to know because they are currently in confusion. For example, a traditional rule of courtship used to be: He chases her until she catches him.

Today that's a problem. Suddenly it seems she could chase him too, if she so prefers. Though she's not entirely comfortable with it and neither is he . . . though he likes the idea of sharing expenses and he finds the thought of a sexually aggressive woman erotic . . . except when he sometimes feels assaulted and finds her pushy . . . though she didn't mean to be pushy, God forbid . . . and now she's tired of being the one to do all the pursuing and wishes she'd meet a man who took charge for a change . . . though those men tend to order her around a bit too much, so she's really not sure . . . and neither is he . . . so they both figure they'll kind of wing it. There we have the current state of a traditional courtship rule.

Finally, whatever the rules of the courtship ritual are, you are not taught them in any formal sense. In fact, it is the ambiguous and unspoken nature of these rules that allows for the changes in courtship that we've seen in the last two generations. The ritual of baseball is about the same now as it was in 1895; courting isn't.

Mostly though, it's our myth of the right person that interferes with the willingness to teach people how courtship works. We don't *want* to know. We love the idea of chemistry and magic. We love the feeling that we are the only two people who have ever felt this way.

For some people, to appreciate courtship as a ritual, instead of as an expression of love, is to take some of the specialness out of the experience. I hope you won't be one of those people. Knowledge *is* power, and love is a miracle however consciously you pursue it. Be a romantic by all means, but don't let it stand in the way of being happy.

For most of us, "Don't take it personally" requires a huge shift in thinking about courtship. Be prepared. You'll probably find it difficult to remember. When you are emotionally overwhelmed by your relationship, you are likely to slip back into fixing the blame, assuming the blame, or deciding it just isn't "right." That's the time to consciously remind yourself

16

not to take the whole thing so personally. Maybe one or both of you are projecting. Maybe you've hit a tough stage that has to be weathered. Give you and your partner the benefit of the doubt. Love is worth it.

"Don't take it personally" is meant to help you achieve a positive attitude, not a self-destructive one. It's not intended to help you rationalize abuse or bad treatment at the hands of your partner. The message is *not* "Put up with everything and maybe you'll find love!" That's a formula for misery. "Don't take it personally" sends a different message: "Step back from the situation and see it more clearly. You'll take better care of yourself if you do."

If you want your courtship to add up to something, instead of constantly starting and then starting again, you need to learn the principles of a fine romance.

A fine romance is one that you handle in the way most psychologically satisfying for both of you. It is the romance that you are able to develop into mature love, in which both parties are able to come to the point of commitment, to agree to share a life together. A fine romance is not a matter of finding the right person but of creating the right relationship. That is infinitely easier to do if you remember—Don't take it personally.

2

A Matter of Motive

A book about courtship is a book about ambivalence.
If you don't understand ambivalence, you can't understand
the craziness of courtship.

Ambivalence means simultaneous, conflicting feelings, like
wanting and not wanting the same thing. It's easy to spot the
moments in courtship when you are experiencing ambivalence. They are the moments when you throw your hands up
in frustration because nothing seems to make you happy.

Dana finds Joe's pursuit uncomfortable. By their third date
he is calling every night and wants to see her every weekend.
She wants a relationship, but Joe strikes her as possessive
and demanding. He already has an air of ownership. Dana
cringes and stalls on making any further plans to see him.
Joe seems to get the message and stops calling. Oddly, Dana
starts to miss him. Ambivalence.

Beth delivers an ultimatum to Brian, with whom she's been
living for six months. "I'm hoping to get a ring for Valentine's Day. If I don't, I'm not sure how long I'll stay around."
Brian produces a perfect two-carat solitaire. Beth awaits the
explosion of joy. Instead, she is swamped with dread. He
seems a stranger to her and now she's trapped. Ambivalence.

Gary can't really find fault with Pauline, who is as lovely
to be with as she is to look at. His friends are urging him on
and his family is holding its collective breath. Gary loves
Pauline, but when he thinks of marriage he feels some kind
of steel doors closing. He doesn't want to lose her, but there
are so many lovely, unexplored women in the world and he
doesn't want to lose them either. Ambivalence.

21

Ambivalence: Courtship's Emotional Tug of War

What you thought you'd feel, if it were "right," was certain. Instead, you feel pangs of occasional doubt punctuated by spells of longing interspersed with periods of tranquil certainty. Some of you are even bothered by the tranquillity, assuming that real passion is never soothing.

Why? Where does ambivalence come from?

It is the irony of the human condition that we crave attachment as ferociously as we hunger for freedom. This essential polarity is the root of ambivalence in courtship.

We crave attachment because we long to be rescued from what Erich Fromm refers to as our "prison of aloneness." Our spirits need closeness, warmth, and love from a secure, continuously reliable source. In our society, the most likely route to satisfying these needs is to couple.

As passionately as we long to be attached, we need to be free. In order to develop to the limits of our capacity, in order to explore the universe without restraint, in order to be available to love others and to connect as the spirit moves us, our soul requires that we be unattached.

These dualities in our spirit—separation and attachment—are a psychological seesaw. In some stages, like adolescence, we tip heavily toward the separation side in order to make the room to develop as individuals. At other life points, like early adulthood, we yearn to reattach, choosing mates and founding families out of that need.

Some people will spend most of life tilted significantly in one direction or the other. You will have more than your share of a craving for attachment or a passion for separation. These psychological biases color your life history because they determine your choices and shape your relationships.

The ambivalent split occurs not simply within an individual, but between the sexes as a whole. We teach each sex to emphasize one of the conflicting needs and then encourage men and women to marry and battle it out between them. Women typically carry the banner of the needs for attachment. They are socialized to seek dependency and intimacy, to provide nurturance and safety. Men stand behind the bastion of separation and individuality. They are schooled to honor freedom, independence, and risk.

Courtship is the first arena in which these two sexes struggle to find a common meeting ground. Each is, to some extent, drawn to further courtship because each has a need for attachment. Each also resists the goal of courtship because of his or her equal craving for freedom. The result is the ongoing emotional tone of courtship: ambivalence.

It can feel awful. When you are on the emotional merry-go-round of ambivalence, it's a blow not simply to your self-confidence but to your self-image. You've been trained to expect certainty. Instead you suffer over the same ground repeatedly. You consult your friends, your family, the stars. Each time one of these sources takes a stand on one side, you find yourself arguing for the other. ("Yes, but . . .") It hurts.

You'll be advised that if you're so uncertain about your partner, you should give up. Alternately, you'll be warned that you've got a great thing going and only a fool would let it go. Sometimes a close friend gets sucked into your seesaw with you and goes back and forth on these positions as a mirror image of your own flip-flops.

No, of course not every courtship represents this extreme. Through the course of a developing romance, ambivalence can be a constant struggle or a brief bad patch from which you both emerge firmly committed. Sometimes the crisis of ambivalence is obvious to both of you, and sometimes it shows itself in only subtle signs easily overlooked.

When ambivalence is low, we are inclined to believe we've met the right person. We believe we're more sure because of who we've chosen. That's partly true, but only partly. We decide to move forward into relationship as much because of what's inside ourselves as because of another person.

It makes sense, doesn't it? Ask a person how or why she fell in love and she will say, "I don't know. It was just something about him. . . ." It was, but she might just as accurately add, "It was also something about *me*, at that moment in my life." That something is called *readiness*.

Readiness is an internal process that acts as a psychological catalyst for commitment. It tilts the scales of ambivalence in the direction of going forward, often before you even meet your partner. The last half of this chapter is a detailed discussion of readiness. You might want to pay special attention to it if:

- You typically turn off the minute you know someone is interested.

- You get caught up in an agony of doubt somewhere in the middle of your love affairs.

- You tend to choose partners who want space, freedom, no expectations, and unlimited options.

Readiness is not the only way to resolve ambivalence. Sometimes this internal shifting of the scales doesn't occur sufficiently to permit both people to say, unequivocally, "Let's move forward." You can love someone very much and yet be paralyzed by ambivalence (just as you can feel only mild affection for your partner and be propelled into marriage by your readiness).

When the internal shift isn't sufficient to reduce ambivalence, people often rely on some external event to tilt the scales. Those events are usually experienced as accidents of circumstance. In reality, they often have a strong element of personal (though unconscious) creation. We find ways to trick ourselves, go behind our own backs, force ourselves to move.

The classic outside event that "forces" a reluctant male or even an uncertain female to move forward is pregnancy. The couple who marry because a child is on the way is viewed with little moral censure these days, but sometimes with scorn. They are disappointed themselves because their commitment came not out of love for each other but because of an "accidental" necessity.

Greg and Mary are exactly that kind of couple. Greg really hated the idea of marriage. Mary really hated her future as a live-in love.

Greg and Mary lived together for a year, fighting most of that time over the question of commitment. They set vague wedding dates, which he always backed out of as the time to make specific plans approached. Greg was quite clear that he loved Mary, and he fought her threats to leave. Mary was

24

always angry, always complaining, but too attached to simply move away and start over with someone new. He felt she was nagging, pressuring, and punishing because he was simply unready. She felt he was harsh, immature, and unwilling to look at the truth about himself. They were deadlocked for months.

Guess what happened? Right, Mary got pregnant. It happened on a night, one of many, when they couldn't wait for Mary to insert her diaphragm. Mary declared her intention to have this baby whether Greg chose to marry her or not. Suddenly, Greg was equally clear. He had no choice. The wedding was on.

There is a postscript to this story, though it is not entirely written yet. Greg and Mary were married in a beautiful ceremony surrounded by friends and family, when she was four months pregnant. Greg seemed happy and relaxed and so proud that you would have never suspected the agonies involved in reaching this point.

It's three years since that wedding, and their daughter is two and a half. They seem, both to the outside world and to each other, to be a firmly committed couple, loving, fighting, and building a future. These days they are deciding on the possibilities of a second child. The ordeal of Greg's ambivalence is beyond them.

But there is a downside. Greg and Mary never totally came to terms with the way in which they made their commitment. Mary worries that she forced Greg to marry her. Greg doesn't like to talk about it, but the truth is he sees it in that light. He is reluctant to admit that he needed to create a situation that would resolve his ambivalence. His inability to accept his part of the responsibility colors their communication. It clouds the certainty of his love for her and gnaws at her sense of security.

Their problem is not so much with the way they came to get married, but with their interpretation of how it happened. They carry unnecessary baggage because neither understood the natural role of ambivalence in courtship.

The accidental pregnancy is discussed at such length because it is the time-honored external situation that tips the scales of ambivalence. It is certainly not the only one.

25

Outside events that can press courtships forward or dissolve them include:

- The ending of a lease
  ("My lease is up. Do I move in with you or do I sign a new three-year lease on my own?")

- The loss of a roommate
  ("I'm going to have to find someone to share the rent. How about you?")

- The relocation of a job or school
  ("I'm leaving town. Do you go with me or stay behind?")

- The illness of a parent
  ("Mom doesn't have an infinite amount of time left. I want her to live to see me married.")

- Family pressure
  ("Both our parents are driving us crazy. What are we holding out for?")

- Career upheaval, job loss, job dissatisfaction
  ("I need stability in my life somewhere. Marriage will give me something to hang on to.")

As with the "accidental pregnancy," sometimes we help unconsciously to create or to exploit the outside event that forces the relationship forward. We overreact to the "emergency" of a terminating lease or a new job opportunity in order to tilt our own scales of ambivalence. Remember, courtship is nothing personal. To the extent that ambivalence is a natural state of courtship, the ambivalence is nothing personal either. It does not mean that the love between you is not genuine, deep, or true. Love is one of the reasons why we attach, but it does not automatically overcome all of our fears of attachment.

What's Love Got to Do with it?

Wasn't love just supposed to happen? Didn't you believe what you were told as a child: "Someday you will grow up, fall in love, and get married.'' You were given an amazingly simple-minded view. The beliefs, the myths, about love, being in love, and true love represent the whole spectrum of possible explanations for courtship behavior.

At one end is the highly romantic (some say sentimental and silly) belief that love is the be-all and end-all of relationships. Love is magical, love strikes, love just happens and when it does, it sweeps aside uncertainty and doubt in its path. The proponents of this attitude believe that when you love someone, ''you just know it.'' If someone doesn't want to marry you, he or she probably ''doesn't really love you.'' In essence, love should conquer all, and if it doesn't, it really isn't love.

At the other extreme is the highly pragmatic (some say cynical and cold) view that love is an illusion. In this view, love is a code word, a simplistic but acceptable cover story for the complicated confluence of factors that lead one to marry, including readiness, anxiety, lust, chemistry, availability, social pressure, appropriateness, emotional neediness. All of these issues push you forward toward your partner. The pragmatist believes that you are merely more comfortable telling yourself that you are in love.

The perspective of this book is somewhere in the middle. Love is not the crucial factor in the ability to complete a courtship. (That crucial factor is mutual readiness.) But love certainly plays a major role. We are moved to form an attachment through courtship because we want to love and be loved. We hope that by making a commitment we will provide a shelter in which love can grow and flourish.

Love is one reason why we begin a courtship and why we continue it. It is, of course, a very special reason. Love's unique role can best be understood if you get a clear appreciation of the other needs and desires that might motivate someone to pursue a courtship.

The question of what, besides love, might cause you to marry may be an uncomfortable one. It smacks of manipulation. That's partly why we prefer to believe in the magic of love, in chemistry, in lightning. It relieves us of the responsibility of feeling that we might use people to satisfy our own needs.

In a couples therapy session, Jim was asked his original

27

reasons for marrying Robin, in the hope that it might shed some light on their current problems. He balked. He wasn't able to look at the question of why he married. "It's funny, because I don't think of myself as a romantic person. I don't read poetry or novels. Just in this one area I can't stand to think that I had a purpose, a need, beyond being in love and wanting to marry her. It makes me feel like I used Robin."

The truth is that we marry who we marry, when we marry, for many reasons. Becoming aware of your needs can only help you to satisfy them. It's not enough to love someone so much that you will marry him or her. You also, to some degree, must feel an urge to be married.

The Motivations of Courtship

There are lots of reasons, besides love, why you might feel an urge to begin or to complete courtship. Some of these motivations encourage commitment and some of them short-circuit it. We are all a complicated mixture of these drives, each with our own unique balance.

The most important of the motivations that encourage commitment is developmental maturity. Reaching this growth point is probably the best reason to complete the courtship ritual and is likely to lead to the best quality relationship. As we grow in age, so we grow psychologically in terms of our ability to connect with other adults in close relationships. As children we are intimately connected to our parents. A big part of the process of growing up is the process of separating from this attachment and becoming independent functioning adults with a sense of identity as separate beings. When we accomplish this task to some degree of satisfaction, we take on the next task of adulthood—namely, the selection of a partner with whom we start a new family and so begin the cycle of life all over again.

The desire to have an intimate and committed relationship, to build a life with another adult, is a normal part of the process of developing psychologically as a human being. Normal, however, does not in any way mean inevitable. We don't all grow into this stage in life, and we certainly don't all reach it at a particular age. Furthermore, this desire is rarely a simple one. We feel the strong wish to be close to someone, but we fantasize that it will be a perfect love that involves no struggle. We feel the urge to settle down, then we feel a surge of desire to kick up our heels, be bad, stay a kid, go home to mother, have sex with a stranger, or any combination of the above. Ambivalence, again.

Developmental maturity is not an endpoint, a pinnacle that you will either reach or not reach. Instead it is a matter of degree. Some of us complete the process of separating from our parents during marriage. Some of us begin the process of separating by marrying. And some of us marry mostly as a fulfillment of our parents' expectations of us, and our marriages are part of a long line of trophies we bring home to lay at our parents' feet.

Developmental maturity, then, is an ideal. There are a number of other motivations that might drive you forward toward commitment including:

- The desire to leave home
- The desire to have a child
- The desire to gain financial support
- The desire for one safe, available sexual partner
- The desire to be taken care of, or to take care of another

All of these motivations push you along through the rigors of courtship toward its ultimate goal. Whether they push you toward a close, crucial bond (like the push that comes from maturity), a functional, enabling bond (like the kind you need to get you that baby, or that new home), or a bond of dependency (like the need to have someone do for you what you can't or prefer not to do for yourself), they all push for commitment to occur.

There are an equal number of reasons to begin courtship that have little or nothing to do with commitment. These motives are satisfied by the earliest stages of courtship. You'll surely recognize yourself in these. If not, you'll recognize them in a previous partner. They include:

29

- Sexual arousal
- Ego satisfaction
- Social approval
- Healing
- Fun

You may find it easy to single out one or two motives that describe your own feelings at this point in your life. It's just as likely, though, that you'll identify several: You think you're mature enough, but you also admit that you date simply because you're looking for attention. You'd love to take care of someone, but you'd never turn down a sexual conquest.

What about your lover? Perhaps you are hoping for marriage, but you can see that your lover is strictly in it for fun. What are your chances?

A thousand love stories, movies, daydreams have been constructed around this dilemma. There is a wonderful romantic allure to the saga of the heartbreaker, the man-about-town, who is tamed by the love of a good woman.

If you are in this situation, you have some chance, but not much. You have some chance because, as we've discussed, the courtship ritual has a life of its own. It has an energy, a drive toward completion, and it is possible to get caught up despite one's intentions.

The man or woman who begins a relationship solely because he wants to have fun does, sometimes, end up marrying. But not very often. And not without an enormous crisis of ambivalence. He or she simply isn't ready.

Readiness: The Essential Ingredient

"People ask me when I knew I wanted to marry Anne. I always say 'the day before I met her.' You have to want to be married before you meet someone you want to marry."

—Charles, thirty-seven, an anthropologist

30

"It was a gradual softening. I saw how wonderful it was to be with James. I didn't need to be so angry, so fiercely independent anymore. I wanted a home and the foundation of a home is a marriage."
—Lily, divorced for ten years before her recent marriage

None of us is the simple sum of all of our various needs. There is an elusive quality in our psychological development that seems to account for how and when we move forward in life. The name for that constellation of attitudes and feelings is readiness. It is a term used to describe the ability to learn, develop, or move forward in some other way, at various stages of life.

When we describe the way a child learns, we rely on the concept of readiness. There seems to be a developmental point when a child can learn a new cognitive skill, like reading. Yes, with much effort and drill you can teach a younger, intelligent child to read. But if you wait until the right age, there is a moment when the child moves quite naturally toward this skill. We understand some, but not all, of the factors that create this openness to learning. We describe it by saying that the child is ready to learn.

From toilet training to abstract thinking, readiness is clearly a factor in development. Parents can certainly insist on teaching ideas and behaviors according to their own schedules. But there is a timing with the child, when he is most apt to acquire certain skills with joy and a sense of adventure.

Naturally, readiness is not a sufficient condition. A child who is ready to read must be shown books and taught the technique, just as a man or woman ready for marriage must have the opportunity and the skills necessary to develop a relationship. But readiness is the essential ingredient.

Readiness, in both instances, means readiness for change, readiness for development, readiness for new, more complicated tasks.

Readiness in courtship means readiness for commitment, for intimacy. Readiness does not mean being without anxiety or ambivalence. You may be ready for a close relationship and still be frightened by it. The child who is ready to read may also fear failure, be scared of parental disapproval, or

31

be anxious to perform well in order to win love. That child may be uncomfortable with the competition in a reading group or spurred by the skills of an older brother or sister. A lot of complicated feelings come up when you are seeking to move yourself to the next developmental level. Readiness is a state of mind, an attitude of approach that helps you to push past the barriers created by these feelings.

Much to the chagrin of your mother (who is telling you that you should be settling down) and of your best friend (who just got married and wonders if you'll ever grow up), your chronological age is only minimally connected to your readiness to connect and commit.

Certain birthdays signal to many people that they are ready, that is, at an appropriate age. Twenty-one signals this to many women, largely because it coincides with the end of formal education and the requirement that they create a home. Twenty-five is another such marker for women and many men, because these people planned to spend a few years playing around, sowing wild oats before settling down. The twenty-fifth birthday is usually an announcement that the few years is up and it's time to get serious.

These chronological markers are statistically reflected. The median age for women to marry these days is 23.3 years. (That's three years later than our mother's generation.) For men, the median age is 25.5 years. Other anniversaries that act as prompters of readiness are thirty for men and women, thirty-six for women who want a child, and forty for the man who is surprised to find himself still a bachelor.

This is not to say that your own psychological clock should run on this schedule. We handle the tasks of separating from our family, establishing a career, and forming an intimate relationship with another person at our own pace and in our own particular order. One woman marries at eighteen, lives two blocks from her mother, and does not even consider the possibility of making an independent decision until she is widowed, while another goes to medical school, establishes herself in practice, and never looks at an available man until her thirty-first birthday. Men certainly have the same variations in the way they work through these issues. One marries in his senior year of college and chooses a wife who will take care of him at home while he wrestles with the outside world.

Another dates, romances, and courts countless women, but doesn't "find one" with whom he can make a life until his late thirties.

Who is to judge which of these people is more "mature"? We can only note that each of them has handled the conflicts of love and work, of independence and anxiety, of freedom and commitment at different times and in different ways. Readiness is more a function of the way these psychological tasks get resolved than of any chronological age.

If you are not yet ready for a committed long-term relationship, you will probably notice a pattern to your romances. You may tend to choose lovers who are not ready themselves or not available. Maybe they tend to be married, or you always find someone who lives out of town. Perhaps you fall in love with partners who are already in love with themselves. You are likely to account for this romantic history as an accident of circumstance or chemistry. ("I can't help it. That's just the type that turns me on.") It could be. But it could also be that you're telling yourself something about your own readiness.

Another pattern that can signal lack of readiness is this: You get involved in long-term romances, but only after you've assured yourself that you could never marry this person. You feel comfortable because he or she is the wrong religion, social class, or educational level. The strong reservation you have about your lover may actually be an expression of your own unpreparedness for marriage.

What if you are not ready? Well, don't worry about it, but be prepared for the effect on your courtships. When you aren't ready, you're likely to be more ambivalent and more out of sync with the pressures of the courtship ritual itself. It will make your romances rockier and probably more painful. Some men and women even get hooked on the emotional intensity of these chaotic love affairs and repeat the pattern forever. Others are exhausted by the hurt and the struggle and withdraw from courtship indefinitely.

You don't have to suffer either of these extremes if you learn to read your own signals and your partner's signals more clearly. How do you know when you're ready?

33

Something Is Missing

You find yourself thinking or feeling differently. You may
begin to find your life as a single adult unsatisfying. Those
party weekends at the beach that used to be so exciting start
to become repetitive. The possibility of a new lover, another
flirtation, a new romance suddenly seems like a chore instead
of a rush of pleasure. You begin to feel that your life is all
motion, no meaning—that you are moving on a treadmill from
lover to lover, apartment to apartment. When you left home,
you were energized with the excitement of freedom, exploration, open-ended possibilities. Now you want less freedom,
more structure. You feel the urge to build something. You
are tired of wondering what you will do on Saturday night,
or next year.

Or, you may feel an unaccountable restlessness, a sense of
no longer being comfortable with life. Sometimes the feelings
take the form of sadness or low-lying depression. One young
woman described seeing herself in the bathroom mirror and
suddenly noticing that she was crying.

Instead of depression, you may feel agitated in a way that's
unlike you, anxious for no apparent reason. Whatever the
presentation, your body and your heart are telling you that
you can no longer be satisfied with life as it is. You feel an
urge to move on to the next stage—from single to very much
attached.

You Start to Like Yourself

You've worked your way out of the agonies of adolescence
and through the muddled floundering of your early twenties.
Sometime between your late twenties and death, you might
begin to feel good about yourself.

This isn't the same kind of good feeling you might
have had in your omnipotent teen years or in your daring,
rule-flouting early independence. It's a solid sense of self-
acceptance that has been tempered by failure and disappointment and enriched by self-awareness. You've developed a
feeling of self-worth, of pride and self-respect. You have
your own limitations, but you can live with them without
crippling shame or self-punishment.

When you start to like yourself, you begin to feel that you

34

there were no line between work and leisure. From time to time, Connie began a relationship with a new man, but he never seemed to fit in with the group. It went nowhere.

All three of these people had to make an interim step before they could progress to developing a committed relationship. They had to loosen their tight bonds to a circle of friends.

In each case, these groups of friends made it more difficult to connect with, to fall in love with, and to work out a relationship with an outsider. Jane's friends were already married. They had passed through courtship and naturally had their emotional energies invested in other areas. Ron's group was like a boys' clubhouse with a sign on the door saying Girls Keep Out. Connie's gang blurred socializing and work to such a degree that she couldn't feel comfortable doing one without the other.

Gradually, undramatically, each of these people pulled away from his or her friends. They became involved with new groups, new relationships. Jane took a share in a ski house and found herself caught up in a whole new atmosphere. Ron began dating a woman and, for the first time, allowed himself to be drawn into her friendship network. Soon he was playing co-ed volleyball and thinking of himself in a different way. Connie took advantage of a job opportunity with a new firm.

Jane, Ron, and Connie were married within three years of their break with the old peer group. None was consciously aware of how they used their friends to avoid relationships nor were they deliberately setting out to get married when they made their moves. But the impetus to move beyond the security blanket of a friendship network was set in motion by their readiness to move on in life.

You Keep Your Own Life on Hold

Keeping your life on hold means not making major commitments in your life that might make it more difficult for another person to fit in. It means holding your life open for change. Unfortunately, people who keep their lives on hold often confuse readiness with neediness.

The difference is one of degree. Readiness is a sense that a person who has made some psychological progress toward independence is now prepared to make progress toward attachment. It's an expression of growth. Neediness has a very different flavor. It feels more anxious and more uncomfortable. When you are needy, you are desperate for any relationship because freedom and independence are scary, empty, or overwhelming. You need a lover to make you feel worthwhile and important, to take care of you, or to give you value in the eyes of the world. Readiness is an expression of the desire to share your life. Neediness is the wish that someone would create a life for you.

The line between the two isn't always perfectly clear. If you're very ready, you might be feeling a bit needy. If you are overwhelmed with neediness, you are likely to describe yourself as very ready.

There are some clues you can watch for to help you make a distinction. If your life is open—that is, if you don't over-schedule every minute of your time, if you are available to meet new people, if you have enough flexibility in your routine to devote time to nurturing a relationship—you are probably displaying positive and productive signs of readiness.

Some people go way beyond this. Excessive neediness seems to be more of a problem for women than for men, though men can certainly be needy too. Some women are afraid to lead their lives for fear that they will not be immediately available to a man.

- Vicky cannot hang pictures in her apartment or purchase a decent set of dishes. She doesn't want to give the impression that she is too settled into her single life.

- Joanne longs to go to law school. She won't let herself, though, because any commitment she makes to her studies could discourage a man she might meet who would want more of her time.

- Anne is bored with teaching. She has the opportunity to travel the world for a year on a university-at-sea program. She's excited by the prospect of adventure but, as her mother has pointed out,

"Who are you going to meet halfway around the world?" She decides to stay home.

It's deadly to spend your life waiting for a man. Many men are longing to marry too, but that fact doesn't paralyze them, doesn't inhibit their ability to live life. Oh, they may spend more of their time at singles functions and on blind dates than anyone would prefer if given a choice, but that's about it. Some women who are ready to marry deny themselves life in order to make room for marriage. It isn't necessary and it doesn't work. It isn't readiness—it's neediness.

You Start to Date Potential Partners

One of the signs of readiness may be change in your choice of partners. You find yourself attracted to, available to, or interested in people who would never have interested you before. The nice man who seemed dull and wimpy suddenly looks stable and warm. The daughter of old family friends who used to be as exciting as your Aunt Grace now has her own kind of sex appeal.

When you are ready, you put behind you the impossible but dramatic love affair you've been having with Mr./Ms. Hopeless. Usually you do it with a tremendous, agonizing wrench; sometimes it comes easier. But you do it because you are ready for something more.

When you are ready, you begin to notice others who are out there and ready themselves. You stop being so critical of a potential partner's shortcomings and begin to appreciate his or her strengths. The world starts to seem full of possibilities because you become more open to finding them. You are not so quick to decide that you hate short men or brunette women. You start to look for the possibilities of developing a relationship, rather than seeking a magical person who will make it all easy for you.

When you notice this kind of maturing in your attitude, you are noticing readiness.

Your Career Becomes Less Important

This shift occurs in both men and women, though it does seem to occur chronologically earlier for women. The work

39

that was so absorbing begins to lose its luster. It's harder to get yourself to the office in the morning. The Frobisher account seems a little bit less like life and death.

This is as it should be. If, as Freud said, there is only love and work, then it is reasonable to withdraw some overinvestment in one to make way for the other. When work begins to lose its edge, you may be signaling yourself that you are ready for love.

You View Your Parents More Realistically

One of the signs of readiness for an adult love relationship is a shift in your relationship with your parents. You begin to see them as adults and yourself as an adult like them. You notice that you don't fight with them as often or cling to them as much. You still see their flaws, but now you can forgive them more. You are not as angry as you used to be. The old battlegrounds are still there, but you feel less need to prove that you are right. While you will always seek their love, you now can make decisions without their approval.

Dad and you have long disagreed politically, but you have reached a point where you no longer have to bait him. You know Mother's Day is sacred to Mom, so you stop refusing to commit yourself until the last minute. When you become more secure in your sense of power, you don't need to test it all the time.

All of these are signs that you have progressed in your development from the role of dependent child to the role of independently functioning adult. That gives you the psychological license to forgive your parents for their imperfect care of you. You are able to take care of yourself. When you stop being the child, you are more ready to have a child. And that is a signal that you are ready to commit.

Courtship is the process by which two people become a couple. It's an emotional process, a developmental process, that involves two essential strangers who become so close, so connected, that, at its end, they agree to live life together. Their motives for forming such a profound partnership are, as we've discussed, complicated and various. Because of the differences in motive, as well as differences in readiness, we may begin courtship with many people but successfully complete it with very, very few.

Whatever your individual motives and however ready you are to find a partner, one point remains the same: Courtship has a life of its own. It is a process, but it is not a completely fluid, indeterminate process. In fact, a good deal of the process is ritualized, codified. No matter whom you choose as your partner, no matter how magical and right or tentative and fumbling you may feel, you will still have to navigate the ritualized process of courtship. The rest of this book is devoted to explaining how courtship works, what you can expect, and how you can best overcome the obstacles in your path.

3

The Politics
of Romance

She is, most definitely, in love. She has been happier, in a quieter, more solid way, in the thirteen months they've been together than at any other time in her adult life. He is also in love, thinking of her as "the best thing that ever happened to me." They are compatible and they laugh a lot. They are no longer oblivious to each other's shortcomings, as they were in the beginning. But their love appears to have survived the light of reality, and they have settled into a deliciously comfortable Plateau. She is buying sheets for his bed. He is doing her taxes.

Somehow, seemingly with a will of its own, the idea of marriage develops. She wants to marry him. She wants them to be married. She wants *marriage*. Simultaneous with her developing desire, a voice is growing in him. He never really heard it before, would have even denied its existence a year ago, but there is no denying its message now. His internal voice is screaming, "No! Not yet! I'm not ready! Don't make me!"

♥   ♥   ♥

They've been together every weekend and most of the weekdays in between since that incredible party when they were introduced three months ago. The two of them feel as if they invented the word chemistry. Her friends are filing missing person notices. He never even bothered to phone his other women to tell them of his change of status. In his mind, they simply ceased to exist. No question about it—this is it!

One Sunday afternoon, he is watching a Celtics playoff when she interrupts to tell him some troubling feelings she had the night before. Even though he really doesn't want to listen, his initial irritation passes quickly.

45

Two nights later they go to bed and, for the first time ever, they just sleep. She makes a joke about it in the morning. A week later he mentions plans for Friday night that do not include her. She says all the right things, but she feels an unaccountable anxiety. He does too: some vague, restless, claustrophobic feelings that he does not choose to examine too closely. She senses his retreat, without his doing anything she can really pin it on. She tries to discuss it. "What's wrong?" He retorts, "Nothing." She breaks out in a full-fledged rash of insecurity and seeks the only medicine that can possibly cure it—reassurance. The more she tries to get it, the more pressured he feels. She insists, he resists.

♥   ♥   ♥

He is Mr. Nice Guy, while she had been hoping for Mr. Magic. Still, Mr. Magic has not appeared and Mr. Nice Guy is preferable to loneliness and isolation. She ends up spending a fair amount of time with him. In return, he fixes her car, nurses her through the flu, and develops a terrific relationship with her kids. To be fair, she has always been open with him about her feelings, always told him explicitly that she wants to be free to date others, to explore other relationships, other men. He tells her to enjoy all the time and freedom she needs, all the while taking her son to ice hockey games and her daughter to the orthodontist.

She does date a little, but none of it means much and no one emerges as a likely contender for the spot he now occupies in her life. He has become a fixture at family functions, a father figure to her children, and a friend to her. It all happened so gradually. The only thing that hasn't happened is her ability to love him, really love him.

He begins to become more demanding, upset if she has a date, unwilling to accept her noncommittal description of "plans" when she is not available to see him. He is entrenched in her life. It has gone way beyond what she intended the relationship to be. Should she settle for their arrangement, or separate, leaving herself lonely but open to the possible appearance of Mr. Magic? Two bad choices, she feels. She decides, for the moment, to do nothing.

♥   ♥   ♥

46

Those three vignettes have several things in common. They each represent typical stuckpoints in courtship. They each involve a good deal of pain to both parties. And the effect of the pain is universally alike: it obscures clear thinking and makes it impossible to see the big picture. The purpose of this chapter is to outline for you the big picture of courtship.

When you can see the big picture, it's clear that becoming a couple is a process, not a bolt of lightning. It's a romantic, traumatic, and marvelous process, but it's really not as haphazard as it seems. Let's lay it out.

The Stages of Courtship

Stage 1: Selection. When you choose, actively or passively, a partner with whom you begin courtship. Selection can be immediate, as when you meet an attractive person and one of you asks to spend time with the other; or it can be protracted, when two social acquaintances fence, flirt, and feel each other out before arranging the first formal date.

Stage 2: Pursuit. What we generally call dating. It's that awkward time when you are trying each other on for size, aiming to achieve some degree of attachment while holding to a minimum the guarantees you make. During Pursuit there is no shared agreement about when and/or how long you will be together. There is no assumption that someone else's time belongs to you. One person has to invite and the other to accept in order for you to keep connecting.

Pursuit can be divided into two Phases. The first, *Seduction*, is that period of time when you and your partner are deciding if your relationship is romantic, platonic, or dead. The second is *The Switch*, that uncomfortable period in so many courtships when the pursuer backs off just as the partner has begun to respond.

Stage 3: The Relationship. When you share some assumptions about the importance of your connection. You have each settled into and acknowledged your increased degree of emotional attachment. You are no longer "dating," you are "going together." During this period you are coping with your individual expectations of what it means to be a couple. You are accommodating less and revealing more of yourself in order to move closer to genuine intimacy.

The Relationship is divided into three often-overlapping phases.

The *Plateau* phase is a brief or delightfully prolonged fantasy land when you are secure as a couple but have yet to conflict as individuals. The two of you have a regular rhythm that no longer requires that one person invite and the other accept in order that you be together. It's important to note that many marriages occur during Plateau.

Negotiation occurs when a couple begins to acknowledge their differences and struggles to develop a decent way to fight about them.

Commitment is the phase of a Relationship in which a couple works out, fights out, or eases into the decision to marry.

As you know from experience, each of these stages has a multitude of nuances, variations, and qualitative differences. There is, for example, casual dating, serious dating, dating-to-pass-the-evening, and sexual buddies dating, each of which is a variation of Pursuit.

There are Relationships in which you see each other every weekend and one of you denies that anything important is occurring, and Relationships that seem to emerge in full bloom at the moment of Selection. Both of these kinds of couples are handling issues in the Relationship phase, but they are handling them very differently.

We're going to discuss each of these stages in detail in the rest of this book. First, there are some general principles of courtship that you need to understand.

Operating Principles

The model you've just been introduced to is a ladder of courtship progress. These operating principles explain the idiosyncratic ways couples have of moving along the ladder. You can use them as a reference point to illuminate some of your own experiences in courtship.

Couples do not progress through the stages of courtship in a straight line. Like most developmental models, the stages of courtship are a lot neater than the couples who live through them.

Freud described a tidy progression—oral, anal, phallic, latent, genital—that define the stages of a child's psychosexual development. But the child moves forward, then back, then forward again with baffling quickness. At one minute the three-year-old is perfectly toilet-trained, and at the next he is suddenly wetting his bed and sucking the thumb he hasn't touched in six months. Freud labeled this backward developmental movement *regression*. He called the lack of forward progress in development *fixation*.

Both of these concepts have their place in a developmental model of courtship. Instead of fixation, which implies a certain pleasure derived from sticking with an early stage, those delays in the forward progress of courtship are called the stuckpoints. Regression is also part of the development of love, which explains why your courtships sometimes seem to lose more ground than they gain.

Instead of a nice straight line from Selection through Pursuit and on to a Relationship, what you live through often feels more like a loop-the-loop. She chases him (Seduction); he gets interested, she loses interest (The Switch); he backs off (his Switch); she regains interest (more Seduction); they make it to a Plateau and begin to quarrel (Negotiation). They break up. Three weeks later he calls her, and they are back to Seduction again.

Sometimes one partner insists on some kind of retreat. For example, they've been monogamous and he is overwhelmed with a feeling that things are going too fast (fear of entrapment, which we'll talk about later in this chapter). He announces his intention to see other people, though he definitely doesn't want to break up and end the courtship altogether. He just wants to take a few steps backward.

Sometimes a couple hits a serious stuckpoint, such as their inability to negotiate time together. For example, he wants a report on every minute they are apart. He also wants most of

49

their free time to be spent together. She will give him regular Tuesday night and Saturday night dates, but she insists on privacy for the rest of her life. This kind of conflict can re-trigger The Switch, forcing her to lose interest or to rethink the courtship.

And sometimes one or both partners act on the impulse to move backward because it's so much safer than moving forward. Early courtship can be fun, romantic, and unthreatening. The stakes are low because the emotional attachment is equally low. The impulse to return to the moments in courtship when all was romance and you couldn't even imagine arguing is a partial explanation of the loop-the-loop of courtship.

Stages are not equal in length. Couples spend different amounts of time in each stage. For one couple, Selection goes on for months. They are colleagues and reluctant to take an emotional risk at the office. Each is uncertain of the other's interest. Does he find me desirable or is he just being friendly? Is she interested in me, or in picking my brain? Another couple meet in a bar and decide to live together a week later. They've skipped right over Pursuit and flung themselves into a Relationship. A third couple lingers interminably in Pursuit, dating most Saturdays, eventually becoming sexually involved, but never really letting each other into the rest of their lives.

The stages you skip say a great deal about your readiness and the readiness of your partner. The stages you get stuck at say a lot about both people's fears of being close. The fact that you may have skipped one stage or never reached another doesn't mean that the stage doesn't exist. It just means it was an especially easy or especially hard one for the two of you.

Stages are not discrete in experience, and progress through them is no longer clearly marked by society. Can you imagine the bliss of always knowing where you stand? It is certainly true that in the not-too-distant once upon a time, there were a dozen clearly marked steps toward marriage. (There even used to be five or six clearly marked steps toward intercourse. Everyone knew what they were, and you were permitted to dally at any one of them indefinitely if you chose to. What a luxury.)

The steps toward marriage were marked by ceremonies like going steady, getting pinned, getting engaged. "Seriousness" was marked by family introductions, sexual intimacy.

This is not the world of today—for better and for worse. Today, as Stephanie Bush says in *Men: An Owner's Manual,* you can be "a little bit living together." The truth is you can sort of have a relationship, be kind of dating, or semicommitted. You can spend every weekend together for months on end and sense that "nothing is happening." Or you can make love once with an old friend and wake up in the morning knowing that something very important has been decided.

Sometimes it's quite difficult for you to pinpoint your own courtship. Some of you will read about a stage and say, "Yes, this describes the two of us exactly." In other cases, you will feel as if you have one foot in Pursuit, one in a solidly established Relationship, and, if you had a third foot, it would be halfway out the door.

As you progress through the stages of courtship, you progress toward intimacy. Yes, you can marry during one of the early stages of courtship and never work further toward intimacy. Intimacy is not the same as familiarity. But you are depriving yourself of something very special in order to avoid taking the risk of being close.

Each successive stage of courtship that deepens the emotional attachment between two people provides a safer, more meaningful climate within which intimacy can develop. In the early stages of courtship, especially during Selection and Seduction, courtship does promote so much role playing and stereotypic behavior that you sometimes feel the last person to know the real you would be someone you are dating. But there is a purpose to such ritualized behavior early in courtship. It helps you to take the risk of becoming involved in the first place. It gives you a safe role to assume and a language to use while you are still dealing with a stranger. These ritualized roles are necessary to the psychological needs of the individuals. We need to keep ourselves intact while we are reaching out.

After Selection and Seduction, each succeeding stage of

51

courtship can be a progressive stage in the growth of a genuine bond of intimate attachment. True, some couples never create the substance of this bond—they just go for the pretty picture. Other couples develop real intimacy after marriage, when they feel safe enough to reveal themselves. Most couples are somewhere in the middle, coming closer to each other as they come closer to marriage. The stages of courtship help this to occur.

Courtship is a paradox: It sometimes progresses of its own accord. It sometimes requires a push from you. If courtship has a life of its own, the individual couple controls its metabolic rate.

On the one hand, the social power behind the courtship ritual appears to take over. Neither of you had anything serious in mind, yet you find yourself shopping for a ring. Both of you expected to meet someone more likely, but you've fallen into living together. It felt as if each next step unfolded before you, and here you are.

On the other hand, paradoxically, some courtships do not automatically progress of their own accord. You and/or your partner make it happen.

It's hard to see how both of these could be true, but they are. To the extent that courtship is a social ritual, you will be carried along by it. To the extent that it is a developmental process, you and your partner will control its tempo.

It's true that in some courtships the effort required to move forward is greater than in others. Some love affairs feel as if they move inevitably from one stage to the next. Neither partner feels the urgency to push forward. Progress feels natural and effortless. The relative ease these lovers experience is a reflection of their mutual readiness and of their compatible motives for beginning the courtship. It is also evidence of the power behind the social ritual. We'd all prefer our romances to progress this smoothly. When they do, we tend to call it true love.

Even in these seemingly effortless courtships, the paradox applies. The romance is progressing because one or both of you is pressing it forward. You are taking the risk of saying "I love you" or making the move to become accountable for your time. Someone still has to dare to discuss a problem or

52

be the first to involve friends and family. It's simply that in some courtships these risks are minimized because each partner is operating out of the same set of expectations and on the same time schedule.

As you probably know from experience, the progress of love is not always so easy. Sometimes one of you has to really push, really insist, in order to get from one stage to the next. It's harder to do, it creates more anxiety, and it won't feel so good to you. You will worry about whether love should require so much effort. Sometimes it does.

Each stage is associated with a central psychological challenge that must be mastered before the couple can progress. This principle is so crucial that we're going to discuss it in detail. The progress of courtship is the progress toward intimacy and commitment. The obstacles to progress are variations in the fear of intimacy. Every one of us is likely to experience this fear to some degree. Each of us is likely to experience this fear most acutely at some particular point in courtship. It helps to know in advance where yours might be. If you can identify your own obstacle or your partner's, you can work to get it out of your way.

Love and Fear: The Intimacy Problem

Intimacy has become one of those catchall psychological phrases that all of us revere but few of us grasp. It has come to represent the Holy Grail of emotional life. We know we need it, we're not sure how to achieve it, and sometimes we don't recognize it when we have it.

Lots of social-science writers have tackled the problem of defining intimacy. Probably the best definition is Erik Erikson's in *Childhood and Society*. "Intimacy [is] the capacity to commit [oneself] to concrete affiliations and partnerships and to develop the ethical strength to abide by such commitments, even though they may call for significant sacrifices and compromises."

As Erikson says, ethics is an integral part of an intimate relationship. It seems that we've wallowed for a decade or two in an ethical system based on fleeting feelings. "I'll be close to you as long as I feel like it, as long as it works for me, as long as you satisfy me." Erikson's definition is a reminder that the ability to be truly intimate with another person is based on being grown-up enough to have integrity. Marriage is empty if you do not have a value system that supports commitment. Intimacy is a sham if you are not comfortable enough to be honest.

To Erikson's lofty definition, author and psychoanalyst Robert Johnson adds a definition of love that captures the joy of day-to-day closeness. He calls it "stirring the oatmeal." By this he means a love that does not require drama or intensity to sustain itself. Love based on intimacy can leave the realm of fantasy and survive in the real world.

It's difficult for many of us to make the shift from being in love to being intimate. Many people are devastated when love changes, frightened or disappointed when the bells stop ringing and the bickering begins. The need for drama and excitement can keep you locked into a miserable, chaotic courtship. You initiate a Switch, are unable to commit, or flat-out leave a lover because "the magic was gone." We can get by fine in life with only occasional patches of magic, but it's a lonely road without someone with whom to stir the oatmeal.

All in all, intimacy is not so mysterious. It means feeling natural and comfortable in the presence of someone else. It means being totally unself-conscious, relaxing into simply being yourself. If you want to be yourself, you have to be willing to reveal yourself. For every secret you keep, you must tense up a bit to keep it from view.

The most simple way to think of intimacy is to think about your willingness to be known. Especially in courtship, intimacy means dropping your social facade and exposing your secrets. It means self-disclosure, revealing your private thoughts and feelings. It means taking the risk of being genuine.

Intimacy is two steps past letting your guard down. After your guard is down, you'll need to take the risk of extending yourself to make contact with someone else.

Intimacy involves receiving as well as giving. Think about what you are willing to reveal and what you are willing to accept. Are you willing to be close enough to tolerate someone else's fears, dependency, character weaknesses? So many of us vastly prefer the sexy, strong, exciting first impressions our lovers make. Intimacy, which means getting close enough to see the warts, is a mixed blessing. We long for intimacy in theory, but we mourn the loss of our fantasies that closeness brings.

Overall, intimacy means the ability to tell the truth about ourselves, receive the truth about our partners, and keep love alive during the process.

It's a very scary proposition.

The desire for intimacy is the desire to be thoroughly loved for who we are, not simply for who we appear to be. We can't discuss the longing for intimacy without appreciating our equally strong fear of it.

Can you continue to breathe as you, if you have to breathe in unison with someone else? This is the ambivalence we began to talk about in the last chapter. Fear of intimacy is a natural cautionary device built into your psyche to help you maintain your individuality, your sense of autonomy. All of us have to quiet these fears in order to take the risk of getting close.

The fear of intimacy is a perfectly normal part of the human psyche. It is a part of our psychological check and balance system which permits us to be separately functioning individuals and deeply attached individuals at the same time.

To be an independently functioning adult you must establish some sense of your own unique identity. Getting close always threatens that sense of self a bit. It's a real worry, even if it's an unconscious one. How can you remain yourself and still be close to someone? Will you be overwhelmed by him or her, will you have to give up some crucial part of you? Getting very close means submerging some parts of your personality that chafe against your partner. It means compromising in order to steer your life on a joint course. It means losing some freedom. Intimacy means obligation, whether it's the burden of making someone happy or of paying someone's bills.

Intimacy disturbs more than your sense of individuality. It also threatens to hurt your feelings, shake your security, or land a deadly blow to your self-image. Intimacy involves these risks for two reasons:

- Your partner is a mirror. You have to see yourself in ways you would probably prefer not to.

  Close relationships do not necessarily bring out our most attractive features. In the context of a developing courtship, you may be forced to notice that you are not as strong as you'd like to believe, or as unselfish. You may discover that you are less rational than you'd prided yourself on being, or less confident. Intimacy forces you to confront the question, "Will I still love myself when I see myself through your eyes?" The answer is not a guaranteed yes.

- You are totally vulnerable to your partner's assessment of you.

  Having revealed yourself, you must confront the question of whether you are lovable. Could someone who is permitted to know you, love you? You can seduce people, con people, or charm people into loving you. You can package yourself in any set of pretenses in order to win love. But you cannot totally fool yourself into believing that you are loved. Only a genuinely intimate relationship can give you that feeling of acceptance. Of course, it's a risk, because you might not be as wonderful as your package suggests.

Fearing intimacy, feeling a reluctance to be exposed or restricted, is therefore something most of us feel to some degree. Again, the key word is degree.

Some of us have fears so great that intimacy is beyond us. We may marry for comfort, social acceptability, children, for any one of a number of reasons, but we have difficulties with a partner who wants genuine emotional closeness. Remember, the goal of courtship is marriage and intimacy. We don't all achieve both.

Some of us have relatively little fear of intimacy. We are

56

freer to open ourselves to a partner, freer to present a genuine face to the world. It's the richest way to love.

Even if you are seeking the most expedient of marriages, the one in which she simply gets to leave home and he gets a mother for his children and a face to frame for the picture on his desk, you will have to grapple with intimacy to some degree. On the other hand, if you are looking for a genuine marriage of the spirit, the true commitment of one soul to another, you will have to challenge your fears of intimacy head-on.

The next section describes each of the variations of the fear of intimacy which emerge through the stages of courtship. You'll probably be able to identify with one or another of the courtship patterns that result from these fears. Where you do identify, don't feel bad about it.

Psychological Stuckpoints

"The course of true love never did run smooth."
—*A Midsummer Night's Dream*, William Shakespeare

When Shakespeare was commenting on the peculiarly bumpy road to true love, he was warning us about the stuckpoints of courtship. If you understand the psychological underpinnings of these sandtraps in your path, you'll be better prepared to handle them. Each major bump is related to a variation on the fear of intimacy.

Every phase of courtship has its own internal obstacle, its own version of the fear of intimacy, that you must overcome in order to successfully complete the task of that stage. You may be all too aware that you have a problem in this area, or you may have an absolute blind spot. You may come to understand the unspoken feelings of your partner, even if a particular fear presents no problem for you.

There are five faces to the fear of intimacy, any one of which may be a problem for you or your partner during courtship. They are:

- **Fear of rejection.** An intense anxiety that prevents you from revealing your interest in or attrac-

57

tion to a new person for fear it won't be recipro-
cated. You are very self-critical and tend to have
more fantasies than relationships.

• **Sexual anxiety.** Awkward, uncomfortable, or ex-
tremely inhibited feelings about sex or its consequences that make you avoid possible sexual
relationships. You end up as everyone's best friend
but nobody's lover.

• **Fear of entrapment.** A crisis of doubt that seems
to develop whenever you get a love affair established. You can't seem to help yourself. Suddenly
you are wildly picky, noticing only the flaws in a
partner who delighted you last month. You end up
with a string of short-term romances, none of
which seems exactly right.

• **The anger taboo.** A dread of dealing with the
normal conflicts of a deepening relationship. You
work to keep a smooth surface and try to sweep
unpleasant feelings aside by denying or ignoring
them. You change the subject, discourage criticism, become preoccupied with work, anything
to avoid discussing upsetting issues in your relationship. It's hard for a partner to get close to
you.

• **Fear of commitment.** The panic or paralysis that
can emerge when you are confronted with the
question of marriage. You are relatively comfortable with your choice of partner but distinctly uncomfortable with the prospect of marrying. You
feel not ready or not sure. You resent being pressured, but you are unable to move forward under
your own steam.

Each of these versions of the fear of intimacy exists throughout courtship. If, for example, you are especially anxious
about commitment, that anxiety will affect you a little bit
even on the first date. But it won't be a serious problem for
you until much later in your romance.

In the list that follows, each of these fears is linked with the stage of courtship that it affects the most. The fear doesn't necessarily disappear in the other stages, but it quiets down a bit. Here is the breakdown:

- Fear of rejection inhibits you most during Selection.
- Sexual anxiety most affects the outcome of Seduction.
- Fear of entrapment is the underlying cause of The Switch.
- The anger taboo reduces your ability to handle Negotiation.
- Fear of commitment makes the transition from Relationship to Marriage a tough one.

Every couple does not have a crisis at every transition point. Some romances progress with enviable smoothness from the first meeting. Two people meet, select, fall in love. They are happy together and within months have easily mastered Pursuit and made a comfortable, inevitable transition to a deeply involved, monogamous relationship. Perhaps within a year they are living together with no anguished holding back on either side. Then, during the second year, one of them begins to talk of marriage. The other does not respond so enthusiastically. They begin not getting along, bickering over small things. The real crisis is the fear of commitment, though the arguments might center on which person should leave work early to walk the dog.

Other romances explode much earlier on. They flow from exciting Seductions through briefly enjoyed Plateaus. The Switch, where one person begins to back off, is dramatically played out.

My own courtship with my husband followed this nail-biting script. For three and a half months, he was wild about me and I was merely very interested. We were together every day, I had already rearranged his furniture to suit my tastes, and I was starting on his wardrobe. We had exchanged ''I love you's,'' though I felt his was more sincere than mine. I was completely secure.

In the fourth month, things fell apart. He got cranky and not so nice to be around. His old girlfriend started to pursue him, and he was wondering if maybe he shouldn't spend a little time there just to be sure he was over her. I had moved in with him by this time (complete with worldly possessions and partly housebroken dog), and he started saying it was too soon for all this. He needed more time. He needed to see other women. He thought I was very nice but really too chubby for his tastes, plus his friends weren't so wild about me. It was the retreat variation of The Switch, in full gory glory, and right on schedule, after four months of togetherness. (See chapter 6 on The Switch.)

It was our only courtship crisis. We battled it out for two months or so, but when we emerged on the other side, it was with a solid, vested Relationship. We cruised from Relationship to Marriage with only a minor anxiety attack on my part when he proposed. (He said, "Will you marry me?" and I said, "I'll have to ask my mother," which will give you some idea of the degree to which my own fears of commitment pushed me to regress. I stalled for four or five days before I could bring myself to say yes.)

Some romances have a crisis at every possible point along the way. One might be a bit skeptical about the viability of such relationships because they often involve battling, dramatic separation, and reconciliations. None of this is fertile ground for love, though it can be a positive Petri dish for passion.

And yes, there are those couples whose courtships have no discernible crises. You might want to attribute it to true love. I prefer the explanation of readiness, availability, and a happy coincidence of expectations.

Some romances run very smoothly, some are catastrophically disruptive. Most are in the middle, with one or more crises at a transitional point along the psychological road to becoming a committed couple.

As you learn more about the obstacles that block the progress of courtship, don't feel overwhelmed. *A Fine Romance* tries to describe most of the possible crises on the road to marriage; you and your honey will probably only have to go through one or two of them. But if the possibility of facing even one could intimidate you, try to keep in mind: Crisis is a mixture of danger and opportunity.

The Timing of Love

It may seem absurd to attempt to describe the timing of a process that some impetuous couples appear to complete over a long weekend, while some hypercautious couples drag it out over a decade. For the sake of discussion, this is an overall impression of the general timing of the stages of courtship. It's an impression based on the experiences of the people with whom I work, rather than on a scientific survey of the development of love.

As a general rule, successful courtships progress to marriage somewhere in their second year. Of course, the individual variation around this average is huge. This eighteen-month to two-year courtship is a typical period of time for a couple to achieve not simply the ceremony of marriage, but the intimacy that is the psychological basis for becoming a couple. You can marry without having achieved intimacy, but those who rush to the altar in the first month after meeting simply do the work of becoming a couple after the ceremony.

This time schedule applies to an adult couple whose life circumstances don't preclude marriage. If you or your partner is awaiting a divorce, the completion of an education, or any similar external event, the length of your courtship will reflect these circumstances.

The eighteen-month to two-year average is typical of courtship in which at least one partner was initially motivated by the desire to marry. If both of you were looking to heal your wounds, to feed your egos, or just to have fun, all bets are off about the time you will dally.

The average courtship has a typical breakdown in terms of time spent at each stage of courtship. Again, remember that the individual variation is very great. One couple spends six months in lingering and uncertain Seduction. Another moves instantly into a short-lived but idyllic Plateau. The time breakdown that follows is a typical one, but you and your lover are not necessarily typical.

61

Selection. Can be instantaneous, as when you meet at a bar, at a party, or on a blind date, click quickly, and decide to date. Selection can also be drawn out, as when you spend time with a work colleague over a period of months before you have your first official date. Selection starts at puberty and hopefully ends with marriage.

Pursuit. Lasts one to six months and is broken into two phases:

- **Seduction.** The decision as to whether this is a platonic or romantic relationship usually takes four or five dates. Some of you are clearly much slower here, and some of you settled this the night you made your Selection. The entire Seduction, in which the pursuer secures the interest of the pursued, lasts one to three months.

- **The Switch.** Comes up generally at the end of three months of courtship. It can take a month or two to resolve, or it might be smoother and shorter-lived. Some couples enter a revolving door of Seduction/The Switch and then back again. For these couples Pursuit can go on indefinitely.

The Relationship. Begins with the Plateau after three to six months of courtship. It consists of three phases:

- **Plateau.** The lovely period when you enjoy each other physically and emotionally, begin to become closer, feel "in love," fantasize about the future. This lasts from three months to a year or so. The timing depends a lot on readiness, on the amount of time you are together, and on the social pressure to which you are subjected.

- **Negotiation.** Begins anywhere from six months to a year from the beginning of courtship. Eventually Negotiation on general differences will begin to focus on one major issue: marriage. At this point, you move into Commitment.

- **Commitment.** Brings you to the beginning of the second year of your courtship. Generally, depending on readiness, at least one of the two partners will begin to consider, or to push for, marriage. This push could begin much earlier in courtship if a couple has zoomed through the earlier stage and reached the Relationship point quickly. It could be considerably delayed if outside circumstances have forced your life into a different timetable.

The amount of time a person will spend pushing a partner toward marriage before he or she gives up and moves to another courtship varies a lot. Some couples stay deadlocked for years. They live together, one wants marriage but the other resists, giving some semiacceptable combination of reasons or excuses. ("We don't need a piece of paper." "If we ever decide to have children, we'll marry." "It's not you, dear, I just never got over my dreadful divorce.") Other men and women are so impatient, so ready, that they push for Commitment at the instant they feel they have a Relationship.

When one of the pair wants marriage, couples resolve that question over varying lengths of time. In my observation, the decision to marry generally occurs during the second year of courtship.

The chart on page 64 will help you picture the overlaps of the stages of courtship. Nobody's courtship looks exactly like this diagram. It's not meant to make you feel that you should follow any precise timetable. But it will give you a sense of general time boundaries and perhaps an understanding of when your own romantic difficulties typically emerge.

There is one more component you need to include in your big picture of courtship. That is the peculiar, awkward, mind-bending communication style we all rely on in romance.

63

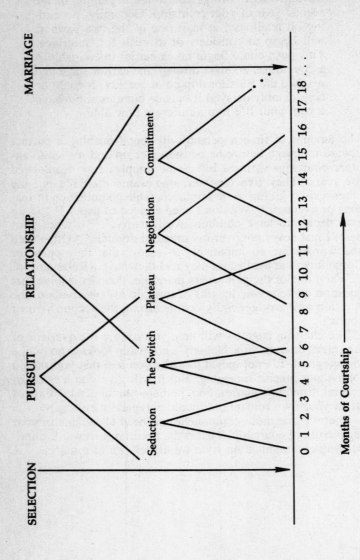

SELECTION   PURSUIT   RELATIONSHIP   MARRIAGE

Seduction   The Switch   Plateau   Negotiation   Commitment

0 1 2 3 4 5 6 7 8 9 10 11 12 13 14 15 16 17 18 ....

Months of Courtship

4

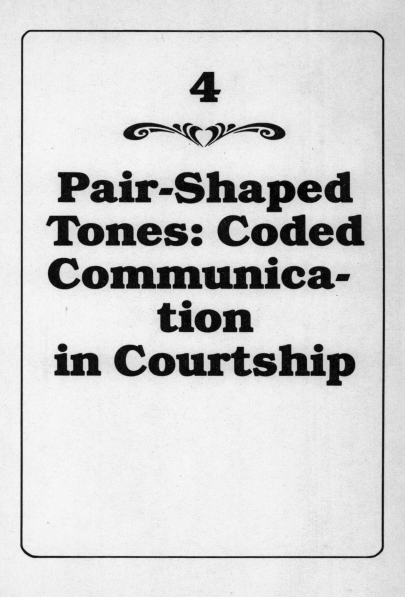

Pair-Shaped Tones: Coded Communication in Courtship

Elliot thought Sarah was nice enough, as first dates go. So far, he liked the fact that she was tall and dark, and he loved the fact that she didn't ask a thousand questions. True, she was a bit plain for his tastes, didn't seem to wear much makeup or make any sort of push to be glamorous. Still, they had enjoyed the movie and he got her to laugh a few times in the bar afterward. Sarah seemed to like him, but she also seemed straightforward—not the least bit seductive. So when he got to the steps of her apartment at the end of the evening, he was surprised to hear her say, "Would you like to come in for a while?" Elliot does not see himself as a man to miss an opportunity. However, he is also definitely not a man to force a sexual issue. What might a woman like Sarah mean by that invitation?

There you have the precise situation that makes dating an activity of captivating interest to those addicted to puzzles and a source of aggravation and exhaustion to the rest of us. You see, Sarah could have meant any one of many different things. And Elliot, concerned with not blowing a potentially pleasant relationship, but equally concerned with not missing a possible sexual opportunity, and especially cautious because he doesn't want to get himself rejected sexually, is left to decipher this complicated message.

For example, Sarah might mean, "I don't want you to leave. I want to go to bed with you." Or she could be signaling, "Let's spend some time talking. I want to check out your health." Or perhaps, "I feel like I really blew this evening, and this is my last-ditch effort to get you to like me," or, "This is a test to see if you're like all the other men."

What bothers Elliot—and the rest of us—is how to *know*

which one she means. Sometimes he gets frustrated with this kind of communication. Why can't she say what she means more clearly? (Why does he say, "I'll call," when he won't? Why does she say no when she sometimes means yes?)

Why, you might groan, does there have to be all this game playing that makes it so much easier for people to misunderstand each other and to feel hurt?

The point of this chapter is to show you that there is nothing wrong with Elliot for feeling confused, and nothing wrong with Sarah for falling back on an ambiguous statement instead of a direct, unequivocal message. Both of these people have just begun the earliest phase of the courtship ritual. In early courtship, and through its difficult passages, communication is coded. Coded means we do not say what we are thinking. Instead we offer certain ambiguous messages that generally convey our feelings and protect them at the same time. The code enables us to communicate about very sensitive and potentially embarrassing topics without being completely vulnerable. It means that when he says, "I'll call," maybe he's saying he'll call, or maybe he's saying goodbye.

We all know intuitively that when we begin the ritual of courtship, we are not free to express our private thoughts. Instead we are left in the peculiar situation of speaking in code and of cracking someone else's code. What makes clear communication so impossible?

The Street Smarts of Love

You may be unfamiliar with all of the subtle rules of courtship, but if you are a female reader there is probably one principle you learned at your mother's knee: *Don't scare him off!*

This is an intuitive expression of the perception that a lover's feelings need to be handled delicately in the early stages of a romance. Men truly want and need to be emotionally involved with a woman. They get caught up in the process of developing a relationship, but they don't always like to dwell on the consequences of that romance—namely, marriage, children, a mortgage, and the severe curtailment of sexual possibilities.

If she brings his attention to these consequences prematurely, she is likely to trigger the kind of anxiety that will swamp love in a second. It's irrelevant to become irritated at such a negative view of love and commitment. It is productive to soothe fears, not to repudiate them. Hence, the origin of her street-smart rule: *Don't scare him off*.

Somewhere in his process of growing up he will have learned how to safely connect with a woman, just as she learned about the male's fear of commitment. He believes, rightly or wrongly, that she is interested in an end result. He has a definite, though poorly articulated, notion that a woman has some awesome power: "She can trap me if I don't watch out!" He's not at all sure how she'll do this. He might be growing genuinely attached, but he doesn't know yet if he wants to end up where she seems to be heading. Therefore, in the interests of protecting himself against the possibility of things going beyond his control, he operates, at least in the early stages of a courtship, out of his unspoken rule: *Don't commit yourself*.

You'll quickly see that "don't commit yourself" and "don't scare him off" are very closely related. Both require tentative, indirect behavior. Both express the need for a natural braking system to withstand the emotional onslaught of infatuation, sexual excitement, chemistry, longing, and God-knows-what other hormonally induced fits you might experience. Both rules dictate caution.

And both rules are interchangeable. You could just as easily be the sort of woman who doesn't like to get too deeply involved, who feels constrained by the limitation of a full-time, serious lover, not to mention the rules and requirements of tending to a husband. As the options for economic independence increase, more and more women are irritated by the sacrifices involved in maintaining a relationship with a man. This woman approaches each man with a keen tally of the costs of being involved. ("He wants too much attention" or "I'll have to constantly build his ego.") She is operating on the principle of "don't commit yourself," though she may tell herself she's just waiting for the right person.

By the same token, some men are very open about and

comfortable with the goal of marriage. They are not simply challenged by Pursuit; they are relaxed about its end result. These men could quite consciously operate on the principle "Don't scare her off."

Sometimes this book will generalize about the stereotypic behavior of men and women. It is more accurate to say that there are always two roles to play and that men and women seem to occupy them interchangeably these days. It's true that women are more likely to feel comfortable with the goal of marriage and that men are more likely to see their wife flash before their eyes. But in a given relationship, and in fact at different times in the relationship, the reverse could also be true.

You'll see this more clearly if you look at the variations on these two central operating principles. Both men and women find themselves making decisions based on these kinds of thoughts:

- Don't look overeager—it frightens them away.

- Don't get in too deep. It's not so easy to turn around and go backward.

- Make her wait. She'll be more interested.

- Don't let him know that you're interested—men always want what they can't have.

- Don't be the first to say "I love you."

- Don't say what you mean until you're sure he won't leave you when he hears it.

The gist of all of these thoughts is simple. Don't make a move—but make something happen! Obviously, if neither of you makes a move or indicates interest, the whole thing will go nowhere. Yet the rules suggest that if you make your move too abruptly or too directly, you will defeat your own purpose.

The solution: communicate in code. Say what you want to say, but say it in a way that isn't quite clear, that doesn't overtly commit you. Say it in a way that would allow you to

70

retract it if necessary. Say it in a way that is ambiguous enough to encourage someone without frightening him or her.

Your relationship street smarts dictate that, at least early in a relationship, it's best to rely on ambiguous signals to get your message across. A woman doesn't tell a man on the third date that she is anxious about her biological clock and quite ready now to have a child. (You *don't*, do you?) However, if the subject of relationships comes up (and it often does around the third date), she might comment that she's reached the point in life where it's more intriguing to take one relationship as far as it will go, rather than constantly staying at the flirtation stage she preferred when she was younger. The former direct self-disclosure targets her as anxious and pressing. The alternative is a fuzzier self-reference. It leaves the possibility for many outcomes. It doesn't scare him off. It tells the truth without terrifying the audience. It's in code.

Nonverbal cues can be especially effective forms of coded communication. They are ambiguous just by virtue of being unspoken. Because they rarely require a verbal response, a couple can have an important shared communication without either person risking overt rejection.

However, nonverbal cues, like all codes, tell you something only if you have the ability to read them correctly. Anxiety interferes with the ability to send or receive nonverbal messages. So, pay attention, but try to keep a leash on your impulse to draw a conclusion.

A person who holds your hand or takes your arm crossing the street immediately increases the feeling of connection between you. But these gestures are typically reflections of personal style, and they are not available to everyone. You can enjoy the contact, without drawing conclusions.

One woman, who is especially sensitive to nonverbal cues, described a gesture on a first date that immediately warmed her heart. While she was in the ladies' room, her after-dinner coffee was served. Her date placed the saucer over the cup so it wouldn't get cold. She said she knew by that gesture exactly the kind of care this man would take of a woman he loved.

Her interpretation was right. He probably was a very nur-

71

turing man. But she should not rush to conclude that she would be the woman this man would choose to take care of.

Part of the process of developing into a couple is to gradually, over time, find a way to communicate directly and honestly your thoughts and feelings. In the earliest stages of coupling, the risk is too great. Communicating in code is the only solution to the mutually conflicting needs to get closer to someone while maintaining enough distance to spare both of your feelings. The ability to handle the code well is a key element in allowing a romance to develop.

Courtship requires a code for three reasons.

A code can reduce anxiety. Your perfectly normal feelings of anxiety and vulnerability are protected by the ambiguous nature of the communication. For example, she is protecting herself when she says, "I'm not ready yet" to a sexual invitation. The truth could be more baldly stated, "I don't want to go to bed with you because I always fall in love afterward and I'm afraid you'll reject me." But if courtships required us to be this exposed, we'd be a lot more reluctant than we already are to enter into them. People need to reduce their anxiety to a manageable level in order to pursue a goal.

Symbolic communication also protects your partner's feelings. We resort to clichés as a way to protect others. Therefore, to the dentist who bores you to death with talk of inlays and bonding, it's kinder to say, "I've started seeing someone exclusively" than to be honest, i.e., "I'm just not that interested in root canal."

A code can reflect ambivalent feelings. Coded communication is crucial because its very vagueness reflects the true state of affairs, especially early in courtship. For the first several months of a relationship, your feelings about someone are likely to be very volatile. The dynamic of a developing relationship is almost always a tentative push-pull, with one person pursuing and the other holding back until the roles reverse. This is the exact process of the first two stages of courtship, Seduction and The Switch. Ambiguous communication serves the needs of these two stages. It is not so much game playing as it is the most accurate reflection of an ever-changing truth.

72

A code can ease communication on sensitive social issues.
Coded communication alludes more than it confronts. Romance
itself touches on the most private aspects of the social world—
sexuality, morality, personal secrets, personal ethics. In order
to be close to someone, it is necessary to disclose one's thoughts,
feelings, and experiences in these areas. But it is not something
to be done cavalierly. The ritualized signals we send each other
during the early stages of courtship lay the necessary ground-
work for these discussions. There is one exception. Only frank
discussion of sex and health can help you choose your sexual
partner wisely. Codes won't work.

Cracking the Code

If you allow yourself to be acutely aware of the symbolic
nature of the messages you are sending and receiving, you'll
be better able to handle the rigors of courtship.

The following exercise is a review of several classic situations with which you may be confronted during courtship.
We'll discuss each one individually later. Right now, take
out a piece of paper and write down *at least three* alternative
interpretations to each of these situations. (Don't turn the
page to get the answers first. It's your own thinking we want
to examine.)

1. After six weeks of regular, amiable evenings together, he has not asked her out for Saturday
   night. This might mean:

2. On the fourth date, she makes a sexual overture.
   He ignores it and goes right into a story about
   the office. He might be saying:

3. After several evenings as a twosome, she suggests an evening at a party with her friends. She
   is communicating:

4. After two dates, he indicates his sexual interest
   in her. She says, "I find you attractive, but I'm
   not ready." She is really saying:

5. Instead of spending a leisurely Sunday as she usually does after a Saturday night date, she announces this Sunday morning, "I have to get going. I have a lot of work to do." She is telling him:

6. She is thirty-six, never married, no kids. In around the fifth month of what's been a comfortable love affair, he begins a theoretical discussion on the importance of children and family. He is fumbling to find a way to let her know that:

Simultaneous Translation

We're going to review each of these situations. This exercise has four goals:

- To give you specific alternatives that you may not have considered about situations that you may confront.

- To demonstrate that most behavior early in a romantic relationship may have one of several meanings. You cope best when you allow yourself the possibility of many alternatives, rather than the comfort of false certainty.

- To school yourself in flexible thinking. Developing a relationship is practicing the art of the possible. Flexibility leaves room for a relationship to grow naturally. Too much uncertainty, of course, will arouse all your insecurity and leave you showing your desperate edge. Too little makes you miss the other person because all you really see is what you expect to be there.

- To draw your attention to the fact that you do get a lot of information about how a person is thinking and feeling about you. It's easy information to overlook because it's indirect, but it's there.

To review the situations:

74

1. After six weeks of regular and amiable evenings together, he has still not asked her out for Saturday night.

When a man keeps his weekends to himself, it's a pretty clear indication that he is withholding potential emotional investment in you. You don't know why. Maybe you're exactly his type, which makes him interested enough to get in halfway but cautious enough to go very slowly; or maybe he's hooked into a passionately unhappy love affair and sees you on Tuesday to prove to himself that he's trying to find someone new. Or it's possible that his style is to see many women, leaving it to the woman to emerge from the pack and arouse his interests.

Your choice is obviously to tell him that you've noticed or to keep it to yourself. You can wait as long as you are comfortable. When you are unable to tolerate the uncertainty any more, you'll have to comment. Don't frame the question as a rejection, or a self-criticism. You don't have to be utterly direct—"How come I never see you on Saturday night?" Instead, put yourself in the frame of mind that invites confidence. Comment that you are aware there are parts of his life that you haven't been let in on. Tell him (or her, if the roles are reversed) that you hope at some point he will be comfortable enough to tell you more about himself and how he spends his time. This is an invitation rather than a confrontation. There are no guarantees that he'll take you up on it. But he might.

One note: This is a situation in which it's best to go slowly sexually. You have a hint that your new partner is not monogamous. Consider the issue of disease carefully. Don't hope that the sexual involvement will advance your status with him. It might, but it's a gamble. Let your importance to him advance first; then, if you feel comfortable, become lovers.

If it's too late for this caution, take some time to consider the costs to yourself. It is hard to go backward, but you do have the option of saying, "I love the time we spend together, but I'm not comfortable having sex. You see, I tend to expect more from my lovers and less from my friends and we seem to be shaping up as friends." Yes, it makes you nervous, because if he's coming around for sex and you say no, that might be that. On the other hand, you could be cutting your losses. You will have to be the judge of when you want to do that.

2. On the fourth date, she makes a sexual overture. He ignores it and goes right into a story about the office.

Permission for a woman to get things going sexually is the legacy of the sexual revolution. Rejection, anxiety, and social awkwardness are the negative side effects of that permission. (There are plenty of positive side effects as well.)

It has *always* been up to a woman to indicate nonverbally her availability for sexual involvement. Only the most brash or overconfident man fails to seek out these signals. Just as some men don't wait for a cue from a woman before they pounce, some women are moved to offer sexual advances toward a man before they have any tacit indication that these advances would be welcomed.

You are certainly free to make your sexual feelings known loudly and clearly if that is your preference. If you are ignored, it's easy to leap to the conclusion that you are with a man who simply doesn't find you physically attractive. However daunting, that's a definite possibility. But it's also possible that he is simply not yet ready to develop the physical part of your relationship. Perhaps he, too, is concerned about the possibility of disease. The simple fact of possessing a penis does not, contrary to some women's suspicions, mean that a man will avail himself of every opportunity to use it.

This man may find you physically attractive, but perhaps he's the sort for whom no amount of sexual arousal can overwhelm his need to be in control. Perhaps he's uncomfortable with a sexually aggressive woman. Perhaps his interest is based on the excitement of Pursuit, and your invitation took the fun out of it for him.

Maybe he's simply obtuse. We all hear what we expect to hear a good deal of the time. Most men expect a woman to await their sexual moves. He may be so blinded by his expectations that he simply didn't get your message.

Regardless of which hypothesis strikes you as the most likely, you really have only three productive ways to cope. You could fall back and restrain yourself, deciding that the ball is in his court. Or, you could move ahead and stage a full-blown seduction dinner, complete with intoxicants, sheer clothing, candles, and fresh bed linens. Finally, gently, you could tell him of your confusion and the two of you could talk about it.

In order to choose one of these options, you will have to resist the idea that you have been rejected. It's easy to feel awful when you have been ignored sexually. It's very easy to take his lack of response personally, to assume it is some reflection on your attractiveness. In the end, a woman who makes a direct sexual play and gets no reaction can feel like a fool—and end up taking to her bed with an entire Sara Lee cheesecake. Don't let yourself overreact.

3. After several evenings as a twosome, she suggests an evening at a party with her friends.

Things are moving along. She is introducing you to her friends. For most people, this is a considered rather than an impulsive move. It could mean that she simply needed a date for the party, but, even so, she's saying she's comfortable with you in that role. What you won't know is to what degree this is a test of your acceptability. Is she announcing to her friends that you two are now a couple? Is she asking her friends for a go-ahead? Or are you merely an accessory, an escort? The truth is probably somewhere in the middle.

Your task is to accept your role as an interested, relaxed outsider. The challenge is to feel self-possessed enough to handle what might be a lapse of attention on her part or a lukewarm welcome on the part of her social family.

If she seems to ignore you at the party, if the conversation excludes you, if you are suddenly left standing alone at the bar fending for yourself—don't take it personally. We are all different with our friends than we are in the privacy of a newly developing romance. Some people feel self-conscious about their new attachments. Keep in mind that there's some anxiety in this situation, whether she has acknowledged it or not. Go back and visit her from time to time during the evening, but don't try to claim all of her attention. Make contact with some of her friends. In this way you will be sending a code that says to her, "I'm not always needy. There's room for the rest of your life too," and says to her friends, "Don't be threatened by me. You won't lose her because of me. I'll add more than I'll subtract."

4. After two dates, he indicates his sexual interest in her. She says, "I really find you attractive, but I'm not ready."

When a woman tells you that she is not ready for sex, it's as confusing as when you refuse to react to her signals. You don't know if it means (a) let's just be friends, I don't find you attractive; (b) I'm being coy—please pursue; (c) I need you to say "I love you" first; (d) never, under any circumstances with you, you fool; (e) I'm anxious about AIDS, about my body, about whether you'll leave me; or (f) I have another lover. She may even mean, "I'm not ready."

Initially your best option is to assume that this is a test of trustworthiness and proceed accordingly. If she wants to know if you are interested in more than sex, stick around for a while and prove your point. A test of trustworthiness between two people who are both sexually attracted and available is usually a short-lived thing. She should eventually be sending you signals that the time is right and that she is physically receptive. (The decision to lose one's virginity is a very different process and follows a timetable entirely different from the one governing the decision to take a new lover.)

What if you follow the low-pressure strategy, time passes, and you are still getting no sexual response? It's time to ask her to be more explicit. She knows by now whether she's simply anxious about sex or uninterested in you. You deserve to know too.

5. Instead of spending a leisurely Sunday as she usually does after a Saturday night date, she announces this Sunday morning, "I have to get going. I have a lot of work to do."

When she leaves on Sunday morning with a perfectly legitimate excuse, don't miss her possible message. She could be deliberately putting some distance between you. She might be telling you something like (a) I've been neglecting the rest of my life on your account. Now I need to catch up; (b) I don't like the pattern we've fallen into where every date is forty-eight hours long. I want to exercise a little independence; (c) I get anxious around another person after too long a time. I need a little breathing room; or (d) I'm used to a man falling into a Wednesday night/Saturday night pattern. Sundays are reserved for brunch with my girlfriends and a very thorough reading of the *Times*. You've been getting in the way.

Your coping strategy here is one we'll go over point by point in chapter 6. For now it's enough to consider that there is a lot of information in any change of established pattern, however subtle the change.

6. She is thirty-six, never married, no kids. Around the fifth month of a comfortable love affair, he begins a theoretical discussion on the importance of children and family.

When a man begins talking theoretically on the subject of children and family, pay close attention. He is sounding you out as delicately as possible. Don't necessarily assume that this is his way of sharing the depth of his feelings for you. It is more likely that he has some anxieties about the future of your relationship and that he's trying to find a way to signal them to you.

First of all, dreadful though it is to confront, he may have concerns about your age. A lot of men in their late thirties through their forties have a strong desire to marry because they are craving children and a family. These men get nervous about women who may be getting too old to reproduce.

When a childless man in this age group meets a woman who attracts him, he may begin to focus on her age as a source of tremendous concern. He certainly doesn't know how to tell her directly that she isn't seriously in the running, but he feels compelled to bring up his anxiety. He is looking for reassurance. He wants to hear that you, too, are aware of the press of time, but that you've been assured that you have a good five years or so before childbearing is impossible, or that you would adopt, or that you don't want kids. Mostly, he wants to know he can be anxious out loud and you won't crumble.

Or he may be wondering about your ideas on child rearing. Would you insist on stopping work? Would you insist on continuing? How much conflict should he expect from you? Men often try to spot and minimize the risks in a relationship much as they would in a business deal.

The point is that when he's bringing this up, it's because he has strong opinions on the topic. He wants to know if you'll fight him and what you'll expect of him. Your first task is to help him express those feelings fully. Don't try to dodge the conversation, though you might be tempted to because it's threatening. He may approach you with a question such as "How do you feel about working mothers?" or he might state an opinion about one of your friends. ("What did she have a kid for if someone else raises it?") Make every effort to resist the pull of a political argument. Tune in to the personal. Try to understand his anxiety and what it has to do with you.

Recognizing Your Deaf Spots

It's clear from this exercise that each of these ambiguous messages has a multitude of possible meanings. The meaning you attach to one of these coded communications is likely to be a reflection of your own expectations. Here is a specific instance of the role of projection in an unfolding relationship. We feel as if we are responding to the other person. In fact, often we project onto this other person our own fears, insecurities, and anxieties. We feel a particular way *about* ourselves, so we assume that someone else feels the same way *toward* us. It is particularly easy to make this projection of our internal world during early courtship because the actual communication is indirect and open to all kinds of interpretation.

For example, when a man ignores your sexual advances and you know he may simply be obtuse, are you most likely to feel that you are not desirable enough? Another woman, absolutely convinced of her attractiveness, would always assume that the man in question was just being dense. You can see how these interpretative biases would strongly affect the reactions of these women. The first feels rejected and perhaps a bit embarrassed. She inevitably backs way off. The second tends to escalate. If she's not yet getting through, she feels she must be louder and clearer.

Neither of these women is more likely to be right or wrong. Both bring to the situation certain expectations that bias their interpretation of coded courtship messages.

When a woman is suddenly busy on Sunday morning, how

are you most likely to construe it? One man will ignore the message completely. He's so self-absorbed that he doesn't bother to wonder. Another man will get anxious. For him, independence in a woman is identical with rejection. A third man will experience sexual jealousy. He'll get angry or sulk because he feels threatened. Each interpretative bias changes the pattern of a developing courtship. Neither interpretation is necessarily more "correct" than any other.

We rarely acknowledge the ambiguity of the situation. Instead, we secretly feel we know what someone meant, though this knowledge is more often based on our self-image and expectations than on a clear perception of the individual in the situation. This kind of mind reading can lead to some real distortions in your interpretations of a partner's words and actions.

Most errors in decoding fall into one of three categories:

- Errors reflecting poor self-esteem
- Errors reflecting rigid social expectations
- Errors reflecting anxiety about intimacy

Errors Reflecting Poor Self-esteem

Some people find it very difficult to believe that they could be loved. They make a fundamental, though often unconscious, assumption that happiness comes to other people, not to them. For this person rejection is an inevitable event in courtship. He or she spends a lot of emotional energy agonizing over when it will arrive. Often this person hears rejection prematurely just to get it over with.

This is not the usual kind of anxiety that most of us feel when we begin to care. Everyone hopes a relationship will be successful, but most of us tease ourselves with the possibility of loss, perhaps as a way to steel ourselves against it.

The feelings that stem from poor self-esteem may be the same in content as normal anxiety, but they are different in degree. The man or woman who truly feels unworthy of love sees rejection in every hesitation. She interprets his desire to be with his friends as an indication of lack of desire to be with her. When he phones and gets her answering machine, he assumes that she's out this very minute with a man she prefers. He figures it's not even worth leaving a message.

They date for months, but she is too insecure to let him know how she feels about him. She's certain that the moment he hears a feeling expressed, he'll leave. He is too unsure of himself to relax into a relationship. He gets an invitation to meet her friends and immediately assumes it's a test of his worth. He goes with a chip on his shoulder, deciding in advance all the reasons they won't like him and feeling angry before he arrives.

- If your partner says you are not invited to be his date for the family party and you tend to hear that you aren't good enough, you are distorting the communication because of your poor self-esteem.

- If your partner admires your best friend's sense of humor and you hear a veiled criticism of your own, you are distorting because of your poor self-esteem.

- If she says she hated the movie and you get a horrible pang because you picked it, you are confusing yourself with your tastes.

- If there's silence between you and you hear the silence as a message that you are boring, you are not responding to your partner. You are responding to your own self-image.

All these are examples of the kind of interpretative biases that operate when you assume that someone feels about you the way you feel about yourself and how you feel about yourself is not so hot.

Errors Reflecting Rigid Social Expectations

Do you assume that a man who really cares calls by Wednesday for a Saturday night date? Do you assume that a woman who pays for you is liberated? Do you find yourself often critical of your friends for the things they will put up with from partners, which you would never tolerate?

Do you find yourself with a very strong sense of right and

wrong over the conflicts that come up in a relationship, only more often you're right and your partner is wrong? Do you have a keen sense of a timetable in which sexual intimacy occurs at a particular point, monogamy at another, commitment another?

Do you have firm ideas on the right way for him to acknowledge your birthday (lavishly), for her to interact with your friends (like one of the guys), for him to talk about his feelings (openly but easy on the criticism of you), for her to invite you to her place (it should include a well-cooked meal)?

In these cases, you are likely to greet behavior that falls outside these boundaries as *wrong*—without being able to view the other side of it. In effect, what you've done is to design a little box into which a romance must fit to be comfortable for you. The box is created from all of your expectations about the way things should be. Where a partner fails to fit neatly in the box, you feel angry or disappointed. Where his behavior conforms to your requirements, you are unastonished.

The problem is that while you have a strict set of rules, not everyone's reading out of your book.

Errors Reflecting Anxiety About Intimacy

- He says, "Let me buy you that book."
  She hears, "I'm going to run your life."

- She says, "Come to my parent's house for brunch on Sunday."
  He hears, "I want to marry you."

- She says, "How was your day?"
  He hears, "What did you do, who did you do it with, when did you do it, were you a good boy?"

- He says, "What do you think I should say to my boss on this?"
  She hears, "I can't take care of myself, much less you."

Each listener is distorting the message because of his or her difficulty with intimacy.

Each variety of the fear of intimacy introduced in the last

83

chapter has its own special interpretative bias. If your fear of rejection is high, you will have difficulty picking up someone else's shyness or uncertainty. If your sexual anxiety is high, you will block out the world's sexual response to you. As one woman described this distortion, "I find it so hard to believe a man could want me sexually that even if he has his hand on my thigh, I tend to feel he's just being friendly."

If your fear of entrapment is great, you will tend to hear the mildest encouragement as a marriage proposal. Partners will often appear to you to be more needy, dependent, or lonely than they actually are.

If you are very uncomfortable with anger, you are likely to completely miss your own hostility. You will have a hard time seeing the passive, indirect ways you express your own anger. Partners will seem "crazy" or "overemotional."

Honesty Games

Honest self-disclosure is at the core of intimacy. But it can't be rushed; it must be nurtured instead. Some people are quite impatient with, or disapproving of, the required coded communication early in courtship. They are eager for honesty and hungry for instant intimacy. In the service of these needs, many of us allow uncensored self-disclosure to take the place of conversation.

In general, you are communicating too directly and revealing too much if you are verbalizing certain kinds of attitudes, feelings, or thoughts in the early part of Seduction. You are on dangerous ground if you:

- Criticize your ex-husband/boyfriend, ex-wife/ girlfriend.

- Express anger toward men or women as a group.

- Tell about the ordeal you've had with your difficult parents, alcoholic brother, or sexually promiscuous younger sister.

- Reveal your struggle with drugs, your battle with your weight, your inability to hold a job.

- Discuss your problems handling money, your history as a compulsive shopper, your IRS difficulties.

- Draw attention to your shortcomings by pointing out that you are a slob or a klutz.

- Agonize over your neglected, troubled, or delinquent children.

- Complain about your physical condition, chronic aches and pains, needs for special diet or care. The emphasis here is on the word *complain*. Necessary information is something else.

- Describe your miserable boss, your disloyal colleagues, or the way you were robbed of a recent promotion.

- List everyone who dumped you, rejected you, or did you wrong.

You know it's appalling when new dates present themselves to you in such a negative fashion. They force you to be wary and unresponsive when you were hoping you'd find a reason to fall in love. But some of you, even though you are exquisitely tuned in to the other guy's presentation, haven't listened in to your own lately. It's a common form of deafness. Each of the previous examples marked an actual first (usually last) date for one of my patients.

Discretion is not distortion. You don't need to present a false image of yourself. You may resent the idea that there are facets of your life better concealed than revealed. As a courtship develops, you will naturally have to disclose all these personal issues and more. Just be sensitive to the time and place.

These revelations are appropriate to, and in fact necessary for, the establishment of an intimate relationship. But intimacy requires time, trust, history. It rarely occurs over the first three or four dates, or the first magical weekend you share, no matter how closely connected you feel.

Genuine self-disclosure is best offered and best received in the context of feelings of warmth, closeness, connectedness.

When you are moving from the period of Pursuit to the establishment of a Relationship, you will find it necessary to talk with sincerity about some or all of the difficult topics listed above. You will take the risk of revealing some of your past failures in relationships. You will be interested in his or her past experiences. You will feel close enough to unburden yourself of family secrets and private battles. And you will be willing to listen to your partner without harsh judgment or intrusive cross-examination.

The problem is that when these self-disclosures occur very early, they are more likely to work against you and the courtship. In fact, in the name of honesty or being up front you may actually be using them to push a romance away. To tell a person you hardly know that other lovers have been rotten to you, drugs were a problem for you, or your family is an unhappy, troubled one is to pin a huge Danger! Warning! sign on yourself.

These premature disclosures are often a kind of test. "Take this and this," she seems to be saying, "and let's see if you will be the kind of bastard who leaves me like all the others did." "Here's the mess I've made of my life," he signals. "Let's see if you're impossible to please like all those other women."

When you test people in this way, they are much more likely to fail the test. They are in the earliest stages of forming a picture of you. In these early stages, our first impressions often become little more than stereotypes. We have nothing else to go on, no way to create the unique, complete image of a single individual that emerges after time and history. To deliberately assist a man (or woman) in stereotyping you as desperate, troubled, or angry, and then to condemn him for doing so is foolish and self-defeating.

In addition to honesty as a guise for pushing a partner away before you get hurt or for testing loyalties, these premature self-disclosures are the offspring of anxiety. Afraid we will be rejected because of some shortcoming or past failure, we rush to get the bad part over with. We are anxious and embarrassed by these less-than-perfect parts of our lives. We want to find out as soon as possible if our partners will tolerate them.

There's a clue you can use to determine if anxiety is pushing you to present yourself in a negative way. You'll notice that the speech you end up giving is canned.

A canned speech is a story, anecdote, self-disclosure, or self-reference that you've told over and over. It's the one that you always find yourself telling by the second date, where you repeat the clever line about your ex that always gets a laugh. It's the cute story designed to get lightly past the question of why a presumably nice person like you never married.

Most canned speeches, rehearsed anecdotes, and well-worn personal tidbits are positive. They are designed to charm your audience, make a good connection, and present yourself in the best, funniest, sweetest light. One of the real delights of beginning a new courtship is the brand-new audience it provides.

But many of us have an automatic negative story. It's the one in which you think you sound amusing, wry, but what you really sound is angry or self-deprecating. Listen to yourself the next time you tell one. Maybe you don't need to bleed so freely, so quickly. This is courtship, not first aid.

There is another version of the honesty game that demands attention. In this version, your date uses it as a way to tell you something mean, harsh, or hurtful about yourself. A woman who is not responding very warmly is told that she's "probably never had a good relationship because she's cold and critical." He gives examples of what she's done to him so far. (All of this after one cup of coffee and a movie.) A man who offers only limited responses to his blind date's inquisition is greeted with a twenty-minute assault of honesty. He's told he is difficult, plastic, and boring. She accuses him of being passive, of waiting to be entertained. If you're single, you probably haven't escaped being this kind of victim at least once or twice. It can hurt a lot to hear yourself so cruelly attacked. This is exactly the moment to remind yourself of the possibility of projection in courtship. Keep repeating: *Don't take it personally*. Then leave.

Finally, the honesty game has a devastating variation. This is honesty used as a come-on, a seduction ploy. This form of self-disclosure involves the pursuer revealing his feelings ("I've never met anyone like you"), fears ("Gee, I've always felt insecure around a woman like you. You're so special."), hopes ("I know this is crazy, but I love you.")—all

87

in an effort to create enough instant intimacy to accomplish Seduction. It very often works.

Even the most sophisticated of us can be taken in by honesty as a come-on. After all he (or she, if she is pursuing) is saying all the right things. You want to believe him. You want to feel close. You want to be loved.

Many of us are especially vulnerable to this ploy because we are only interested in courtships that begin with a bang. If the first few dates are not intense emotional experiences, we lose interest. If someone is slow to express his or her feelings, we feel nothing. By contrast, the man who leans across a table on the second date and says, "I've been lonely and empty for years. I have a feeling you're going to change all that," lights a firecracker. We feel we are on our way to being in love. Actually, we are on our way to being seduced—and probably abandoned shortly thereafter.

The Language of Love-at-First-Sight

There is one circumstance in which premature self-disclosure feels almost inevitable. That is the magical love-at-first-sight phenomenon.

You meet at a party and feel miraculously comfortable. There is a rapport, a sympathy, you haven't felt before. You leave the party together and go to sit on the steps of the Art Museum. You talk until the sun comes up—and talk some more over breakfast. The sense of connectedness extends way beyond a verbal rapport. It's a feeling of recognition, a sense of instant familiarity. This is a perfect fit, a harmony, a completion. The feeling you have is very strong, however irrational. The two of you are a couple—you belong together. You feel secure and intimate. It's a feeling people struggle for months, even years, to create, and here it's been handed to you.

You speak of things you've never told anyone. You both tell the truth about yourselves. It *is* magic. This is such a special and rare experience that it is absurd to suggest that you exercise any degree of caution or self-discipline when you are presented with this kind of opportunity.

These are the circumstances when it feels natural, even blissful, to confess to a stranger that you've always felt ashamed of your pitted skin, or that you wonder if you're even capable of feeling love. Under these circumstances, she can tell you about cheating her way through college, he can reveal that he drank his way through half a dozen women, and both of you feel compassion instead of alarm.

"You" and "I" become "We," an instant couple. As such, "We" might skip the restrictions of coded communication that operate in most courtships. There are pluses and minuses to this acceleration. The enormous plus, of course, is the intense joy of fusing with a near-stranger instantly. This is the extreme version of the fireworks beginning for which most of us long. No work, no anxiety, just a headlong dive off a cliff.

The downside of a courtship that begins with this kind of explosion is that it often ends with a fizzle. Over the next few weeks or months, the miraculous, instantaneous sense of "We" will dissolve. You will again become aware of each other as two separate people who are compatible in some areas, conflicting in others. When you begin with the utter enchantment that temporarily erases all barriers, the reality of your separate identities can be overwhelmingly painful. It's difficult enough to slowly develop a loving relationship that eventually breaks through each of the obstacles to intimacy. It can be unbearable to suddenly uncover conflict when you had allowed yourself the fantasy of perfect and immediate love.

It can seem impossible—but it doesn't have to be impossible. In the same way that communication began in an especially easy fashion, it will now probably have to weather an especially difficult period. Many couples are able to do this, making the transition from being wildly in love to being solidly in love. For others, reality is too severe a shock for the relationship to tolerate. It fizzles, explodes, or dissolves and often neither partner is quite sure of how or why. "It was just one of those things."

The overview is complete. You have a picture of the general goal of courtship and a menu of motives that might explain your date's hidden intentions and shed some light on your own.

You have an outline of each of the stages of courtship, and you've been alerted to each of the likely sources of stress associated with each stage.

We've talked about each of the key themes that run through courtship:

- The essential attitude of courtship: *Don't take it personally*
- The nature of courtship as both a social ritual and a psychological developmental process
- The importance of readiness
- The inescapable tug of ambivalence

And you are prepared for the peculiar language of courtship—communication in code.

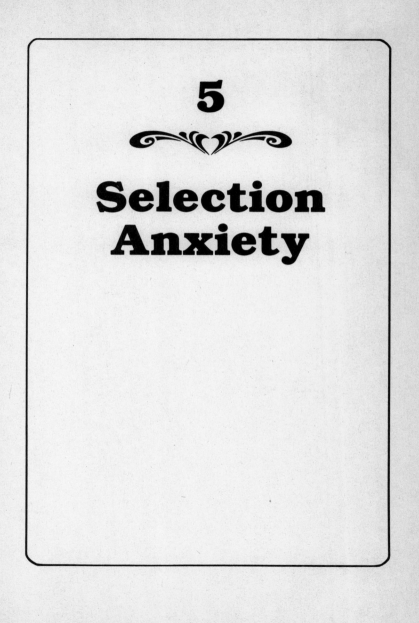

5

Selection Anxiety

Nathan is preparing for a blind date. It's his fourth such meeting in the last six weeks, thanks to the list provided by a dating service. He climbs into what he thinks of as his "first date uniform": blue blazer, gray slacks, loafers. Nathan feels the outfit communicates that he's made an effort without going overboard. He's a veteran of so many first dates that he has mastered the technique. His conversation is long since prepared—heavy on movies and books, light on his passion for basketball; strategic questions to get her talking; rehearsed responses to convey an attractive impression. Nathan is so practiced at first encounters that he notes ruefully, "I could turn in a first date without even being there."

♥   ♥   ♥

Marjorie (please, not Margie), has once again yielded to the persuasions of her friend Sharon to spend an evening at a singles event. Marjorie *hates* the very word "singles," never even thinks of herself as single. In Marjorie's mind, you might just as well substitute the word losers. She doesn't consider herself a loser, and she looks down on the kind of man who would attend such a gathering.

Tonight proves her point again. It's another symposium, this time on "Singles and Money." None of the men interests her enough even to speak with. They all look short to her, or wimpish—losers one and all. She feels half guilty about her reaction and half depressed. She and her girlfriend leave shortly after the program. On the way home, Marjorie makes her familiar pronouncement: "There was no one there."

♥   ♥   ♥

It is Wednesday evening and the local singles bar is packed. Elaine stops in alone, hoping to run into some friends. She does, of course. Everyone from the agency where she works uses this bar as a hangout. Elaine is quickly a part of a group. She feels good around her friends, though she knows that none of the men is a potential partner. Of the two single men in her crowd, one does not interest her and she's already had a brief fling with the other. That connection went nowhere, and Elaine is back to relating to him as "just a friend." It took her a few weeks to accomplish this emotional feat, and she's rather proud that she conquered her feelings of rejection so readily. Still she hangs around him a bit, surveying the bar from the security of her friendship network. She'd like to meet someone new, but she finds it very difficult to approach a stranger on her home turf. On vacation Elaine is a whiz at approaching new men. At home she is paralyzed. She can't understand why.

Matthew has been nursing his beer on the other side of the bar for an hour. For most of that time, he has been eyeing Elaine, enjoying her animation and warmth. She seems so attractive, so at ease. Matthew is a bit stiff himself. He has always been drawn to Elaine's type, bubbly and sure of herself. He'd like to meet her, considers buying her a drink and having the bartender deliver it. He rejects the idea as corny. He can just imagine the group she's with picking him out of the crowd and laughing together. Besides, it looks to him like Elaine is with someone. There's one guy she talks to a lot, seems to like. He could never cut in on something like that. He'd only make a fool of himself trying. Finally, Matthew leaves, comforting himself with the fantasy that he'll return next Wednesday and maybe she'll be there. And maybe she'll be alone, and maybe she'll talk to him. And maybe . . .

♥   ♥   ♥

In order to begin a courtship, all you have to do is connect with another person long enough to indicate your interest and come to some agreement that the two of you will deliberately meet again.

That's it. You don't have to make a wonderful, witty, first impression. You don't need to come up with a reason why the two of you might meet. You don't have to worry about

94

coming on too aggressively or too passively. You don't need to do it well or do it right. You just need to do it.

It's not worth planning a great line or perfecting seductive eye contact because it's almost impossible to predict a stranger's response. What is gauche to one woman is reassuringly boyish to another. What is offensively aggressive to one man is blessedly assertive to another. You cannot tailor your persona to guarantee success. You don't have the necessary information and, if you did, you might feel foolish using it. Don't rearrange yourself, just present yourself.

Sounds perfectly simple, doesn't it? Actually, for some people it is. If you are one of those blessedly self-confident and relaxed individuals who enjoys meeting strangers, Selection will be one of the delights of courtship.

You are someone who generally does well at big parties, blind dates, and body bars. You are probably attractive enough to arouse interest and comfortable enough to handle the interest you arouse. You may be eager for a long-term relationship, but until one comes along, you find life satisfying in a lot of other ways. This sense of satisfaction frees you from the frantic need to find someone who will love you. You can afford to be open to people because you aren't going to be devastated by the ones who reject you.

These are all wonderful attitudes and most of us are able to think and feel this way—from time to time, say, every other Tuesday or during a particularly happy life patch. The rest of the time, we're apt to fall a bit short of this standard of superb self-acceptance. When we do, and to the extent that we do, Selection can be a difficult moment.

A stranger might not be able to break your heart, but the process of selecting among and being selected by strangers inflicts so many little ego bruises. You may have one for every woman who refused your offer to buy her a drink, or every man who took your number and never called. You can suffer minute but constant erosion to your self-esteem for every pair of eyes that continued to survey a room while you were looking into them. And worst, you can, bit by bit, lose those essential components to the spirit—hope and anticipation—as you attend party after party, class after club, and fail to meet someone who excites you.

All of us experience these wounds to some degree. You

95

could reduce the potential for pain in Selection by means of a small change in attitude. All you need to do is to see it for what it is: *An entry point to courtship, not an endpoint.*

You've been taught to overemphasize the importance of Selection. It stems quite naturally from that myth of romantic love that we've discussed at length. You have been lured into the fantasy that all you need to do is to find the right person. Is it surprising that when you begin with that belief, you are likely to exaggerate the importance of your first reaction? You are hoping to feel excited, stirred, to hear at least a few bells. It's your practice to quickly reject a possible partner as soon as you spot a flaw. You believe that Selection is far too important to waste time and energy with the wrong choice.

We want to know in advance that we've found the perfect person instead of accepting that we create relationships and develop love. We certainly do fall into love, but we do not fall into commitment.

In fact, Selection should be the least selective stage of the courtship ritual. Remember, Selection in particular is nothing personal. You have very little information, and what you do have isn't worth much. We're all stuck operating from stereotypes, prejudice, and pure assumption when we make judgments based on initial impressions. Certainly sometimes you are justified in making a negative judgment. But if you decide no too quickly, too often, you are stacking the odds against yourself.

Besides, when you aren't frozen with the concern that you choose right, you'll have a lot more fun with your choices. Beginning a flirtation is fun if you aren't worrying about where it's going to lead. Some people can always enjoy the attention and appreciation of an admirer. Others get bogged down in the feeling that attention from the wrong source is as disappointing as no attention at all. Selection to begin a courtship could be a casual, open-ended process. You just have to be willing to be surprised. Your orientation should be toward spending time with many potential partners. As you move through courtship, you keep refining your relationships until you form that solid bond with one person.

De-emphasizing the monumental importance of beginning courtship only with those people who seem right will make the Selection stage more relaxed. This is an attitude change

96

that requires only a minor adjustment in your thinking, but it will yield a major change in your behavior.

Your attitude is not the only reason why Selection is often a difficult part of courtship. The Selection stage also brings with it an inevitable anxiety and awkwardness because it forces us to meet each other as commodities. Commitment requires that we meet as human beings. It's a long road to travel.

The Consumer Mentality

The worst part of this stage of courtship is not your attitude about Selection, but your attitude about yourself and toward your potential partners. In order to select someone, and be selected in turn, you must market yourself. It is ugly, odd, inhuman, and inescapable.

Marketing yourself means doing exactly what the manufacturer of breakfast cereal does to his product. It means creating an attractive package, displaying yourself strategically among the competition, and hoping to attract a whimsical shopper.

Marketing yourself may mean detesting the imperfections of your jaw line, or refusing party invitations if you've gained five pounds because you feel no one would want you.

It may mean obsessing over your clothing or your hair, or practicing clever introductions that you are unable to deliver unless fortified with alcohol.

Marketing yourself may mean scanning every room to get a sense of the competition and hating, really hating, every great-looking person of your own sex who is present. It means developing an acute sense of your own flaws in order to better disguise or eliminate them. It means, whether you are male or female, making every effort to appear thin, fit, groomed, relaxed, poised, interesting, funny, and sexy, while you are really feeling nervous or vulnerable or fat or boring.

The result of all this packaging is disastrous in two ways: It can hurt how you feel about yourself, and it can ruin your ability to select someone else.

No matter how successful you are at packaging yourself,

the marketing aspects of Selection can give you an almost poisonous sense of self-consciousness. You are constantly aware of the impression you are making, constantly tuned in to your need to sell, sell, sell. You may be successful at it, but it's hard, inside, to forget where you started.

Almost as serious as the wounds to self-esteem is the damage to courtship itself. The pressure to package makes good Selection very difficult. It focuses your attention on all the wrong things. Although you are buying the goods inside, all you really have to go on in Selection is the wrapper. It's even more of a problem in courtship than in the supermarket, because in romance there is absolutely no law that requires truth in advertising.

You may realize this, but you feel unable to redirect your behavior. Proper packaging is such a heavily emphasized value in our society. You may come to love someone's true self, but if he or she looks wrong or acts oddly, you may be embarrassed about associating yourself with such an unattractive package. Unless circumstances force you to, you will not allow yourself to get into this dilemma. If a person's package is not immediately attractive to you, you will probably reject him or her out of hand. You may know intellectually that what you need is inside the package, but the social pressure to overemphasize the wrapping is very powerful.

For a more detailed discussion of the problems created by this social emphasis on status and the consequent concern of single adults that they may have to settle for second best, see *How to Stop Looking for Someone Perfect and Find Someone to Love*. It describes techniques for reorienting your thinking so you can avoid these problems in Selection.

To recap: Three attitudes interfere with your ability to make the Selection stage either comfortable or successful. They are:

- An overemphasis on Selection as the crucial stage of courtship

- An exaggerated sense of self-consciousness

- A tendency to be overly influenced by someone's ability to package himself or herself well

Most of us hope that we will miraculously avoid each of these problems. What we are hoping for is the miracle of chemistry.

The Magic of Chemistry

Before we discuss the way Selection actually works, we need to talk about the way you hope it works. There is one universal explanation for why two people get together, how they choose each other, what makes them click. We call this chemistry.

Chemistry is the elusive phenomenon we rely on to explain why that perfectly nice man who treats her better than anyone else does not excite her. "No chemistry." Chemistry accounts for his raging lust for the cold, critical brunette who will never let him relax into love, but refuses to definitively let him go.

Chemistry is the magic that makes one person exciting to you and another irrelevant. It is an awesome force in Selection, because we feel it is essential but unreliable. You must feel it to connect, but you can't control where you might feel it—or for how long.

Chemistry can mean the click that occurs when two personalities intrigue each other. It is a mutual exchange of sexual appreciation, plus a genuine liking. Chemistry is the magic of sensing the potential in someone else, an often instant awareness that you could get close to this person, drop your guard. It's a special feeling of comfort, based on no substantial interaction—just intuition. It's also a feeling of excitement that someone has come into your life who could change it forever.

A large element of chemistry is sexual arousal. In fact, some of us use chemistry as a synonym for lust. You know you're feeling that kind of chemistry when you notice that you don't especially like or admire someone, but you want him or her anyway. This is a disconcerting experience that, if repeated too frequently, leaves you despairing for your stability while impressed with your sex life.

When all the elements of chemistry are present, the lust

99

and the liking, and especially when they are mutual, you are probably headed for that most delicious life experience, falling in love. When none of these elements is present, not much is going to happen between the two of you.

So, the crucial question is: How important is chemistry? The answer is: It all depends on what you mean and how often you get the feeling.

If you mean something like the first definition—a sense of connection, liking, comfort, interest, and sexual attraction—then chemistry is essential. You do best to begin a courtship with some degree of attraction and interest, and not every available person is going to stir this.

If, on the other hand, what you mean by chemistry is an electric flash signaling *this is it!!* and an uncontrollable rush of passion, the instant dizzying connection you've read about, the glance across the crowded stadium that makes you long to run off together—well, don't hold your breath.

I'm not saying that such experiences do not occur. They most certainly do, and they are real dazzlers. This kind of chemistry occurs when you are presented with someone whose package might have been designed by your unconscious. As profoundly exciting as this experience might be, it is not the kind of chemistry that is required to have a successful courtship or to create an intimate, committed relationship. On the contrary, since courtship is, essentially, the unwrapping of the package and the exploration of its contents, this kind of chemistry can result in a vastly disillusioning experience.

On the other hand, if you've got good chemistry with a lot of the potential partners you meet, chemistry could be your sole criterion. That is, if you like a lot of people, find many of them sexy and attractive, are interested in most of those who cross your path, and find it easy to feel comfortable and relatively unguarded, then you've got lots of people to select to begin a courtship. If almost no one gives you that feeling of chemistry, you've got a problem.

If you rely entirely on the magic of chemistry, you can impede Selection more than you assist it. Some people unconsciously use chemistry as a way to avoid courtship. They feel it for all the wrong people, or in only the wrong situations. Only married people, or the boss, or exotic foreigners on winter vacations ring bells for them. Available, appropri-

100

ate partners are just "not my type." If you're stuck in this dilemma, it can leave you with a helpless feeling. You believe you need to feel chemistry, and you believe that it's impossible to control when or how you feel it.

Later in this chapter, when we discuss the psychological issue of the Selection phase, we'll try to identify where you might have a problem responding to people, and how you might overcome it. Chemistry is something you can experience more often if you can overcome your own inhibitions and anxieties. You don't have to rely on luck or a better crowd of people to inspire you.

Where Do I Go to Meet Someone?

The two questions asked most often about courtship are: Where do I go to meet someone? And how do I make contact once I'm there?

These two revealing questions point to the all-encompassing pressure to meet Mr. or Ms. Right and to your assumption that, once you do, everything will magically flow toward love. The most important questions come up *after* you've met: "What makes him back off when I get close?" "Why does she get angry when I tell her I reserve Sundays for squash?" "How can I keep him around but stall on sex?" "When should I expect to be included in the rest of her life?"

Still, the two common questions are important too. The answers have more to do with attitude and approach than with strategy and technique. It's the way you approach Selection, not where you go, that makes the difference. The more open you are to liking people, to seeing their virtues rather than their flaws, the more likely you are to be successful at Selection. The more open you are to talking with, smiling at, making contact with the world, the more possibilities for Selection the world will deliver into your lap. The more frequently you turn off your television, leave your apartment, or take a break from your office, the more likely you will be to make contact with new people. To the degree that you are willing to connect with people, the best place to meet someone is everywhere.

101

Of course, some places *are* better than others. They are not necessarily better by virtue of giving you more people from whom to choose. They are better because they are environments in which it is easier for you to have the right attitude, easier for you to be open and available, and easier for you to make better judgments about the people you are meeting.

Using this definition of a good place to meet someone, you can see why the singles places to meet are not very productive. Yes, the people are there, but you are forced into your most self-conscious, defensive, critical posture when you meet them. You feel an intense sense of competition; you are forced into your consumer mentality.

There's nothing inherently impossible about developing a serious relationship with someone you've met at a bar. I met my husband at one. I consider it a fluke in that it was during a period when I was enjoying an attack of supreme self-confidence. When you are feeling that good about yourself, it's an easy leap to enjoying most of the people around you.

But generally it's harder to feel good about yourself in an environment designed to have people treat each other impersonally and judgmentally. Unless you are feeling fabulous about yourself, sexy, alive, positive, and relaxed, skip the formal singles institutions—the bars, dances, networking parties, and special events designed to facilitate instant Selection. They don't work very well.

The best place to meet someone is in any environment that (1) helps you feel your most natural and relaxed so that you don't need to ward off everyone around you and (2) puts you into prolonged or repeated contact with new people so that you have a chance to get beyond the package.

There's some research that supports this. Psychologist Leonard Jason and associates report that the average duration of contact in singles bars is seven seconds! Their research also suggests that natural settings like beaches are more appropriate for establishing dating relationships than are formal, structured settings, like mixers or lectures.

The solution? Don't go to a bar, have a bar. Having a bar doesn't mean owning one, it means having a neighborhood hangout that is public but comfortable. It means knowing the bartender and some of the other regulars. It means being in a place where you feel that you can meet strangers while you are among friends. When you have a bar of your own, you have a place to share companionship and pleasantries. You are not desperately on edge, hoping to make a connection.

If the idea of spending time in a bar is unappealing, you have lots of alternatives that can accomplish the same task. You are looking for any situation that will provide you with the same structure the local bar does: an environment where you are comfortable within a circle of friends, but where that circle is a fluid boundary that invites new people to enter it all the time. A tight clique of friends keeps new people out. A solitary venture into the social world makes most of us feel vulnerable and anxious. The solution is to be part of a loose association that continuously introduces you to new faces. It could be the local political committee or community theater, a share in a beach house or ski house.

What makes these good situations in which to meet someone is not increased opportunity. You really have as many people to choose from in your local meat-market singles bar as you do when you are playing co-ed volleyball at the beach. The volleyball is better because you feel freer and more relaxed about noticing your opportunities and taking advantage of them.

You also may feel a bit more likely to develop something serious with one of these opportunities. Different behavior is expected when you meet someone among friends rather than in a sea of strangers.

Wherever you go to participate in Selection, you are apt to be worrying over question two: How do I go about it?

The Selection Sequence

Selection means that two people have agreed that they have enough interest in each other to deliberately meet again. This usually takes a relatively short period of time, though the range might be from minutes to months.

The classic version occurs over the space of an evening. You meet, chitchat, gauge each other's response, exchange

103

phone numbers. One of you actually calls, a date is arranged. Voilà, Selection.

The comfortable version takes more time. You meet repeatedly due to circumstance. You work together, play at the same beach, both attend choir practice. You strike up an acquaintance, then a friendship. There is some sexual interest plus some camaraderie. Eventually one of you invites the other to spend some time outside of the normal circumstances that would bring you together. A date is arranged. Voilà, Selection.

The romance-novel made-for-TV-movie version occurs instantly. He wins the Indianapolis 500, the polo championship, or the marathon. She is the beautiful but elusive movie star/princess/tycoon selected to hand him the trophy. Their eyes meet. They know. In the next scene they are making love in a stable. Voilà, Selection.

Whichever situation you are selecting in, you will have one of two roles to choose from. You can be active or passive. Usually people try for some middle ground between the two. The best option is to develop a stance that is comfortable for you and try it out. If you are not successful with it, adjust yourself up or down the scale a notch.

Male or female, if you tend to take a very passive role in Selection, you limit yourself to those who've picked you. If you are satisfied with the range of opportunity that presents itself, fine. If the only people who approach you are not those you are yearning to meet, you will have no choice but to take a more active role in signaling your interest. It's a risk, but it's a must.

Conversely if you take a very aggressive stance, coming on strongly to anyone who excites your interest, you are limiting yourself as well—by leaving out the other person. You aren't taking the time to read the other person's signals. The man who assaults a woman with his interest often turns her off. She sees him as an insensitive boob, when he may be a perfectly nice guy who is anxious. The woman who makes her interest in a man all too plain, in all too heavy-handed a fashion, sets herself up to be seen, at best, as a casual sexual partner. At worst, she is seen as desperate. In neither case does she get what she wants, the beginning of a courtship.

These men and women need to tone themselves down a

peg. Don't squelch your personality, just control your impulses. Selection is the height of coded communication. Make use of it.

No matter which two people are meeting or flirting, no matter how passively or aggressively you play your role, five events must occur in sequence in order for Selection to be successfully completed. These events were observed and described by anthropologist Timothy Perper in *Sex Signals: The Biology of Love*. Here's how it works:

- **Approach.** One person must approach, or move next to, a potential partner.

- **Turn.** The potential partner turns slightly, or looks at the person who has approached.

- **Talk.** When the turn occurs, the two people will begin a conversation. While they are talking, if Selection is to proceed they will continue to turn, gradually, until they are face to face.

- **Touch.** While the talking and turning are occurring, touching will begin. These are usually light, fleeting gestures—she touches his hand, ostensibly to make a point; he squeezes her shoulder in appreciation.

Over time, if Selection is proceeding successfully, two people will continue to talk, continue to turn toward each other, touch each other more frequently, and look more constantly at each other (as in "I only have eyes for you"). While all of this occurs, one final, rather amazing process begins:

- **Synchrony.** The two people begin to mirror each other's movements. For example, each lights a cigarette, inhales, puts it in the ashtray, leans forward, sips a drink, and leans back, all simultaneously. This synchronization, which occurs quite spontaneously, is, according to Perper, the best indicator that two people are mutually involved. The two have, for that period of time, built something of a private world.

105

The whole sequence—approach, turn, talk, touch, synchronize—can last anywhere from a few minutes to several hours. Naturally, not every approach leads to a successfully completed sequence. You know that only too well.

Each point in the Selection sequence where one person makes a move to increase his or her involvement with the other is known as an *escalator*. If he touches, however lightly, he has escalated. When she turns more on her bar stool, she is escalating. The continued success of an encounter depends entirely on how each person responds to an escalation. If he touches and she responds positively, say by turning more or touching back, chances are excellent that this pair will complete the entire sequence. If she turns to face him and he fails to continue to turn, the connection probably will dissolve, and Selection will not be accomplished.

It seems quite commonsensical. You may not have been able to analyze this precise sequence of events, but you certainly know intuitively that you are making a stronger connection if someone turns, looks fully at you, and touches you.

This analysis of the mechanics of Selection will probably leave you with two questions: Why does it work this way? What can I do to guarantee more frequent positive responses?

Perper provides an elaborate discussion of why the sequence works in the way it does. You might wish to refer to his book for a complete explanation. It's important here to note that this observable sequence is presumed to be an outward expression of each person's internal feelings. Two people do not turn and touch because they know that it's the next appropriate thing to do. They turn and touch because they are feeling something, some arousal, interest, sense of connection, warmth, and they turn or touch to express these feelings. This is not meant to be a description of a mechanical process, at which you can improve your skills. It is the outward description of an emotional unfolding that you might appreciate more, or feel more comfortable with, if you are more sensitive to it.

This begins to address your second question: What can I do to guarantee more successful responses?

Some of you would like to handle your anxiety by having some surefire "scientific" techniques on which to rely. It's a false comfort. The effect of consciously trying to synchro-

106

nize your movements to someone else's can only make you feel a bit more foolish and awkward than you might already feel. When you are concentrating on technique, you are not listening to your intuition, not sensing another person's responsiveness, not allowing your feelings to be your guide. Your internal information during Selection, your sense of timing and spontaneity, is your most important tool. Don't put anything in the way of listening to yourself.

That having been said, some conclusions drawn from Perper's research may be useful in helping you complete the Selection process more successfully. The first is that more than half the time women initiate the approach. This means that they physically put themselves next to a man who interests them. They are also often the escalator—for example, touching first or turning more first. Women can use this information to give themselves a lot of permission to approach. It is a relatively low-risk action, at least as compared to, say, asking for the first date. A willingness to approach gives you more control over the pool of people you have from which to complete Selection.

Second, Perper points out that the sequence's successful completion depends not simply on sending verbal and nonverbal signals, but on how "intense" those signals are, how intense they appear to the potential partner, and how "intense" that potential partner needs them to be. This could make you crazy. He might feel that "Can I buy you a drink?" is simple politeness (i.e., a low intensity signal), while she might hear it as a pushy, brash attempt to monopolize her time (i.e., a very high-intensity signal). We are once again demonstrating the difficulties of coded communication that play such a frustrating role in courtship.

Conversely, she might turn to welcome the drink but turn away in an attempt to appear casual. This low-intensity signal might not be enough of a response to reassure a man who needs a stronger signal to proceed. He drifts away, feeling unappreciated.

All of this confusion seems to illustrate two points.

First, it is further support for the central courtship maxim, *Don't take it personally*. It is so easy to take someone's response personally, to assume that she turned away because she noticed your bald spot, or he drifted away because he

107

saw someone prettier. These are the kind of foolish and self-destructive projections that can make the Selection stage an ordeal.

The second point is more crucial. As Perper suggests, and, as you may have already experienced, many more approaches end in failure than in success. Failures to connect are frequent in the Selection stage for reasons as complicated and varied as there are people. What's important is to determine how your own failures affect you.

These inevitable failures can create the central challenge of the Selection stage of courtship, namely, how you handle rejection.

Fear of Rejection

Rejection can be defined very simply: Someone you want doesn't want you. It's one of life's lousiest experiences. At best it hurts, it's embarrassing, and it makes you angry. At worst it is a devastating psychological blow that is permanently crippling. Every time you straighten your tie before the door opens to reveal your blind date or check for lipstick on your teeth before you brace yourself to make a party entrance, you are probably coping with your fear of rejection.

If you are interested in beginning a courtship, it's impossible to avoid rejection. You are in the business of selecting strangers. Some of them are not going to respond. It's going to hurt. The problem is not that rejection exists in courtship. The problem is how you handle it.

The best indication of how much your fear of rejection interferes with your ability to Select potential partners is to scrutinize your actual behavior. Your fear of rejection is interfering too much if:

- You wouldn't think of approaching an attractive man or woman you noticed at a party. You'd be far more likely to stay on the sidelines and admire from afar. You limit your courtships to those who approach you.

- You rely on drugs or alcohol to loosen up enough to talk to strangers.

- You tend to stick with a group of buddies and actively avoid meeting new people. You'd probably turn down an invitation to a party because "I won't know anyone."

- You refuse to try a new game or sport for fear of looking foolish. In fact, you are inhibited in lots of social situations because you worry about appearing silly or incompetent.

- As soon as you do meet someone, you go into a dreadful panic. You begin to obsess. Should you call? Will you seem too available? What should you wear? Should you have sex? Is it too soon, is it too late? The beginning of a courtship is agony because you are sure you will mess it up and get rejected. Eventually, you do get yourself rejected, just to put yourself out of your misery.

- You can't bring yourself to walk into a bar or a party unless you feel perfect. If you gain five pounds, you'd rather not leave the house. Oddly, you frequently find yourself going on a binge just enough to add the five pounds and keep you from going out into the world.

- You conduct intense love affairs, but they mostly occur in your fantasy life. There's a terrifically interesting woman in your MBA evening class, or an incredible man whose path you cross every lunchtime at the coffee shop. You put a lot of energy into thinking about him or her, noticing small details of dress and behavior. You make elaborate plans for a conversation, an accidental encounter. They never occur, but there's a lot of excitement in just the imagining. In the meantime, you have a few dates with other people who come along. None of them really interests you.

Fear of rejection is not exclusively the problem of shy people. It can incapacitate even gregarious men and women. If many of the above patterns of behavior sound like ones you've been stuck in, you are probably significantly inhibited by your fear.

The most painful part of fear of rejection is the way it feels. You suffer wincing inhibition that can give you unaccountably clammy hands, cause you to utter a horrified "I could never!" when you imagine asking for a phone number. Fear of rejection makes it impossible to walk up to someone who mesmerizes you and introduce yourself.

Sometimes it's not that panicky, apprehensive feeling. Instead, you may experience the opposite of anxiety—namely, a depressed apathy that makes you feel it's not worth the bother to leave the house. You may be listless, too tired to exert yourself to socialize after work, or too overwhelmed with life's maintenance to plan fun. You may be binge-eating, getting high, or drinking yourself into a moderate buzz, all to blot out your discomfort with yourself and the world. This entire range of feeling, from anxious to apathetic, can be an expression of your fear of rejection.

Fear of rejection also sponsors thoughts like these: "I'm not attractive enough." "I won't be able to think of anything to say." "I'm dressed all wrong." "He/she would never be interested." "I can't compete here—I'm too old, too young, too dull, too anything. . . ." You'll notice that the majority of thoughts that reflect fear of rejection are self-deprecating. You just aren't good enough.

These negative, self-hating thoughts are what we've come to describe as poor self-esteem or insecurity. They can be so overwhelming that you never venture beyond the realm of your safe network of friends and family. The notion you've probably read about, that you need to love yourself before anyone can love you, or that you need to feel good about yourself in order to feel good about anyone else, has direct application here in the Selection stage. In order to feel confident enough to approach someone, you must feel good about yourself.

There is another set of negative thoughts that reflect, less directly, the fear of rejection. These thoughts involve putting down the people around you instead of disparaging yourself. They include things like "Oh, she'd be attractive if she wasn't

110

wearing so much makeup," "There's no one here worth talking to," "All the men here look so wimpy," "All the women here are so shallow." You get the strategy, right? Reject them before they can reject you. It's the psychological equivalent of "the best defense is a good offense" when what you are defending against is your fear of rejection.

Be careful not to draw the conclusion that, if you have either of these negative thought patterns, you automatically have a self-esteem problem. Everyone has these kinds of negative thoughts, at one time or another and to some degree or another. The key word is degree. How much and how often do these thoughts get in your way?

When rejection occurs, most people cope in the usual way. You call your friends, tell them the gruesome tale, take to your bed, and administer strong doses of whatever you use to escape: television, drugs, music, food, alcohol, romance novels. If it only lasts a night or two and if you have the self-confidence to try again next weekend, you're OK. You've managed to find a way to cope with rejection. It hurts, but it doesn't devastate you.

Others are not so fortunate. If you're in this group, you find even the possibility of being turned down a horror. You feel you must avoid it at all costs. You haven't yet developed an ability to cope with rejection. When it does occur, you suffer for months or years. You're still smarting over a man who said he'd call four months ago and never did. You remember for weeks the woman who told you to get lost. And a speech that started "I like you, but" could stop you in your romantic tracks for an entire season. You let rejection knock you right out of the game.

Permitting yourself to be devastated by rejection is like standing in your own way. The potential for rejection is never going to go away as long as you are participating in courtship. It's a built-in part of the ritual. What *can* go away is your incapacitating fear of it. Your goal is to reduce your fear of rejection to the point where you are able to increase the number of approaches you make. That's all.

You can't eliminate this anxiety altogether. Like each of the other varieties of the fear of intimacy, some degree of anxiety over rejection is an inescapable part of courtship. You just need to lower yours to the point where it is tolerable.

111

Rx: Make It Safe to Take a Risk

Take this business of overcoming a fear seriously. It's a challenge from you to you. Your goal is not simply to start a romance. It is the larger personal goal of freeing yourself from one of the psychological limitations that has interfered with your happiness. We all have them. Developing as a person is largely a matter of pushing past your individual barriers and getting on new psychological ground. Yes it's work, and yes it can be scary. But the reward is opening your life to an infinite set of possibilities.

If your barrier is a personal fear that other people will reject you and hurt you, think what your life will be like when you reduce that fear. You'll be able to enjoy the social world, be free to approach when you choose and to withdraw when it appeals to you. You won't be plagued with the constant awareness of how other people might be judging you. You won't really care. You'll feel comfortable in many different social groups and atmospheres. You won't have to worry about making a fool of yourself in a new situation because it won't matter if you do. Best of all, your romances won't be such potentially lethal weapons because they'll lose some of their power to hurt you. If he stops calling after the third date, you'll remember not to take it personally. If she breaks up with you in favor of someone older and richer, you'll be able to be philosophical where once you were suicidal.

If you hold onto your fear of rejection, what you'll have is anxiety. If you take the risk of letting it go, what you'll have is fun. To reduce the disability caused by your fears, make it safer to take a risk. You can do that in a variety of ways.

First, make yourself conscious of your fear. Identify it, label it, and confront it. If you have overtly panicky feelings, this will require no great leap. You already know you are suffering.

But many of us don't recognize our fear of rejection. When you are feeling depressed or apathetic, it's easy to miss the fact that what you really feel is afraid. You focus all your energy on Someday. You figure that you aren't anxious, you're just waiting until you finish up at Nautilus, or get a great job, or write the prize-winning novel.

You could free up a great deal of energy if you faced the fear today, instead of trying to ensure ideal conditions that would protect you from rejection. You see, this protection is largely a fantasy. If you are going to be a part of the world of love, sex, and romance, you are going to get your feelings hurt. We all do. We live.

That last part is most important. We all live. No one ever died from a stranger who wasn't interested. Usually it's not nearly as devastating as you fear it will be. The problem is that if you spend your life avoiding rejection, you never learn that you can survive it.

Next, you have to act to face down your fears. This means you have to put yourself in social situations where you have a possibility of being rejected. In the language of Selection, you'll need to initiate some approaches. When you've decided you are ready to take this on, give yourself a break. Put yourself in settings in which you feel most comfortable meeting new people. Do you do better hosting a party or being a guest? Are you more comfortable surrounded by friends or totally on your own without an audience?

You'll need to take an active role in creating opportunities that are best for you. "Most comfortable" does not mean easy. Selection isn't easy for everyone. It just doesn't have to be impossible.

Your next goal is to ease up on the negative thoughts you have about yourself so that you can reduce your anxiety enough to act. Don't wait around until you aren't anxious at all. If you are alive, you are a little bit anxious about something!

There are a variety of techniques, designed primarily by cognitive therapists, to get a handle on your inhibiting negative thoughts. You might read Philip Zimbardo's very thorough book, *Shyness*. He's done more work on this problem than anyone.

You are ready to act. You are naturally scared. After all, most of your energy has been directed toward avoiding the very situations you are now plunging into. It's OK to feel scared. It's just not in your interests to let your fear stand in the way of taking this risk.

Here's an assignment. Gather as many rejections as you possibly can. Set a goal for any given evening. Let's say you are going to a party where you know very few people, or it's Wednesday night and you've decided to take yourself to the local singles bar. Before you leave, set a goal of, say, three rejections. This means you must initiate the Selection sequence and approach at least three potential partners, each of whom does not respond warmly.

Actually, in order to reach your goal of three rejections, you will probably have to make more than three approaches. You can't guarantee that each will reject you. If he or she does respond positively, you will have to move on until you've met your quota. Some of my patients have had to approach seven or eight people before they could reach their goal. Persevere. It's important that you go out and get rejected and live to tell the tale.

Beyond sheer bodies, there are no restrictions in this assignment. You achieve your goal as long as you approach and get rejected by someone who might be a partner. Don't bother to screen beyond that. Rejections count if you get them from the most gorgeous creature in the room or from the little mouse in the corner. Try to get rejected by the widest possible pool of candidates. You will have the interesting experience of discovering that you can't always rely on being rejected, even from people you deem the most likely.

You won't automatically lose your fear of rejection once you pass beyond the Selection stage of courtship. But as you move closer to love and intimacy, your fears should be quieted. Intimacy depends on trusting that your relationship with your partner is secure.

Eventually you will select a partner, whether haplessly or deliberately. When you do, you've begun courtship.

6

Pursuit

Congratulations. You've made a Selection and you're in Pursuit.

You were probably hoping that what you'd be in was love, or that you'd be leaning in that direction. You may at least insist that you be in heat. Rock bottom, you may have been willing to select someone out of a sheer inability to say no. However you identify your emotional state, what you've actually fallen into is the Pursuit phase of courtship.

The process of Pursuit is just what it sounds like: One person acts to narrow the emotional distance and the other person reacts.

The intricacy of Pursuit revolves around the need for both people to feel comfortable with the degree of attachment they develop. This can be a difficult business. You'd like to open up, but what if she or he uses the information against you? You'd like to get sexually involved, but what if you get too attached, too vulnerable? You'd like to spend more time, but what if the other person takes that to mean more than you intend? You think you're in love, or at least infatuated, but this time you refuse to allow yourself to go beserk. You've been hurt before, how can you trust someone new? You'd like to simply say, "I know this is crazy, but I love you already," but isn't this a guarantee that you'll scare the other person off?

All of these conflicting uncertainties and threats to your emotional well-being make the process of Pursuit a cautious one. Frankly, you'd like to skip this whole stage. You'd love to be able to know, at the moment of Selection, that there's something serious going on here.

In most courtships, we feel the full ambivalence of Pursuit. Pursuit is sometimes passionate, sometimes a dead bore,

117

sometimes a flattering source of comfort, and sometimes an unnerving assault on your self-esteem. What makes Pursuit so peculiar is that the very same courtship can offer you all of these extremes and more.

Fear of rejection, which might cripple your ability to Select and therefore begin courtship, is also a major factor in the way you will handle Pursuit. In order to play the role of pursuer, you must risk rejection. There's no way to avoid it.

This hard truth is such anathema that some people will make every effort to pursue in a way that eliminates the risk of rejection. How? They try to pursue and keep it a secret.

On the face of it, this defies logic. How can you indicate your interest in someone and keep it a secret at the same time? You can't but you can pretend to. Some of you choose exactly this strategy, inventing elaborate excuses for your invitations. (''I just happen to have these tickets.'' ''We need an even number at the dinner.'' ''I was in the neighborhood, so I . . .'') You are trying to protect yourself from rejection. How can someone reject you when you weren't even interested in the first place?

It doesn't work. Pursuit is just what it says it is. The object of your attention will probably get the message, however coded. You will feel just as rejected, however disguised your interest.

There is nothing desperate or undignified about a direct expression of interest. In fact, it's rather sexy. A simple statement—''I want to spend some time with you,'' ''I'd love to get to know you,'' or ''I find you so attractive, I'd like to see more of you''—is the mark of a self-confident person. Try it. Risk it. It will give you a very good feeling about yourself. It will also free up all the energy you are currently expending trying to think up cute one-liners or clever repartee.

Your fear of rejection will largely determine how much and how quickly you need a positive response in order to continue your pursuit. There is no perfect way to know when you should keep trying and when you should give up. If you are not getting the response you'd hoped for, consider interrupting the enterprise rather than abandoning it. Back off for a few weeks. Don't call. Disappear. Then initiate contact again. This won't ensure a positive response. But it will keep you in the game without being so interested, or so available, that you devalue yourself.

Classic Pursuit

The classic model of Pursuit might also be called the Ninety-Day Wonder. In fact, Pursuit usually lasts from several hours (they call it true love, I call it very ready) to about three months. In the classic model, Pursuit begins with Seduction, which involves one person (usually the male) coming closer, showing interest, making sexual overtures, while the other person (usually the female) is either backing off or holding her ground. He is calling, touching, complimenting, showing his feelings. She is a bit cool, noncommittal, and possibly sexually withholding. When she maintains this degree of distance, she makes it more comfortable for him to pursue. He has come closer but she has not, so he's still safe.

Eventually, if the courtship is to continue, she starts moving closer too. Perhaps she expresses it by being willing to become sexually involved. Perhaps she simply tells him her feelings. Maybe she begins to make plans that express her expectations. Whatever form it takes, he gets the message. She is now closer to him, more attached. She is available to proceed even further.

How does he handle all the anxiety this might stir up, all the ambivalence? No matter what motivated him to get into this courtship, whether it was pure sexual arousal or a fervent hope for a wife and children, he'll probably have *some* anxiety, *some* ambivalent feelings. It is simply the nature of courtship. Naturally, there's only one thing he can do. He backs off. He reestablishes some degree of distance, some lessening of attachment. He initiates the second part of Pursuit: The Switch. Suddenly, the roles are reversed, the power balance shifts. She is pursuing, he is less available. She hates it. Actually, so does he.

Because, in the classic Pursuit, he's in the role of pursuer, he is the one mostly likely to initiate The Switch. For the sake of simplicity, the rest of this section is written describing the sex roles of courtship traditionally.

119

Of course, today the sex roles of courtship are a blur. It's one of the confusions that prevents your learning the simple rules of the ritual we discussed in chapter 1. The truth is, she might be pursuing and he might be resisting. She may even be pressing for sexual intimacy, while he is demurring because he isn't ready. It's certainly true that women often initiate The Switch.

In many courtships the role of pursuer and pursued are exchanged with each date. Each person might advance a bit, set a limit somewhere else. She might set sexual limits, but make all the time in the world available. He might pursue sex, but ration the time he's available to see her. So keep all these possibilities in mind as you read on. The next two sections, Seduction and The Switch, are meant to help you get courtship off to a running start.

Falling in Love

You might have assumed that a book about courtship would have a great deal to say about falling in love. After all, to fall in love is possibly the most powerful experience one could have with another person. We long for it, and we assume that courtship is our passport to it.

Instead it appears that the purpose of courtship is to bind two people into a firmly loving and committed couple. Along the way, some of these couples enjoy that emotionally intense, all-consuming, time-limited experience of falling in love.

If you are many dates into Pursuit and you have not yet fallen in love, you may be tempted to cut your courtship off right here. At the least, you are apt to be feeling disappointed. It's true that a courtship that begins with falling in love is a very special one. It has special assets and special problems.

The magic of falling in love is that you both feel as though you've automatically reached commitment. You two are so instantly close that you fuse. You read each other's thoughts, finish each other's sentences.

Your intimacy was achieved without the negotiation, struggle, anger, or compromise that usually accompany courtship. It just happened. In this sense falling in love is more wonderful than anything real life has to offer. You two are existing in a private world of your own creation. You are transformed. You are also probably having an unsurpassed sexual feast. You can't get enough of each other. You never knew it could be like this.

One of the great benefits of falling in love is that you get to speed through the early stages of courtship. These couples breeze through the briefest Pursuit, pausing only to make Seduction memorable and romantic. They often get to skip The Switch entirely. As you'll learn in chapter 6, The Switch is an adjustment to intimacy. It's stirred by the fear of entrapment. A couple falling in love is temporarily excused from any entrapment fears. They've gone beyond entrapment—they are entirely engulfed in each other. They feel as one.

Later all the issues of separation, individuality, and personality differences, which are waiting on the sidelines, will reappear. Negotiation for the couple falling in love can be particularly fierce. The contrast between real life and early romance is a bitter pill.

Yes, falling in love is a magical, momentous life event, all too rare. No, it's not necessarily true love. Couples who "know" instantly, who rearrange their lives with joyful abandon in order to accommodate each other, are having a unique experience. But they are no further on the road of developing real love than those who are more cautious. You don't have to fall in love in the first week in order to love someone. You don't have to think "This is it," the first time you kiss in order to find true love. True love is created. The bells only get the creation off to a fast start.

The important question is not how much love there is at the beginning of a courtship, but how much there is at the end.

PURSUIT

Seduction

They were introduced at a charity telethon. "Val, I'd like you to meet Alexander Whitefeather."

Val: What a beautiful name.

Alex: If you like it, you can have it.

Val and Alex left Val's bed two months later just long enough to get married. She says they married because "When you know it's the real thing, what else can you do?" He says they married because they wanted to announce to the rest of the world the importance of their feelings for each other. I say they married because when you are experiencing the excesses of love that can accompany the Seduction stage of courtship, you are moved to extravagant gestures.

♥   ♥   ♥

Michael, thirty-six, asked Renata, thirty-six, for her phone number after a half hour of chatting at a single-professionals function. Their first date was dinner and a movie, but somehow they ended up talking half the night at her apartment. Several dates followed, with Michael growing more and more interested. He had never had conversations like this with anyone. Renata was so bright, so intense. He couldn't wait to be with her, and he couldn't wait to touch her. Renata was more guarded. She liked Michael but she was skeptical. He was calling all the time, wanting to be with her. She finally told him that his eagerness bothered her, that she needed to go slower. He took it with pretty good grace. He cut down on his phone calls, but he let his interest be known loud and clear. Michael told Renata that he was a man who wanted a relationship. He felt ready for a wife and maybe a child.

Renata was torn. On the one hand, here was this perfectly nice, relatively attractive, single, available man who, oddly enough, seemed to want her. What was the matter with her? Why wasn't she happy, excited? Does she, as her therapist has been hinting, really run away from available men? Or is Michael not what he appears? After all, he's thirty-six and never been married. (Neither has she, but she still wonders about his reasons.) And, while he's not unattractive, his looks don't really fit her picture. All in all, she decides she doesn't know how she feels so she'll "give him a chance." Renata is approaching Michael by inches. As long as she does, Michael feels comfortable pursuing wholeheartedly.

♥   ♥   ♥

Martin is a forty-one-year-old salesman. He is quick, witty, with a passion for old cars and older movies. Martin loves women, but he feels he's loved enough of them now to want to marry one.

Every morning when Martin leaves for work he passes Lisa, who is walking to her office. He describes Lisa as "absolutely adorable" and quickly decides to give chase. They smile as they pass and Martin begins a few, short, innocuous conversations ("Do you believe this weather?"). Lisa responds in kind, with a twin smile, eye contact, and a willingness to walk a block or two in synchrony. Selection is completed. Seduction begins.

One morning Martin says, "Look, I'd like to get to know you. How about dinner?" "Why?" Lisa wants to know. "Because I think you're cute," Martin responds. Lisa pauses and delivers a rejection. "That's not a good enough reason," she says. She walks away.

Most pursuers would be cowed at this point. Martin is enjoying himself. They start to cross paths around town, on the street, at the grocery, in the video store. Each time they meet, there's pleasant conversation, initiated by Martin, who swears that he is so charming in these encounters even he can't believe it.

Finally, Martin reissues his invitation. "Look, about a month ago I asked you out and you said no. I feel you've had a little time to get to know me now, and you can see that I'm not a rapist or some insane person. So unless you find me grotesquely ugly, how about it?" Lisa explains herself a bit. She's seeing someone, not living with him, but she's very involved. Thanks anyway.

Martin goes into high gear. He must get a date with this woman. He flirts a bit more directly. "You know," he smiles, "I wait around every morning just hoping that you'll pass by." That's a difficult compliment for Lisa to ignore. She's interested despite her situation. Martin follows up with an offer. "There's a new Woody Allen movie I'd enjoy seeing with you. We can go just as friends, or it can be a date, whatever you're comfortable with. I think it would be fun." He gives Lisa his phone number and tells her to think it over and call whenever she feels like it, no strings attached.

Martin was betting Lisa would call. He saw her with the guy she's going with. His description was succinct. "Skinny, losing his hair, not as cute as me. They look like they are dragging through the where-are-we-going, should-we-live-together stage. I'm offering a little romance. She won't be able to resist." She calls and they begin to date.

♥   ♥   ♥

When we say Seduction, do you think of music, cognac, candlelight, and cleverly transparent clothing? Do you envision a woman who will take the cigarette from between your lips, draw on it, and then murmur that she wishes it were you? Are you hoping that the man you've been staring at across the restaurant will fling his napkin aside, nibble on the base of your thumb, and whisper that he has to have you?

If so, you'll be a bit disappointed with this chapter. Generally speaking, the Seduction stage of courtship is slightly less dramatic than you've been anticipating—less dramatic, but no less exhilarating.

Seduction includes that entire period in which one person is trying to entice the other into a more intimate connection. Part of the task of Seduction is to define the relationship as either platonic or romantic. This is accomplished by establishing sexual intimacy, whether through an instantaneous leap into bed when the time is right, or a gradual, ever-increasing, oh-so-slowly-drawn-out series of physical intimacies. As you can see in the previous examples, the emotional tone of Seduction varies. It ranges from only the mildest interest ("She seems all

124

right. Nothing special.'') to the purest excitement (''This is it. I'm in love.'').

Your emotional connection is most often tender and fragile. Yesterday you were aroused, intrigued. Today a poorly timed gesture or graceless compliment on the part of your new partner and you are emotionally flat for hours or days.

During Seduction, the tentativeness of most couples' connection is expressed by their limited expectations. Two people in this stage cannot assume that they will necessarily be together Saturday night, not to mention, God forbid, New Year's Eve. Generally, Seduction requires some formal invitation in order to ensure time together in the future. One person initiates this contact, and the other person agrees to it. This is known, in the Western world, as ''making a date.''

The First Four Dates

In a sense these early dates are an extension of the process of Selection. Your purpose is to answer this question: Who is this person and is he or she worth my time?

If you answered the latter question affirmatively when you made your Selection (''Of course, this is worth my time. Look at those dimples!''), then the first dates will be an attempt to get the other person interested in you.

In either case, you spend the first few dates assessing chemistry, the invisible signal that this Seduction should be furthered. This signal depends on two factors: conversation and physical attraction.

Easy conversation with a stranger over a several-hour period is one key element in the desire to further Seduction. She is magically comfortable and chatty. Miraculously he seems to find her witty and informative. Even more astonishingly, she responds similarly. They are halfway there.

To handle the strains of conversation, many of us have developed a standard repartee to cover the first few dates. Some have prepackaged this aspect of early Pursuit to an enormous degree. Remember Nathan (of the first-date-uniform strategy) who said that he had his first dates down so pat that he could ''turn them in without showing up''?

125

He's describing the boredom of repeating to new women his story: The where-I'm-from-where-I-work-what-I-like-to-do-what-I-thought-of-that-movie conversation that occupies the hour and a half over that first dinner. It is difficult to maintain a fresh approach to Seduction, especially if you've had a lot of experience with it. In fact, the boredom that accompanies this repetition is one of the motivating factors for furthering courtship.

Besides conversation, the other half of chemistry is a tingling feeling in some sensitive private part of your body. These two elements are, unfortunately, highly independent. All of us have known the irony of enjoying wonderful conversational rapport with someone for whom we feel not the slightest sexual tug. Or worse, we get caught in the somewhat embarrassing awareness that we feel overwhelming lust for a creature with whom we cannot conduct even the briefest conversation.

Beyond the chemistry of easy conversation, a couple uses the first few dates (or the first few minutes) to experience the pull of physical attraction. If you feel it, the next job is to let each other know. Letting someone know that you're sexually interested is an erotic pleasure, but it has its risks. Some of us rush directly to it, some of us approach it with agonizing caution. Most people take a middle-of-the-road approach. They use a verbal and nonverbal code.

The nonverbal code is a matter of initiating and responding to a variety of physical moves. You are reaching out to touch, hold, or caress your date, or you are keeping yourself apart. You are responding to casual contact in a positive, prolonging way, or you are shying away from it. Each of you is carefully reading the other's approaches and responses. If your reading is in the direction you'd hoped, you are starting to have a very good time.

The other way a couple signals sexual interest is in the subjects they talk about. Second and third dates tend to reflect, by the content of the conversation, the slight increase in intimacy that is developing. The focus shifts from things (his job, her job, the movies, politics) to people and feelings (his past love life, her former marriage, his thoughts about sex and love, her thoughts about passion and commitment).

126

This move to more personal material sets the stage for physical closeness.

At this point a couple still tends to stay away from the here-and-now ("Who else are you dating now?" "Does he have more money?" "Does she have a better body?"). But these issues come up in philosophical discussions of love and sex or possibly in an exploration of each other's past relationships.

The Sexual Watershed

If your courtship has progressed to the fourth date, *something* is happening. Very few of us will invest more than two or three evenings with someone in whom we feel no interest.

The fourth date, whether it takes one week or more than a month to achieve, signals interest and possibility. Usually, the primary possibility at this point is sex.

It's easy to be confused about the courtship process here. The possibility of a sexual relationship raises three issues: *desire, morality*, and *limit setting*. The first two usually receive a great deal of attention, while the third is often misunderstood.

By the fourth date each of you knows whether or not you feel sexual desire. Many of you decided in the first fifteen minutes. Some people are more willing to let lust develop. Whichever is your style, by now you know if you are aroused. Your question is when and whether you'll act on it.

Morality plays a role in that decision. Your personal ethical code might be as simple as, "If it feels good—do it." It might be as restrictive as prohibiting sexual intimacy before marriage.

The biggest issue in the decision to become sexually intimate is limit setting. Remember, during Seduction one person is pursuing and the other is defining the boundaries. Sexual intimacy is a main arena of limit setting. The decision to become lovers is not just whether you have the desire, or feel morally justified. It's a decision about whether it is emotionally and physically safe to change the limits of this relationship.

127

Therefore, assuming traditional sex roles, at about the fourth date each partner is conducting an internal dialogue.

He is adding up their previous physical contact, assessing the possibilities. Is it too soon? Should I make my move? Will she invite me to her place after dinner? Should I invite her here? What will she be like? He's excited.

She is thinking—The question is going to come up tonight. How do I want to handle it? If I say yes, is it too soon? Should I go to his place so I can be the one to leave in the morning? Wouldn't I rather be at my place where I feel more comfortable? How can I ask him if he's healthy? What's the best way to tell him I want to wait? If I announce it over dinner, I'll feel presumptuous. If I tell him after we've started something, I'll feel like a teenager. What if I never hear from him again?

You'll notice that she does about twice the obsessing that he does. This is as it should be. He is in Pursuit, she is setting the limits. She has more to think about. If the roles were reversed, he'd be equally cautious.

At this point you are answering the crucial courtship question: What are we going to be to each other—friends or lovers?

Before you make love, you have any one of a number of possible connections to each other—strangers, aquaintances, friends, colleagues, tennis partners—all of which can mean anything or nothing vis-à-vis romance. After you make love, you are lovers.

You have all the rest of courtship to determine what being lovers is going to mean, but for most of us it means something. Lover is a defined role in someone's life. It comes with feelings, hopes, vulnerability. It is definitely accompanied by expectations, though the nature of these is not always shared by both partners. Furthermore, sexual intimacy is an escalation from which two people find it difficult to retreat. After he has spent the night, it's almost impossible to end the next date with a kiss at the door. After you've made love, it's hard to maintain the posture that you are just friends with no rights or prerogatives to each other's time and attention. The feelings of sexual interest propel courtship. Acting on these feelings changes that courtship forever.

The fourth date is not an arbitrary time nor is it universally

128

significant. It is likely that concern over AIDS will change this figure dramatically. Many people will delay sexual intercourse indefinitely, or at least significantly reduce the number of partners who might be considered potential lovers. At present, the fourth date is typically the moment when physical intimacy is initiated, if it has not begun before.

Physical intimacy does not necessarily include sexual intercourse, though that's a strong possibility if your age, attitude, morals, comfort with your body, and feelings of attraction encourage it. Physical intimacy on the fourth date might simply involve touching, holding hands, or kissing. It's not the consummation that is important but the initiation and the indication of feeling.

The fourth date is not a hard-and-fast rule for sexual intimacy. It's more of a consensus from the single adults with whom I've worked. There are many exceptions. Yes, there are still lots of men and women who become sexually involved almost instantaneously. But they often report that these affairs fail to evolve into full-blown courtships. They tend to remain one-night stands, though that might not have been what both partners had hoped for.

The reason that very early sexual connections frequently fail to progress further is that sometimes after sexual conquest the person who was pursuing tends to back off a little. If there has been some emotional investment, it helps the pursuer to return. When he pulls back from a woman who is still a stranger, there's very little invested to encourage him to return. Oddly, great sex is not always enough to keep a courtship going.

On the other hand, there are many men, and even more women, who would not consider becoming sexually intimate with someone they had known for a mere four dates. Some of these are people who believe that sex before marriage is morally wrong. Of course this group will still need to make the psychological transition from platonic to romantic. Even if they are morally constrained to limit their physical intimacies, they will still kiss, touch, and hold each other to define themselves as romantic partners.

Other people have different reasons for taking a bit longer, especially these days. There appears to be a cultural shift away from the early, "easy" sex of the 1970s. This shift is

129

attributed partly to the growing concern over disease and partly to a growing disillusionment with casual sexual encounters. Single adults today express a need for more meaning, more connection, more caring in their sexual experiences. They also need to feel safer about their partners.

Whereas five years ago you might have gone to bed immediately, now many of you are holding back. You both want some return on your investment of vulnerability. You are looking to establish a substantial relationship, and you sense that making love may prematurely raise the emotional ante before you are ready to handle it.

Perhaps you are no longer interested, or never were interested, in sleeping with someone who is not important to you. Maybe you've done a lot of that, and you're over it. Maybe a voice within screams, "wrong wrong wrong!" Maybe you're constrained by the possibilities of disease or deception. It will be especially true for you, then, that physical intimacy marks some very important advance in your courtship. You may insist on delaying your full sexual involvement until you have a relationship. One woman put it very simply: "I'm not going to bed with anyone anymore until I know I can depend on him."

For the sake of understanding the big picture, let's reiterate that sexual intimacy is a part of Seduction and that after it occurs, something changes. You can't prevent the change from occurring by delaying sex indefinitely. You can only set up a climate where you feel more comfortable handling it.

Sexual Anxiety: The Challenge of Seduction

You might be among the many for whom sex is a joy. If you are, Seduction will probably be one of your favorite parts of courtship. If, on the other hand, you are not so sexually at ease, Seduction will be one of your challenges.

Sexual anxiety is a tough fear to understand intuitively. We can all appreciate the fear of rejection—rejection hurts. But sex feels good, and it can make you feel very good about yourself and toward someone else. Why should it also make some of us so uncomfortable that we'd really rather skip the whole thing?

The answer is found in understanding the risks that sex represents for some people. These risks go far beyond the fear of disease, though that is certainly an increasing contributor to sexual anxiety. Sexual intimacy represents a tremendous emotional risk. For some people, it's just not a risk worth taking.

The emotional risks arise in two areas: the sex act itself and its possible consequences.

Our society has come a long way in making people feel better about and more comfortable with the act of sex. But that doesn't mean that you as an individual might not have a feeling which, succinctly stated, means, "Oh, no, do I have to?"

That is, Do I have to get undressed in front of this stranger? Will I be good enough? Will I have to perform? Will he think I'm experienced enough? What if I can't get it up? . . . The dreadful, anxious thoughts go on and on. The act of making love involves exposing yourself physically and emotionally. Some people feel distinctly uncomfortable contemplating such exposure.

If you are just a bit anxious, but you have enough experience and/or desire, you'll probably go ahead when you feel the time is right, despite your sexual inhibitions. You may adopt the "hold-your-nose-and-get-this-over-with" approach to the first sexual encounter with a new person. That's not so bad. You won't experience the mad, abandoned passion you'd like to feel, but some people are just too inhibited to let go early with a stranger. Over time, you will relax and enjoy your partner more. Your anxieties are real but they are also temporary.

If your sexual anxieties are more severe, you are likely to avoid even the possibility of an encounter. You might have an experience similar to Phyllis's.

Phyllis, thirty-two, and Adam, twenty-eight, have been close friends for a year, living in the same apartment building. At the time they met, Adam was involved with someone else. As that relationship began to dissolve, Adam started spending time with Phyllis. They would rent videos together

131

and use Phyllis's VCR, keep each other company at the laundromat, that kind of thing.

Adam thought Phyllis was terrific, like a sister. Phyllis thought Adam would be the quintessential lover, but she didn't dare admit it. She fantasized about him endlessly, but she never felt she could approach him sexually because "it might ruin our friendship."

Phyllis dated other men, but never more than one or two dates each. She said they didn't interest her. What she meant was that she'd rather be with Adam.

Phyllis is uncomfortable with the loss of control sex requires. She is not a virgin, but her sexual experiences have not been especially extensive or satisfying. She's ashamed of her lack of sexual responsiveness. It makes her feel "not normal." In fact, her platonic affair with Adam is a plus. It provides her with all the companionship and warmth she hungers for, plus it's safe. As long as she "doesn't want to ruin the friendship," she can stay involved without confronting her own sexual fears.

Like Phyllis, you might have some difficulty being fully conscious of your own sexual anxiety. The pressures in our culture to feel comfortable with sex are very great. We are free to admit many fears and shortcomings and expect support. You can tell your best friend that you cheated on your taxes, your résumé, or your ex-wife and expect a sympathetic hearing. But tell someone you don't like sex, and you are apt to raise an eyebrow.

The simplest way to handle a fear that is not socially acceptable is to deny its existence, even to yourself. If you fake your orgasms well enough, even you will be convinced they're real. If you make yourself unattractive enough or abrasive enough, you can get yourself to believe that you want sex but no one wants you. There are a thousand ways to trick yourself into believing that your avoidance is due not to your own fear but to some outside circumstance.

Your anxieties about the act of sex might be revealed by some of the following behavior patterns:

- Your courtships end around the third or fourth date. You are never interested enough to get sexually involved. You don't identify yourself as sexually anxious. It's just that no one ever seems to turn you on.

- Most of your relationships are of the platonic variety. You tend to get deeply involved with people who are "Just friends." You believe that you'd like to be sexually involved, but no one seems to respond to you that way. Instead you play the confidante, the big sister or big brother.

- You don't feel comfortable saying no to sex. You end up in bed because you felt you had to, not because you wanted to.

- You have strong negative feelings about your body. You believe that no one could find you attractive as you are. But someday, when you lose the fifteen pounds, when you finally work up some muscle at the gym, you'll really enjoy sex.

- You find it difficult to become sexually aroused and/or to reach an orgasm. Sex has never been a source of enormous pleasure for you. It's hard for you to understand what all the shouting is about.

Sexual anxiety is as apt to be linked to the consequences of making love as to the act itself. The changes in a relationship that often follow becoming lovers are not always welcome changes. Couples such as Peter and Tina in the next example, who dread these consequences, often get stalled in their courtships.

Tina, thirty and divorced for seven years, has distinctly mixed feelings about Seduction. She likes sex but often dislikes herself afterward. "I always fall apart once we become lovers. I turn into a groveling fool. I'll do anything to please him, whether I like him or not. You can't say no to men at that point, or they leave."

She's been through what she calls "my promiscuous phase," and she's made two decisions about sex. The first is that the next man she goes to bed with will be "the man I marry." She doesn't mean she'll wait until the wedding, just that she wants to be sure this relationship means something.

The second is that she'll never again be the one who initiates sex. "I'm tired of doing the inviting, maintaining the conversation, making the pass. It always makes me feel insecure, like I talked him into it. Why can't a man act like a man and show he wants me?"

Peter is thirty-five and floundering. He's been divorced for a year and a half; his career is uncertain. He needs to make a job change, but he can't seem to focus on the right direction. He doesn't think of himself as sexually anxious, just not sexually aggressive. He couldn't handle a rejection, and he finds that most women will pursue him sexually if they are interested. Peter likes it that way.

Tina and Peter met in a night-school class. Their courtship began over coffee, and both relied on these regular meetings to avoid formal dating. Eventually though, coffee became dinner and dinner became shopping for dinner and shopping started to include all of Saturday afternoon as well as evening. They like each other. They touch each other, though very casually. Neither is sure whether the other's interest is sexual or simply friendship. Neither will make the first move.

Peter talks a lot about sex. He's setting the stage but Tina is too uncomfortable to take the lead role into which he is casting her.

Eventually, their interest in each other peaks and passes. Neither one was willing to risk a sexual encounter or a sexual rejection. Their reluctance left them "just friends." But the friendship fades when it does not evolve into a courtship. They both move on to start again with other people, each hoping to find someone aggressive enough or self-confident enough to overcome their sexual anxiety.

Tina and Peter are each afraid of the possible consequences of making love—rejection, insecurity, dependency—a triad of exceedingly unattractive psychological states. Each is unwilling to risk the emotional vulnerability of a sexual attachment. Each hopes the other will risk rejection first, show neediness first. When both partners are very anxious about the consequences of sex, it's easy for courtships to stall.

Your own courtships might be slowed by your concern for the consequences of sexual involvement. These concerns might lead you to avoid sex with partners who are available for long-term relationships or cause you to feel anxious, lost, abandoned, or guilty after making love. If you have these

134

kinds of concerns, you might notice the following behavior patterns:

- You always fall in love after you make love. No matter how objective or in control you felt before sex, after sex you feel one down. You lose your perspective. Sometimes you find yourself longing for someone you don't even like.

- You may not fall in love after sex, but you may fall apart. You become anxious, insecure, frightened that the relationship will deteriorate. You may experience sudden jealousies or become hypercritical of yourself. Sexual involvement leaves you thinking, "Things always fall apart for me. I wonder when this one will?"

- You get sexually involved, but only with people who "don't count." You feel sexually comfortable with married men, older women, foreign exchange students, anyone, really, who is not available or appropriate for marriage. You are less vulnerable to rejection because you have less invested emotionally in these relationships. When you care less, your sexual anxiety may be less inhibiting.

- You find that you overreact to the possibility of a sexually transmitted disease or an unplanned pregnancy. Even taking reasonable and appropriate precautions does not soothe your anxieties. It's hard for you to enjoy sex when you feel you could be punished for it.

- You feel a sense of being trapped or obligated once you've become lovers. You enjoy the sex, but afterwards you feel burdened in some indefinable way. The reaction might be immediate—you just can't share a bed with someone, or you don't like the feeling you get in the morning when you see that he or she is still there. The trapped feeling might take a few weeks to develop. In either event, your reaction is unpleasant enough to make you

135

avoid sex when it might be linked with expectations.

Rx: Turning On to Sex

Whether you are uncomfortable with the act of making love
or with its consequences, you are apt to fantasize that the
right person will automatically remove your inhibitions.
That's not likely. The solution is not to find the ideal partner
to turn you on. You need to turn on to sex itself.

Turning on to sex does not mean that you will have to be
especially sexually active. You can act on your sexual feelings according to your own morality. But there's no reason
why you shouldn't free up your ability to *have* those feelings—about yourself and the world around you.

There's been an enormous amount written in the last ten
years about sexuality, from fantasy to performance. You
might want to spend some time educating yourself and practicing some of the sexual development exercises in these
books. Check the bibliography for references to the works of
Dr. Lonnie Barbach, which combine how-to techniques with
excellent overall education.

You might consider working with a psychotherapist or sex
therapist to explore these questions further. This is not a subtle way of telling you that you are sick. Quite the contrary.
Every part of us does not grow at the same pace or to the
same degree. You may be highly developed socially, physically, and intellectually. Perhaps you could use some help to
get to the same point sexually.

What if the problem is not yours but a problem of the
partner you've selected? During Seduction there is only a
limited amount you can do to allay someone else's sexual
anxiety. You can give him or her plenty of time. If you're
willing, you can also deliver lots of emotional reassurance.

You can talk with your partner about his or her reluctance,
assuming your partner is willing to discuss it. Unfortunately,
during Seduction the bonds between you are weak. Your partner is more likely to convey the impression that you are not
sexually attractive than to identify himself or herself as anx-

ious about sex. When someone tells you that he's not turned on by you, it can put a real damper on a conversation. Remind yourself yet again: *Don't take it personally*.

If your inhibitions about sexual involvement have more to do with the consequences of sex, you'll have to ask yourself a different set of questions. You might wonder, "Am I really as eager to be involved in a relationship as I think?" "What does it mean to me to become someone's lover?" "How do my expectations change?"

If you are a man who has had very few sexual relationships, could you be avoiding sex in order to avoid emotional obligations? Maybe it's no accident that the only women who excite you are the ones you can't have. Maybe it's safer that way.

If you are a woman with few sexual experiences, could a lover represent a threat to your sense of independence? Some women maintain a firm sense of self only when men are at a distance. A man who gets close can threaten that hard-won autonomy. For many women, making love means losing independence.

Sexual anxiety is stirred by our fears of entrapment, our conflicts with dependency and identity, as much as it is stirred by anxiety over the act of sex itself. When you've asked yourself these questions, try to focus on the issue that a sexual relationship has come to represent for you. When you are avoiding sex, are you avoiding obligation? When you collapse emotionally after sex, have you simply given yourself permission to feel dependent? Does it work for you?

Sometimes the only way to get yourself on higher psychological ground is to act. Risk becoming lovers and force yourself to control your dependency crisis. Or, conversely, risk refusing to be lovers until you're sure that if you collapse momentarily, your partner will be there to catch you. Choose the alternative that breaks your own pattern.

Risk making love to an available partner. Force yourself to spend the night or the weekend, and notice your own anxiety or discomfort as it emerges. Find something sexually attractive about nearly everyone, so that you can no longer rely on your old standby, "I'm not turned on." Exercise the erogenous zone in your brain. It will give you many more opportunities.

137

If you have the opportunity to act sexually when you'd ordinarily back off, act on it. It won't necessarily feel comfortable. After all, it's new. Promise yourself one thing: Whatever feelings come up, don't blame them on your partner. Don't say, "I'd be happier/ sexier/more aroused/more satisfied/less anxious/more interested if only my partner were different." Remind yourself that you can be and feel all these things—but only when you are different.

Seduction Tactics

Assuming that sexual anxiety is not an insurmountable obstacle for you, you will want to proceed with a successful seduction. Whether you are the pursuer or the pursued, you have a number of tactics from which to choose. The following discussion is not a comprehensive list of all possible tactics. (You've probably used some the rest of us couldn't begin to imagine.) It includes the classic approaches to the task of Seduction:

- Playing hard to get
- Accommodation
- Love tests
- Asking someone to do something for you

Playing Hard to Get

This traditional Seduction strategy has clearly fallen out of political favor. Do people still play hard to get? Do women still turn down a date for Saturday night if he hasn't called by Wednesday? Do men still act mysterious about their night out with the boys? Do people still deliberately try to make you jealous just to get you interested? Yes, they still do.

Does it work? Well, that's another question.

A 1973 study by psychologist Elaine Walster asked if men preferred hard-to-get women. The survey divided the perception of "hard to get" into two categories: 1) how hard the woman is for you to get and 2) how hard the woman is for other men to get.

The results tell a lot about successful Seduction strategies for women. Men preferred women who were easy for *them* to get but hard for other men to get. He prefers a woman who appears to be popular, attractive, and desirable and who makes it clear that from her other possibilities she has chosen him.

This puts a different cast on the hard-to-get tactic. Perhaps it's not something you should play, but something you should be.

Playing hard to get is offensive because it implies manipulation. It smacks of coy female ploys and phony sexist role-playing. Many of you, male and female, spurn the idea of putting on an act to win love. You say, "I have to be me. I'm not going to play a game. I have to be honest." You are right to insist. There is something vaguely revolting about setting a trap to snare an unsuspecting male (or female, now that the roles in Pursuit are so much more fluid).

However, in your passion for honesty, you may have forgotten to wonder about something important. How come when you tell the truth, the truth is that you're easy to get? How come you are always so available? How come you are so ready to disrupt your life to fit him (or her) into it?

Easy-to-get women in the Walster study are scary to men and therefore a turnoff. A man perceives an easy-to-get woman as desperate. He gets the feeling that she might make too many demands or get too serious. He's afraid she'll get clingy and suffocating. He's often right.

If you are an easy-to-get person, you probably hate to admit it to yourself. It's nothing to be ashamed of. It's no reflection on your worth as a person. You may simply be very, very ready for marriage. Some people, male and female, are in a panic about finding someone. You believe there are not enough men around. You believe the kind of woman you want would never want you. Time is passing. You are lonely. All this could make anyone easy to get.

Unfortunately, your panic is getting in your way. You are communicating your desperation, your neediness. You are calling too often, sending cute cards too frequently, and dropping everything else in your life too loudly. Or perhaps the problem is that you have nothing else in your life to drop.

It will help if you get some control over your panic. You

139

may not be able to change your hunger for a relationship, but you can mask its more damaging side effects. How? Don't *play* hard to get, *be* hard to get.

This doesn't have to mean that you turn down dates or pretend to be uninterested. Remember the research: Men (and probably women too) prefer partners who are easy for them to get but hard for others. That means we are most attracted to someone who appears to have a full life, including interests, friends, and the possibility of other lovers. Then we want to know that this person is attracted to us. To convey this impression, and counter your easy-to-get tendencies, keep these behaviors and attitudes in mind:

- Don't put your life on hold. (We discussed that in chapter 2.) It's one of the negative signs of readiness. When you have very little interest in your own life, you are waiting to collapse into someone's arms. Your prospective partners sense this. It scares them. Also, it makes the wait for a committed relationship a long, dry patch of life.

- Don't rush into monogamy. Don't announce after you make love that you'll be faithful forever more. If you don't approve of sexual intimacy with more than one partner, then wait a lot longer before you have sex. At the least, keep your fidelity to yourself.

- Don't hang around someone's apartment until he or she throws you out. Set your own timetable. Don't dawdle on Sunday morning hoping you'll get an invitation to spend the day. Get yourself out the door. You may feel needy, but you don't have to stand there with your tongue hanging out.

- Control the number of little adorable gestures you make on his or her behalf. This includes cards, notes, clever messages on the tape machine, home-baked bread, dropping a rose at the door, volunteering to drop off his laundry or her garbage, or any of the other gestures which announce, "Take me, I'm yours." You can certainly make a few of

140

these moves. If they accumulate, you can bury someone under their weight.

- Don't call every night! Just don't. It's suffocating, unless it has been acknowledged that the two of you are officially In Love (then you can call every hour). Let an evening or two elapse. Give a person a chance to think about you.

These strategies are not dishonest or manipulative. Instead, they are behavioral controls designed to help you keep your dignity intact when your anxiety threatens to get out of hand.

Accommodation

So often in couples therapy we hear one person accuse the other: "But you weren't like this when we first met," or "I want you back the way you used to be." What these partners are bemoaning is the loss of accommodation that made their love such a delight initially.

Accommodation is the desire to present your best, easiest, nicest side in order to win someone's love, or to maintain it. It is the attitude that says, "I'll be what you want me to be in order for you to love me (or go to bed with me)." Accommodating means making your needs and preferences secondary to someone else's. At this point in courtship, we don't count the cost of this kind of flexibility. We are only focused on the goal of Seduction.

While you are relying on the strategy of accommodation, you are more willing to attend the ballet even though it usually puts you to sleep. You are more complimentary, able to view someone's shortcomings as endearing rather than obnoxious. You read up on current events to make yourself an interesting conversationalist. You clean your home to make a good impression, spend more money than usual to communicate generosity. You have sex at dawn, though you'd prefer death. You adjust your hours, your temperament, your sleep cycle, and your wardrobe to win the heart of your beloved.

Accommodation naturally changes over time. You may continue to focus on pleasing your partner, but you try to do so at less cost to yourself.

141

One of the effects of new love is to create a passionate interest in every detail of your loved one's life. In the first months of my love affair with my husband, I read the sports pages every day. It was no chore. For a brief time, his love for baseball and my love for him sort of blurred together. Likewise, this man, who has nothing but contempt for television, watched Mary Tyler Moore reruns with me. Now it's eight years later. I encourage his friends to come over to talk baseball. He tapes Mary Tyler Moore shows so I can watch them alone. It's a different form of accommodation.

During Seduction, the pursuer is likely to be at his (or her) most accommodating. He doesn't insist, doesn't get angry, doesn't criticize. His message is, "I'm an all-around terrific guy. Try me." He listens more patiently than he might ordinarily, doesn't chew with his mouth full, asks after the health of her dog, and generally polishes up his company manners on her behalf. As you'll see, when The Switch occurs, the role of the accommodator may also switch. He asserts more of his own needs and interests, and she tries her best to change to meet them. Whoever is the more aggressive in pursuit, at different points in the courtship, is also likely to be more accommodating.

Love Tests

The emotional theme of Pursuit is uncertainty. The pursuer is not convinced of his or her success. The object of the pursuit is not positive of the intentions of the pursuer. Pursuit is a seesaw, with two people inching forward, then pulling back.

Uncertainty is a nagging, anxious state of affairs for most of us. We do what we can to reduce it, short of taking the risk of disrupting our romances. The most efficient way to know where you stand in courtship is to ask. It's also the riskiest method. We fear that a direct conversation about the state of the relationship could be potentially damaging. We reserve this tactic for later in courtship.

Meanwhile, you need the information. How much does he really care? How serious is she? There is a simple, time-honored intimacy tactic designed to answer these questions: a love test.

142

In their research on secret tests for lovers, Leslie Baxter and William Wilmot describe a variety of techniques for getting information about your relationship. The first two are not secret at all. You can ask a direct question ("How do you feel about me?"), though most of us won't risk this during early Pursuit. Or, you can use the old standby of asking a third party, a friend, a roommate, or sibling of your partner for information.

The secret tests are less direct routes to the same information. The first group includes "Trial Intimacy Moves":

- Test by making a physical gesture, a touch or embrace, and judge the response.

- Test by disclosing something about yourself in the hopes that your partner will respond in kind.

- Test by publicly presenting your partner as your boyfriend or girlfriend and seeing how he or she reacts to the label.

The next group, the "Taken for Granted" tests, are a bit riskier:

- Make a joke or teasing remark about your future, to see if the topic makes your partner uncomfortable.

- Deliberately don't call or arrange a meeting to test whether your partner will take the initiative.

- Make a negative comment about yourself to see if your partner will tell you how wonderful you are.

- Just plain hint—about a date, about sex, about living together—and see whether your partner gets the message.

"Endurance Tests" are the next level of risk:

- Make your partner give up something for you. You ask for attention when you know he has to study or she has to go to work. You want to find out whether you come first.

143

- Stage or take advantage of a physical separation to find out how your partner handles your absence.

- Test the limits of your partner's love by acting obnoxious, bratty, offensive, or worse. You are testing to see whether you can show your worst side and still be cared about.

In "Jealousy Tests," you

- Talk about a potential rival.

- Actually date a potential rival, and make sure your partner finds out about it.

Finally, though it sounds like the plot for a situation comedy, some people are moved to stage "Fidelity Tests," in which they leave their partners alone with an attractive roommate or sexy friend and come back to see how he or she handled it.

These love tests might be performed throughout courtship, though they are most common during Pursuit, when the two of you are not yet intimate enough to have a direct conversation. They are also not uncommon during Negotiation, when you might be feeling especially uncertain about the bond between you.

Love tests can provide information for you and, as such, they function to increase your sense of intimacy. But you shouldn't rely on them too much. The problem is that very nice lovers often fail our tests. He doesn't know he was supposed to get jealous, and even if he does feel jealous he might bend over backward to keep you from knowing. Your test backfired and you feel uncared for.

When you test her by waiting to see if she calls on the day you return from a business trip, you could have a long wait. She's insecure too. She could be running the same test.

Not everyone hears your self-disparaging remarks as an invitation to a pep talk. Sometimes you'll convince your partner that this version of you is the truth.

Secret tests are an inevitable part of Pursuit. But they are no substitute for asking directly for the information you need.

144

Ask Someone to Do Something for You

During Pursuit, one of you is trying to draw the other closer. One of you is pursuing while the other is holding back, be it ever so slightly. Quite often, part of the pursuer's strategy is to do nice things for the other person. These gestures go beyond asking someone for a date and then planning a special evening. That's very nice in and of itself, but some pursuers go one step further. They start doing nice things that make day-to-day life easier or happier for you.

He might offer to take her car into the shop or fix her stereo, drop off her dry cleaning, or help her choose a stockbroker. If she is pursuing, she might clean his apartment (yes, she *still* might), take him clothes shopping, tape a playoff game he had to miss, watch his cat while he's traveling on business.

Candy, flowers, compliments, small gifts, plus being treated wonderfully, are the traditional benefits of being seduced. They are as much fun for the pursuer as for his or her partner.

But the opposite might be used to draw someone closer. Instead of doing something to make your partner happy, ask him or her to do something for you. When a woman asks a man to fix her air conditioning, he is drawn a bit closer to her. When a man asks a woman for a lift to the airport, she is just a bit more involved with him. You see, these are the small favors we do for friends. Just the act of performing the favor subtly defines the two of you as connected.

Asking someone to do something for you is tricky. You don't want to be presumptuous and you don't want to impose. You do want to express the feeling that the two of you are establishing a mutual bond. Small favors are one of the ways we express such a connection.

The favor should not involve money. When you are pursuing, it is inappropriate to borrow money or ask someone to lay out money on your behalf. Monetary favors are emotionally loaded, however small the amount of money involved.

Instead, involve your partner in your life by asking for help with a minor chore. Ask him to walk your dog, ask her to help you repot a plant, ask him to help you paint your living room, ask her to help you plan a menu for brunch with your parents (do not ask her to cook it!).

None of this is meant to take the place of the more traditional strategies of seduction. You should still be thoughtful, generous, and creative as a way to express your interest and affection. When you help to create an opportunity for the object of your pursuit to reciprocate, you advance your cause even further.

The Shoulds

There is a particular kind of Pursuit especially likely to drive you nuts. It's a burgeoning love affair between Shoulds.

A Should is any person who is exactly what your mother wanted for you. A Should is a catch by your Aunt Mimi's definition. He or she is the package you *should* want and who *should* want you back.

A Should is a nice Jewish (Italian, Catholic, Presbyterian, Mormon, fill in your own blank) girl or boy from a nice family. A Should is a doctor, lawyer, business owner, banker, or corporate executive. A Should is single, the right race and age. He or she, ideally, has no children from a previous marriage cluttering up the scene. A Should is reasonably attractive, tolerably dressed. She knows how to talk to your father; he brings flowers to your mother.

Shoulds are not sexy, at least not to you. A nice Jewish doctor finds Italian women wildly erotic. He finds Jewish women stifling. A nice Presbyterian banker thinks Jewish women are glorious. To him the CEO's daughter is a flat bore. Wasp debutantes lust after Catholic jocks. To them, Ivy League stockbrokers are unbearably predictable. And so it goes.

All these obstinacies of the spirit are not so mysterious. The Should is automatically less sexy because he or she is too familiar. It's like lusting after your brother or sister.

146

Shoulds are not fun. You feel you have to be on your best behavior around a Should. You automatically act as if you are with a friend of your family. You believe you know what's expected. You censor yourself, lock yourself into the role of nice boy or nice girl. You'd like to make love, but you're more cautious because you don't want to blow your image. You like to drink, or party, or dress in jeans, but you don't because you feel inhibited. You edit your conversation to give a Should what you feel she or he expects to hear. None of this is fun, because it's so inhibiting.

Shoulds cause anxiety. A Should reeks of the message, "I am marriage material." Every fear of intimacy that is dormant in you will be aroused by a Should. Every part of you that is longing for marriage will be triggered by a Should.

Shoulds are stereotypes. The most difficult part of beginning a courtship with a Should is that you can't see the person. You are blinded by your stereotype. These are the boys and girls you grew up with. You feel you know them. Possibly what you believe you know of them, you don't like.

You've classified this date before it began. You are bored before it started. You imagine you already know his or her lifestyle, preferences, attitudes, feelings. You will continue to stereotype throughout the evening. Everything that fits your picture will register. Unexpected data will be overlooked. You know what you're expecting to find and, undoubtedly, you'll manage to find it.

Your responses to a Should will have little to do with this individual person and a great deal to do with your feelings about the stereotype. If Greek restauranteurs or corporate lawyers who jog bore you, so will this one. If lady doctors or female MBAs are, in your opinion, cold and tough, you will perceive this date in the same fashion.

It will take you a while to let go of your expectations and meet the person in front of you. Many of us cut the courtship short or frantically press it forward long before we know the person. What we are responding to is *should*.

Seduction's Fatal Mistake

You could probably list a hundred Seduction mistakes you've made. You recall the times you called too much or not soon enough; the man you slept with when you shouldn't have; the woman on whom you spent too much money; the times you were too accommodating; the times you were too difficult; the times you were wrong for taking your best friend's advice, the times you were wrong for ignoring it.

No matter how long your list of mistakes, there is only one mistake that can really hurt you during Seduction: being too attached to the outcome.

Don't get too attached to the outcome means try not to focus so entirely on the end of courtship. Try to appreciate, to enjoy, the steps along the way. You'll make a much wiser marriage.

You don't sing a song in order to get to the end. You don't read a book in order to get it read. If you approach Seduction like a song to be sung, perhaps you won't be in such a hurry to get it over with. Seduction is a dance, not a race.

A race is a perfect way to describe the way some men and women handle Seduction. You are desperate to get Pursuit over with and get on to the Relationship! You don't want to waste your time on a date that's just a date. You want a date that's going to go somewhere—to bed, to Paris, to marriage, to New Year's Eve, anywhere.

If your readiness level is high, you will be especially prone to make this error. You will focus so much attention on the question of possible marriage that you'll ruin your chance to enjoy lots of Seductions. You may start many Seductions, but you won't enjoy them much. You'll be too busy judging marriage potential. For example:

- Mark discards woman after woman. It's the third date and he's already thinking, "She's not the one. I couldn't spend the rest of my life with a woman who is so quiet."

- Larry describes the error perfectly. "My problem is that I always want to rush things. I'd do any-

thing to avoid *dating*. If we have a nice time at
the movies, I want to ask her to move in.

- Gerry describes a man kissing her while she's
  thinking, "He'll ruin my day tomorrow. Oh God,
  he could take over my life." At the first show of
  interest, Gerry is swamped by her fears of commitment. She's too attached to the outcome in a
  negative way.

- Dana announces in sepulchral tones, "I don't think
  I'd want to marry him." After three dates, perhaps
  the question has come up a bit prematurely? Dana
  laughs but she can't stop herself. If she doesn't
  feel she'd want to marry a man after a month with
  him, she's let down. After all, she doesn't want to
  waste her time.

Being too attached to the outcome means beginning every
Seduction with the possibility of marriage or at least a Relationship foursquare in your mind. You don't want Seduction,
you want to know it's love. It's a serious attitude problem.

There are two mistakes you will make if you hold this
attitude. You will either rush forward too fast or drop out
prematurely.

When you are paying too much attention to the question
of where this relationship is going, you will not get much
pleasure out of getting there. You'll be too anxious to make
a decision, too anxious to allow things to unfold at their own
pace, too anxious to tolerate the natural uncertainties of
courtship. Your decisions will be expressions of this anxiety,
instead of reflections of good judgment.

It's true that courtship, as a social ritual, is goal-oriented.
It is designed to take you to marriage. That doesn't mean that
you have to worry prematurely about whether you'll ever get
to that goal. You will. Nearly everyone does, at one time or
another. You want your marriage to be the most sound, most
solid, most loving bond you can develop. It's in your interests to do it slowly, to believe in yourself. Besides, when you
eliminate all the questions about future potential, you will
have much more fun in the present. You may have forgotten,
but Seduction is fun in and of itself.

149

PURSUIT

The Switch

If your romantic relationships frequently end after three or four months, you will want to read this chapter carefully. If it's your partner who usually loses interest, it could be because you are doing something to make his or her anxiety worse. If you are the one who ends things, it could be that your own unconscious fears are standing in the way. In either case, you are a victim of The Switch.

The most common victim of The Switch is the woman. She was being actively pursued when, suddenly, he turns off just as she turns on. Because this is the traditional and still most frequent scenario, this chapter is written as though the male initiates The Switch and the female reacts to it. Today, however, sex roles in courtship are much more flexible. It is therefore increasingly likely that she may pursue him until she captures his interest and then—whammo—she pulls a Switch and he is the victim. So, male or female, you will need to be prepared to handle The Switch if you want to enjoy courtship.

Hooked

During Seduction, one of you was avidly pursuing while the other was holding back. Seduction continues until (a) it proves fruitless or (b) it succeeds.

If Seduction appears fruitless, the pursuer will eventually give up. This is the case when one is interested and one is not. She might not give him a clear cue ("Look, I just don't think this is going to work"), though that could be the kindest approach. Instead, she's "busy" a lot and can't seem to make time for him. Possibly she'll resort to the standard explanation, "I'm seeing someone else" and be both polite and definitive. In any event, if the pursuer doesn't get enough response, he ends the courtship.

If Seduction succeeds, the object of Pursuit will drop her guard, stop backing off, and take a few steps closer. Many events could trigger her increased attachment. Five are most common:

- **He says "I love you" and/or mentions their future.**
  Both of these telegraph sincere and sustained interest. They encourage her to believe that she doesn't have to be so defended against him. He cares, so why would he hurt her?

- **They make love.**
  Many women and some men describe themselves as immediately emotionally vulnerable when they become sexually intimate.

- **They see each other in new settings.**
  She's been putting him down as a wimp and there he is in his fancy office. The wimp is instantly transformed in her eyes into a successful professional. A different background works for him as well. When his female colleague pursues him, he sees a buddy, not a sexual partner. But when she invites him home for dinner and dresses for the occasion, he sees someone entirely different.

- **She gets the approval of a friend.**
  She's been viewing him as a way to pass time. One afternoon, her girlfriend meets him and tells her she's crazy. This man is delightful. He's sexy. She must be a fool to hesitate. She takes another look. He would, too, if the situation were reversed.

- **She discovers competition.**
  The man who was so-so suddenly looks spectacular the moment she discovers that another woman wants him. Competition, with the jealousy it can

inspire, helps to create the aura of hard-to-get for
both men and women.

Whatever the trigger, the result is the same. She moves closer.
As she does, an unnerving event occurs: He backs off. The
Switch has begun.

The task of The Switch is to slow down courtship, to loosen
the developing attachment, so that both people can feel more
comfortable about their evolving relationship. The challenge
of The Switch is for each person to overcome the anxiety
stirred during this readjustment.

You are likely to feel anxious no matter which role you are
playing in The Switch. If you've come to care for a man who
seemed to want you and suddenly he seems to want you a little
bit less, you are likely to feel awful—angry ("What's going on
here?''), panicky ("I know I'm about to be dumped.''), or depressed ("Everyone always leaves me. . . .''). Any of these
feelings might make you behave in a way that is pushy, clinging, or hostile—exactly the sort of behavior that makes The
Switch worse.

If you are doing the backing off, you are also grappling
with your anxiety. You are anxious about losing your freedom, getting overly involved, hooking up with the wrong
person. Your anxiety could make you back off so far that you
end the whole relationship, even if it had the potential to
make you happy. You might be feeling guilty ("I hated to
hurt her, but . . .''), pressured ("I just felt I couldn't breathe
any more.''), or irritated ("I even started to hate his laugh.'').
It's true that it's easier to leave than to be left. But easier is
not necessarily easy.

The Switch does not occur in every courtship. Some couples fall so deeply in love that when they look up they are in
the middle of Negotiation. Sometimes both partners are mature enough to have mastered their fears of intimacy before
the courtship ever began. In other couples, both partners are
so ready for marriage that they sail right through The Switch
and confront their fears later, during Commitment. The intensity of The Switch varies too. It can range from a slightly
let-down feeling that is easy to ignore to the sense that you
have suddenly and completely turned off.

The Switch is usually most acute when one partner begins

courtship for reasons other than those that push toward commitment. You'll recall that these include seeking sexual satisfaction, social approval, an ego boost, or just plain pleasure of the chase. In three or four months of courtship, most of these needs have been satisfied to some extent. This woman or man senses that the courtship is going beyond original intentions. He or she slows things down or brakes completely to reassess the situation.

The Switch may not occur immediately after Seduction is successful. A couple often enjoys a delightful period that they may identify as being in love. They want to be together all the time. They withdraw from the rest of the world and focus on each other. They clearly feel some special connection has been developing, and they may both be awed by its intensity and excitement.

Sometimes, the period between Seduction and The Switch is a milder, more cautious exploration. Something serious could be developing here, but couples are reluctant to identify it as yet. In either event there is usually some excitement involved, some increase in the feeling of attachment. She begins to plan around him. He remains responsive, for a while.

They are likely to be enjoying their sexual relationship. Having mastered sexual anxiety, they are now freer to relax into enjoying physical intimacy. It's new enough to be easily exciting, familiar enough to be increasingly comfortable.

Oh, if things could only drift this way forever. A lot of people expect them to, which is why the ensuing events of courtship throw you for such a loop. Instead of a greased slide from love into marriage, here is what often happens: Either subtly or dramatically, the behavior of the pursuer changes. He or she might be acutely aware of the change or totally unconscious of it.

Retreat or Stalemate?

The Switch takes two forms: retreat and stalemate. During **retreat**, your partner seems to take a step backward, away from the bond that was developing. You begin to notice that the courtship seems to be going in reverse. A woman (or man) who is a victim of retreat might get any number of coded signals:

- During the time that she has started to assume was "theirs," he is suddenly unavailable. He announces that he's spending Friday night with friends, or that he's busy this Sunday and has to leave early.

- He suddenly makes a few critical remarks about her when he had initially been all compliments.

- Their sex life diminishes and/or he gets a little less physically affectionate.

- He seems to be in a bad mood, but he doesn't care to discuss the source.

- He becomes less interested in her descriptions of her thoughts and feelings.

- He mentions the future less instead of more.

- He makes a highly independent gesture that she cannot legitimately protest because it's "too soon": he plans a weekend away without inviting her; cancels a date because he's tired; or flirts with someone in front of her. She can't exactly complain, but she's bothered.

In a **stalemate**, instead of taking a step backwards, your partner freezes in place. He (or she) just doesn't make any more moves to increase your attachment. Stalemate signals are subtle. Some people get to a certain point of involvement, usually after a sexual relationship has been established, and linger there. They don't back off or pursue, they just stick with a routine.

Progress in a relationship has many indicators: greater self-disclosure, the ability to tolerate anger, increasing feelings of trust, of commitment, for example. Some indicators are less ambiguous than these emotional ones. When couples are more involved they spend more time together, speak more frequently when they cannot be together, introduce each other to significant friends and family.

A man or woman who stalemates erects a barrier that seems to have a legitimacy of its own and against which a partner cannot push without appearing demanding, desperate, or something equally unattractive. The stalemate barriers are usually other romances, family, work, or friends.

Joseph's barrier is other women. He is always involved with several simultaneously. These women serve a variety of functions for Joseph, from purely platonic to strictly sexual. When he begins a courtship with a new woman, he always finds a subtle way to let her know that much of his time is already taken. The new woman may be, at this moment, the special one, but he does not wish to give up his other involvements. Joseph doesn't tell the special woman how he is spending his time. He waits for her to ask.

Joseph has protected himself in two ways. First, he's never lonely, never has time to really miss the special woman because she gets lost in the emotional crowd. Second, he sets up the new woman to become anxious and demanding. Then he has a good reason to be glad he didn't make any sacrifices on her behalf.

Grant is a junior attorney, hoping for partnership in five years. In his eyes, he didn't decide to invest all his time in work—it's just something you have to do. Grant usually withdraws from work a bit when he begins a Seduction. He takes longer lunches, makes his weekends free. When The Switch occurs, Grant suddenly becomes anxious about the way he has been neglecting his job. He doesn't see himself as backing off. His need to stay at the office until nine or to leave her Sunday morning in order to complete a legal brief is just something he has to do. The right woman would understand. If she's very understanding, she ends up making all her plans around him, holding her Sundays open in case he's free, staying awake until midnight just so he can come over, have sex, get a hot breakfast, and go back to the office. She starts to complain. He starts to feel that she is unsympathetic to his needs.

Mai is divorced with joint custody of two small sons. She has an endless series of family obligations, including a complicated but necessarily ongoing relationship with her ex-husband. Mai believes she wants to remarry and start a new life. But each time she begins a relationship, the obligations of her old life seem to interfere. Suddenly the boys begin to have difficulties, the ex-husband needs to be consulted, and the new relationship must be put on hold.

Whether retreat or stalemate, when these signs of The Switch occur, a woman (or man if the roles are reversed) notices. She is astonishingly sensitive to his emotional withdrawal, even if they are still seeing each other quite regularly, still having a happy time in bed, still laughing. She tends to be very tuned in to signs of his increasing involvement with her. She made herself vulnerable when they went to bed, she has begun to care (though often not without serious reservations about him), and she notices any slight shift in the intensity of his pursuit. Is she going to be hurt? Does he really care? Where is this relationship going? Is he losing interest?

At precisely this point, where the pursuer freezes in his progress or backs off a step or two, and the pursued gets nervous and starts to push, The Switch has occurred.

The Challenge of The Switch: Fear of Entrapment

What happened? How come the pursuer who was so excited, so attracted last month, is suddenly putting on the brakes?

What happened was that she stopped backing off and started responding. Her response narrowed the emotional distance between them. For a short time (a few days to a few months) he enjoyed their closeness. Then, inevitably, he got scared. The Switch is usually triggered by the fear of entrapment.

It is possible that fear was only a minor factor in his change of attitude. Maybe he was attracted to her initially, but two or three months in her company proved to be enough. Maybe life interfered (his job fell apart, his father had a heart attack, he lost a fortune in the stock market), and he doesn't have the energy to continue a romance. Maybe he miraculously met the woman of his dreams and all other budding courtships must be swept aside. Maybe.

If you are having this three-month change of heart for the first or second time, it might be attributed to external circumstance. But if you have a pattern of losing interest after three or four months, you would do better to look inside yourself.

You are probably struggling with your fear of entrapment if:

- You have a pattern of becoming obsessively picky after a few weeks or months of dating.

- Your romantic interest tends to evaporate after three or four months.

- You juggle lots of different men or women simultaneously, waiting for the right one to emerge from the pack.

- You are involved with so many different interests and obligations that you can't give time and attention to a serious relationship.

- You tend to become involved with unavailable or unsuitable romantic partners.

- You begin each relationship with a giant mental reservation, a big but . . .: "She's very attractive, but she's not bright enough for me." "He's sweet and funny, but he's not that sexually exciting." The "but" is your built-in escape hatch when your fears of entrapment are stirred.

Fear of entrapment affects men and women. It comes up when you've been dating for a while, and probably sleeping together for a while, and you are confronted with the need to commit more time and energy to one person. You get the wild sense that you've lost control, that this is all going too fast, that you could be getting in deeper than you ever intended. You are suddenly burdened with all kinds of obligations and expectations. You are threatened with being accountable for your time, your activities. You are asked to

157

consider being sexually exclusive, and the idea gives you a choking sense of missed opportunity. You worry, "How can I be sure that he/she is the one?"

Luis, forty-one, a divorced architect who feels eager to settle down and have kids, describes his Switch perceptively. "In the beginning I'm always very interested. Sometimes I'm even fantasizing marriage, seeing her as my wife, envisioning Lamaze classes. I mean, I think I'm pretty ripe for the whole thing. Then we'll be together for a month or two, and she'll seem pretty crazy about me and, I don't know, it's like I click off. I always know it's happening, because I'll find myself making her wrong.

"Like with Angela (a recent romance), the truth is, she can't do much right in my eyes lately. We went grocery shopping and she bought margarine, and I thought, 'God, doesn't she know enough to buy butter? Where did she grow up anyway?' I hated the way she made coffee (doesn't grind the beans), and I hated the movie she thought was so terrific. I know I'm doing it again, making her wrong about things that aren't even important. But I want to be with a woman who I think is just adorable. I want to see her walk into a room and feel like rushing over to hug her. Right now when Angela walks into a room I'm thinking, 'I hate those shoes.' It's crazy."

Luis is describing the thoughts that can be associated with fear of entrapment. He avoids the trap by criticizing Angela. He probably doesn't even identify his fear as having something to do with his reluctance to become involved. He has some suspicions though, because he does notice that this "always happens."

Further evidence that this is an expression of Luis's fear of closeness: He is generally a pretty easygoing guy. He has many friends, male and female. It's comfortable for him to be around people and he readily accepts their shortcomings. On the whole, he is loyal and loving, the sort of man who has maintained friendships since his high school days. It's only with new women who seem interested in him that he becomes ruthlessly evaluative. It happens against his will.

Many of us feel a moderate amount of anxiety when our courtships progress into the possibility of something. Some

158

of us are paralyzed by it. The best description of this kind of man or woman was given by Daniel Goldstine et al in the book *The Dance-Away Lover*.

Doesn't the name say it all? The Dance-Away Lover is a genius at Seduction. He is loving, charming, and cherishing. Once she lets down her guard and begins to enjoy all his warmth and attention, he retreats. She got too dependent. It gave him "this smothered feeling that I'm being expected to fill this great vacuum."

All of the features of fear of entrapment are at their most extreme with the Dance-Away Lover. He becomes highly critical. Every blemish on his partner in his mind becomes an indictment. He may not voice specific complaints. He just becomes increasingly faultfinding until he has to put some distance between them. He doesn't want to be associated with such a loser.

Listen to Goldstine's description: "The Dance-Away's repeated romantic disillusionments are the consequence of his discomfort with the intimacy and commitment love entails. The Dance-Away Lover is preoccupied with the fear of being trapped. He clings to his independence lest, in her eagerness to possess him, someone succeed in sucking him into a web of obligations and responsibilities."

Coping with Your Own Fear

If you feel that your fear of entrapment is interfering with your courtships to a significant degree, you will want to take steps to rid yourself of it. You'll need patience and perseverance, because this can be an especially tricky anxiety to overcome.

The toughest step is identifying your problem. If you are caught in the pattern of fear of entrapment, you probably won't know you have the problem. Almost invariably, you will feel as though the fault lies with your partner. If you are losing interest, becoming highly critical, or choosing unavailable people, you are most likely to think that you just haven't found the right person and that you should move on. After all, you don't want to settle for second best. You want to

159

feel good about your choice. It takes a long time to see that feeling good about your choice has more to do with *you* than with the person you've chosen.

Fear of entrapment is not identified in any individual relationship, but in a pattern of relationships. To detect it, you will need to become aware of your own romantic patterns. This is difficult for most of us to do on our own because we lack the objectivity to stand back and see the overall picture. You may want to seek professional psychological counseling to get some help in identifying your pattern.

Once you've seen it and identified it, how do you get past it? This is the jackpot question for which there is no formula answer. But there are suggestions. For some people, just the awareness that a fear of entrapment affects your romantic relationships changes a great deal. It shifts the emphasis from outside yourself to inside yourself and helps to control your tendency to project and to distort your partner.

For others, awareness is not enough. They will need to delve further into the meaning and origin of their fear. Psychotherapy can be helpful with this, as can some books on the topic such as *The Dance-Away Lover, The Peter Pan Syndrome*, and *The Hearts of Men*. Unfortunately, each of these books describes the fears and anxieties of men. More and more women today are also shying away from relationships, ending romances because they aren't perfect, and resisting the constraints of courtship. The literature hasn't caught up with this trend.

Remember as you grapple with the fear of entrapment that you don't have to erase it. You don't have to get to the point where you never become critical of a new lover or where you'd never consider backing off. You only have to tolerate the flaws you find in your lover a little bit more or back off a little bit less. Your partner and courtship itself will get you over the rest of the hump. It seems impossible that someone you are so critical of today could be someone you love deeply tomorrow. It seems impossible, but it happens all the time— if you let it. Your faultfinding, your doubts, your wavering interest are all a normal part of working your way toward commitment.

160

Handling Your Partner's Switch

Keep in mind that The Switch is an expression of normal anxiety. It is not an indictment of your desirability. The cardinal rule, once again, is: *Don't take it personally.*

When The Switch occurs, you will notice your partner's retreat or stalemate. The crucial factor in determining courtship at this point is the way in which you handle your new role as pursuer.

The timing and manner in which you cope will depend largely on your individual characteristics. The more anxious you are, the more likely you are to confront the situation early. The more direct your personal style, the more likely you will be to talk about the problem. Your own degree of readiness will be a factor in how hard you push. If you feel very ready for marriage, you are likely to spend less time in uncertainty.

Partly your reaction will depend on the kind of Switch he's made. He has either retreated or ceased to come closer.

The Initial Response to Retreat

When she notices his retreat, however subtle, she gets anxious. When she gets anxious, she feels pressured to do something to relieve her anxiety. She believes there is only one thing to do.

She asks "What's wrong?" He responds, "Nothing."

There are few exchanges in a relationship more frustrating than this one. She *knows* something is wrong. She sensed it immediately when he said he'd call at seven-thirty and didn't get around to it until ten. She got the message of retreat when the kiss with which he greeted her was a shade less warm than usual.

Most people are correct when they sense withdrawal, even if it's based on the flimsiest and most intuitive of cues. Yes, some people, especially some women, have an excessive need to be close and an abnormal sensitivity to a partner's autonomy. But that's the exception. When you begin to invest love and caring, you can become quite sensitive to the response you are getting.

When he has retreated during The Switch, why is it so hard

for him to acknowledge it? Why must he deny that it is occurring? There are several possibilities:

- It was an unconscious retreat. He moved backward automatically in response to her starting to come closer. He really *doesn't* know it occurred.

- He doesn't want to increase their intimacy at this moment by discussing his thoughts and feelings. When he says, "Nothing," he means "Go away."

- He is aware that he's pulling back, but he's not ready to put it into words. He doesn't want to lose her, doesn't want to push her away or make her angry. He doesn't want to participate in a confrontation. He can't tell her his true thoughts because they're too critical. He'd rather handle his mental reservations about her privately. Maybe they'll go away.

She is left with the problem of handling her intuitions. She presents them ("What's wrong?"). He denies them ("Nothing"). Where does she go from here? She has a few options, none of them perfect.

She can drop the whole discussion. If he stops retreating shortly thereafter, they will have weathered The Switch successfully. It's rarely this easy, but it does occur in some courtships. The Switch can be simply a mild realignment of the relationship that doesn't require any response beyond tolerance.

If she drops the whole discussion and he continues to retreat, she'll probably need to make another stab at confrontation.

She can ask again, more pointedly. "Hey, I was upset when you didn't spend the night." Or, "I don't feel like you're really listening to me." Or, "Quit picking on me. You're hurting my feelings." She may present herself as hurt, rejected, and uncertain, or angry, righteously indignant, and demanding. Frankly none of these presentations of self is enormously attractive to him. She ends up sounding anxious,

162

dependent, and clingy. If she's hurt, he may feel guilty. If she's angry, he may feel intimidated. Neither of these feelings inspires love.

She can answer the question for him. She tells him her idea of what he really means when he says, "Nothing." She tells him what he is really feeling (scared); what he's really doing (backing out); why he has this problem (his mother); and how he ought to handle the situation (turn off the TV and talk about it!).

Some men respond very positively to this translation of their internal states. They may be drawn to a woman largely because she speaks this language of feelings so fluently. Also, she's paying him a lot of attention and that's hard to resist.

Other men find it offensive. This man hates to be analyzed, is offended when she tells him how she thinks he really feels. Her psychological approach won't bring them closer. It will make him furious.

She can stage an angry, upset scene. Often this occurs on the telephone. She was upset by the time their Saturday date was over. She didn't like the way he talked about his old girlfriend. (True, she asked first. But she hated his answer.) He made an offhand remark about her profession ("You teachers really have it easy") that annoyed her. She broods about the evening all Sunday and Monday. By Tuesday, when he finally calls, she's angry. She's not even sure she likes him anymore. She knows she doesn't like the way he's treating her. She lets him know her disapproval in no uncertain terms. She is all justifiable outrage. He is all misunderstood innocence. It is not a good call. Nothing is resolved.

She can strike back. This woman fights fire with fire. If you think about it, it's not necessarily the best way to put a fire out. When he gets critical, she gets critical. When he pulls away sexually, she distances herself even further. If he is busy Friday, then she is busy Saturday. Basically she handles his retreat by upping the ante. Backing off in response to someone's anxiety about closeness can be an excellent approach. But there are ways to do this. If she meets him, tit

163

for tat, in an angry unavailability, they are embroiled in a struggle without a way to communicate about it.

She says nothing and bends over backward to accommodate. When they are in the Seduction stage, he was accommodating, complimenting, and supporting. When he looks as if he is withdrawing, she will probably, for a while, step into his abandoned role of the accommodator. She will make every effort to be sweet, nice, understanding, fun, and easy. It rarely resolves a Switch.

She can initiate the O.R. (Our Relationship) conversation.* Most of the earlier responses to retreat have one thing in common. They are attempts to initiate a conversation about Our Relationship. No matter which variety of The Switch a couple is confronting, its resolution involves some form of this O.R. conversation.

Of course, the two of you have been talking for months now. You've probably discussed your work, your families, your interests, your friends. Moving somewhat closer on the intimacy scale, you may have reviewed past relationships, past sexual experiences, or past personal failures. You may even have discussed your mutual admiration and your fantasies about a future with each other.

In order to respond to the sudden shift in your relationship brought about by The Switch, you will probably escalate the intimacy in a traditional fashion by attempting to introduce the O.R. conversation. You want to talk directly about the status of your relationship. This is a high-risk endeavor, to which some of us will resort only when all our love tests have failed to reassure us. For others whose style is more direct, the O.R. conversation will be a first resort, risky though it may be.

The O.R. conversation has many variations, but all of them have certain structural similarities. It is precipitated by a complaint or concern on the part of the person introducing it. ("What's wrong?" "I'm upset that you . . ." "I need to talk about . . .")

The theme of the O.R. conversation is, "Where is this

---

*This term was coined by Dr. Brian Gould of American Medical International.

164

relationship going?'' No matter what the content of the complaint, the underlying question being addressed is, "What's going on between us? What are you thinking and feeling? Are you serious?''

Like all of the above responses to retreat, the O.R. conversation usually doesn't go very well the first few times around. This is a big step in increased intimacy. Both people are anxious, and the feelings involved are often anger, hurt, rejection, guilt, or claustrophobia. You are too new a couple to handle these powerful feelings perfectly your first time out. Don't feel bad about it. You'll get better with practice.

You can see that none of the customary responses to retreat has a high success rate. Each is a strategy for seeking reassurance. Sometimes you'll get what you need, but more often you'll become more anxious. Your next step is necessary and difficult: *You need to learn to back off*. It's exactly what you'd have to do if you were confronting a stalemate.

The Initial Response to Stalemate

The O.R. conversation that is precipitated by a stalemate is a slightly different variety of confrontation. This is a talk that is probably partially rehearsed by the person who introduces the conversation. She (or he, depending on who is now in the role of pursuer) has been wondering about the relationship. It seems to have stalled, though everything is pretty much the same when they are together. Yet she senses that some essential emotional contact is missing. She wonders if he is seeing other women or how he's spending his weeknight evenings. She may notice that he doesn't say much about their mutual future, or that he tends to say "I" but rarely, if ever, "we." They have a good time together, but she wonders if there will ever be more to it.

It's important to note that she will wonder about all of these questions, even if she has serious reservations about the relationship herself.

Pat was dating an accountant. She thought he was bright and attractive, but pretty boring overall. He was tired a lot and he would always rather stay home than go out and play. Pat had a lot of doubts about how satisfying he could be over the long haul. Still, she needed to know if he was serious about her, if the relationship had a future in his mind. Her reservations didn't keep her from being concerned about his.

James finds Gloria irritatingly irresponsible. She is congenitally unable to be on time, she forgets to call him when she's supposed to, and she hops from job to job. He doesn't see himself living with this forever, no way. Still, he is nuts about her body, and she can be sweetly affectionate. He wants to know if she has any genuine feeling for him, or if he's just the rebound cure for her ex-boyfriend.

Ambivalence—the snake in the meadows of courtship—rears its two heads again. Yes, you can certainly be in active pursuit of someone that you're sure you don't want. Yes, you can feel a need to clarify someone else's feelings even though your own are not a bit clear. It isn't logical, but it is courtship.

Why do people who don't yet care deeply about their partners often care a great deal about the relationship? It's another example of being too attached to the outcome, which we discussed in the last chapter. If you are totally focused on the goal of courtship, you can become very upset by lack of progress in a relationship, even if it's a relationship you aren't enjoying much. Once again your attachment to the outcome of courtship will stand in your way. It will make you more anxious than you need to be and less able to handle a stalemate successfully.

The timing of the O.R. conversation in response to stalemate is generally a bit slower than one precipitated by retreat. Retreat makes you acutely anxious because you sense a change, a reversal of feeling. Stalemate makes you vaguely concerned. You are more likely to put some time in waiting "to see how things work out." You may be hesitant to rock the boat because you sense the conversation could tell you something you don't want to hear. You may be reluctant to voice your own reservations about a partner, or to state your own muddy and confused intentions. However long you hesitate, if things do not naturally unfold to give you the answers you are wondering about, you will have to ask.

Here's how it unfolds:

166

They've been dating three months, have been lovers for two. Things seem to go well when they are together, but they are not progressing much. Finally, she introduces the topic over dinner one night, or after they've made love. She asks, "How do you feel about me?" or "What do you think about us?" He probably counters with something general. "I think you're terrific," or "I'm really enjoying being with you," or something to dodge the issue, "Why, what do you mean?"

He knows what's coming. He hates the conversation, but he's had it before. She's nervous too. She's afraid she's going to precipitate the speech that begins, "I like you very much, but . . ." Still the time has come when she needs to know. She persists.

"Well, I'd like to know if you are seeing other women," or "Do you think there's anything special about our relationship?" She is asking, in many ways, "Are you going to get serious about me, or is this all there is?"

It's rare, but it does happen, that he will look up and say, "I love you. I'm very serious. I stopped seeing everyone else the moment we kissed." It's rare, because if he felt this way things probably wouldn't be stalled.

He may deliver a clearly defined "I like you, but . . ." speech that closes doors. He may say that he enjoys her company, but doesn't have anything long-term in mind. He may take this as an opportunity to announce firmly, "I don't think we have much in common," or "Our timetables are very different," or even "There's something wrong with me. I can never have a relationship past this point."

Wherever he places the blame, the message is pretty clear: *This isn't it.* She might take offense and they will agree to stop seeing each other. She may hang on because she wants the companionship, the sex, the escort, or because she hopes he'll change his mind. Most likely though, the courtship won't progress much further.

More often, his response to this first O.R. conversation is more open-ended. He cites reasons that interfere with his involvement but indicates he wishes to continue developing the relationship. He says something she finds disappointing, couched as gently as he possibly can. "Yes, I'm seeing other women, but you're important to me and I want to spend time with you." "I'm so busy with work now that I just don't

167

have time to get heavily involved, but I'd like to keep seeing you when I can." "I need a lot of time to myself and I don't think it's fair for you to need to hear from me all the time." "I'm not ready for a heavy relationship. I hope you understand."

It's not *what* he says that shapes the outcome; it's *how she handles* what he says.

The reaction most women have at this point is to fall apart. She is disappointed, hurt, feels rejected. She lets these feelings show. She might express them angrily ("How dare you lead me on!") or contemptuously ("You really don't like women, do you?"). Most often she is devastated and turns to him for comfort.

One man told me that after this inevitable conversation his relationships tend to go into a "holding pattern." "I mean that quite literally," he explained. "After she finds out that she's not the only woman I see, she kind of collapses into uncertainty. I have to hold her a lot, reassure her. Even our sexual relationship takes a backseat to the hugging and cuddling she seems to need. It's too bad, because it never makes me want to spend more time with her. I hang around because I think it's the right thing to do. But the more she gets upset, the more I start thinking of other women."

He's right. Most women, and most men when the roles are reversed, handle the limits set by the other person very badly. They become clingy and anxious and need oceans of reassurance in order to restabilize. They become constantly available, fall over backward to rearrange time in order to make contact with the elusive person. They become quite reluctant to say no to anything, because there's a sense of being on probation.

All this dithering, undignified behavior comes about because she took stalemate or retreat personally. Don't. Remember, people stall or retreat as much because of their own issues over intimacy as because of their reactions to you.

Your Best Response to a Switch

When you have the first O.R. conversation and you got a hesitant answer, don't fall apart. *Back off.*

168

This is the best advice you'll ever get on courtship and the hardest to put into effect. When you are feeling insecure and rejected, you will need to behave with confidence and serenity. When you are feeling desperate to be with someone, you'll need to loosen up and resist some opportunities to be together. When you are concerned that if you let go, nothing will be there, take the risk of finding out. If it's true, you need to end it.

Back off means exactly what it says: Stop being so available, stop expressing your interest so dramatically, stop being so accommodating, stop trying to win his or her interest. Start reestablishing some degree of independence.

There is a trick to this strategy. If you do it in an angry or dramatic way, it won't work. If you get upset and say, ''Well, if you're going to see other people, you can just forget about me,'' it won't help at this point. Remember, it's early in courtship. It's too soon for this ultimatum. It presses too hard on a partner struggling with fears of closeness.

If he's working every night until eleven and he's in the habit of calling you then because he'd like a warm meal and a warm bed, don't confront him about it. Don't tell him he's a selfish user who ought to be ashamed of himself. Don't cast yourself in the role of righteously indignant victim. Instead, refuse to allow yourself to be used. Stop answering the phone after ten. Put your tape machine on. Go to sleep.

If she loves to have you do things for her, but she insists it's too soon to commit herself to one person, stop being so accommodating. Don't help her get her car fixed. Take a wonderful vacation, but leave her home this time. You can keep telling her you think she's wonderful, but don't let her exploit your feelings for her. You increase your value when you step back a bit. When you stand very close, it is often difficult for someone to focus on you.

Back off also means don't talk your problems to death. The O.R. conversation was an opening, a beginning vehicle for communicating each of your thoughts, feelings, and reservations. You will have many hundred such conversations through the length of your relationship, especially if you marry.

Some people try to have all these conversations in one week. You make desperate phone calls seeking reassurance.

169

You pick fights just to get a conversation going. You wake your lover at 2:00 A.M. to discuss your feelings. You cry, carry on, and generally whip yourself into an emotional tornado that anyone would run from.

This is not the moment in courtship for protracted analysis. Later, during Negotiation and Commitment, you should not back off from an issue. At that point you may have to talk and fight and rage and cry in order to work it out. But at that point your attachment to each other is stronger. It can handle more emotional strain, more upheaval.

During The Switch, your partner is afraid that he or she will be trapped and suffocated by you. He is afraid you will be a huge dependent burden who will collapse on him. Tears, rage, and endless talk do not reassure him.

To handle The Switch, you need to remind yourself and your partner that you can function without this romance. You need to convey the attitude that you are a person with many options and a full life. You will not wither and die if things end, and you won't become a dependent leech if the courtship continues. You have self-confidence, and your partner's current hesitations about you do not alter those facts one iota. You don't take them personally.

What makes it so hard to believe this? Why do you feel fine about yourself right up to the moment when someone you aren't even sure you want announces that he isn't sure he wants you?

What Makes It So Hard to Back Off?

Yes, you'll probably find it hard to carry out the edict to back off. You may even be angry with the suggestion. It sounds like some dumb game your mother told you to play. You want your relationship to be past all that charade. You wonder how you can ever get close to someone if you have to be a fraud with your feelings. Why can't you just tell someone how you really feel and go from there?

People often say that they hate the idea of deliberately being less available because it's a phony waste of time. That's

170

only part of it. We also hate the idea of deliberately backing off because we're scared.

It's scary to let go of a relationship. What if it disappears? What if you tell her you can't take her car in to be fixed and she gets angry? What if you tell him you are busy on Friday and he never asks again? The Switch can make you so anxious that you are afraid to assert yourself in any way. You can get scared that if you don't make everything (especially you) as easy as possible for your partner, he or she won't want to make an effort.

Backing off is hard, too, because it's not what you feel like doing. You want to be with him. You want to be the one she calls on for her it's-so-nice-to-have-a-man-around-the-house type chores. You want him to come to rely on you, and you feel you must be utterly available to make that occur. Maybe you feel you are miserable when you are apart, happy when you are together, and you can't deny yourself the short-term bliss.

The hardest thing about backing off is that you need to act strong at a time when you are feeling weak. You need to act self-confident when you are feeling insecure. You need to be light when you are laboring under a heavy sense of loss.

The anxiety you feel when you sense a Switch is unavoidable. What you can change is the way you handle it. Instead of turning to your partner to make the bad feeling go away, you can handle your anxiety on your own. You need to click back into the functioning, independent person you were before The Switch began. Your friends can help. So can your work. Do whatever you need to do to reassure yourself. Your partner can't do it for you right now.

Remind yourself that you are lovable and that your partner is going through a crisis of his or her own. Remind yourself not to take it personally.

Janice described this internal process perfectly. She's been dating Alan for three months. At first, he was such a Should and he came on so eagerly, that she was put off. Gradually, after they become lovers and after two of her girlfriends swore they'd take him if she didn't want him, she got more interested. She began to feel he was retreating when he canceled a weekend trip twice in a row because of work. When they stopped making love frequently and he started leaping out of bed in the morning to rush to the shower, she got anxious. Although he called just as frequently, Janice began to feel that something was wrong.

Finally, naturally, she asked. She pressed for a day or two until he admitted to feeling uncomfortable with her. Alan said, "I don't know why. I just feel pressured around you. I still want to see you, but maybe not so often."

This conversation took place on the telephone. When Janice hung up, she was devastated. She started on her downslide of negative self-accusations. (I've lost him. I knew I would. I always do. It's my fault. . . .)

In therapy Janice has come to realize that this monologue is her own projected self-accusation. These are not Alan's thoughts. They are her own.

This time Janice was able to recognize those thoughts as her own automatic expectations. She pulled herself together and forced herself to change her thinking. "My whole attitude changed from one minute to the next. I saw how needy I was getting and I just thought, "Wait a minute! I know this man cares about me. He's just feeling pressure and he wants a break. I'm fine. I don't need to see him every minute to be reassured."

Janice was clear about her own patterns of behavior. "I always know when I have one of those insecurity attacks. I just sit on my couch and do nothing. I'm totally unproductive. I need reassurance. My own life doesn't matter. If I can get back to myself, it's wonderful. If I can bring myself to be with friends or have another date, even with someone I don't care about, my whole attitude is lighter."

In this courtship, Janice was able to interrupt her unraveling. She understood that her anxiety was internal, less in response to her lover's retreat than in response to her own self-image. Images can be changed.

"I knew I'd survive if he chose to leave. And I also knew that he hadn't made that decision yet." She didn't freeze by the phone until he called. She didn't work herself into a rage directed at him. When he did call a full week later, she wasn't silently angry or measuring every word. She was light, glad to hear from him, and comfortable with the distance. The courtship progressed.

Not all of us expect to fail in relationships because of a

negative self-image. But it's the case for many of us, male and female. And when you spend lots of time with single friends who are telling you how awful men are, how difficult women are, or how impossible romance is, it increases the likelihood that you'll fall apart over The Switch. You will need to protect yourself against these erosions to your self-esteem if you want to be able to back off when you need to.

Take the risk of backing off. It's true that it's a gamble. The romance might disappear before your eyes. Chances are, if you don't back off, it's going to disappear anyway.

When The Switch occurs, it does not have to spell the end of your romance. Unless you or your partner has a serious developmental problem, like the Dance-Away Lover, your courtship has every possibility of surviving this rough spot.

Don't forget, The Switch can occur in all kinds of courtships. It occurs for people who thought they were in love and for people who were slow to make a second date. It can occur when you two are a match made in heaven and when you are the oddest of odd couples.

Men and women who were desperate to marry can surprise themselves with a sudden anxiety attack about commitment which can precipitate a Switch. Those who swore they'd never marry will probably have to wrestle with themselves at the three-month mark.

The point is that most people will eventually make it through The Switch and progress through courtship. They don't move forward because the right person appeared and the anxiety disappeared by magic. They progress because they are willing to confront their fears and because they've found partners who make it safer to do so.

When you resolve The Switch, the two of you have accomplished the tasks of Pursuit:

- You have gotten closer physically and emotionally and you both feel comfortable with it.

- You expect to be together on a regular basis, whether it's Saturday, every night, or something in between. One of you might continue to issue a formal invitation, but it's really not necessary.

- You have started to talk to each other about your

173

intentions and expectations in this relationship. Probably you two have made it through some anxious moments, some feelings of anger or annoyance. You are closer and you mean something to each other.

Pursuit provides an opportunity for two people to grow closer. When Pursuit is complete, you emerge at the other end of it as a couple. You've developed a relationship.

7

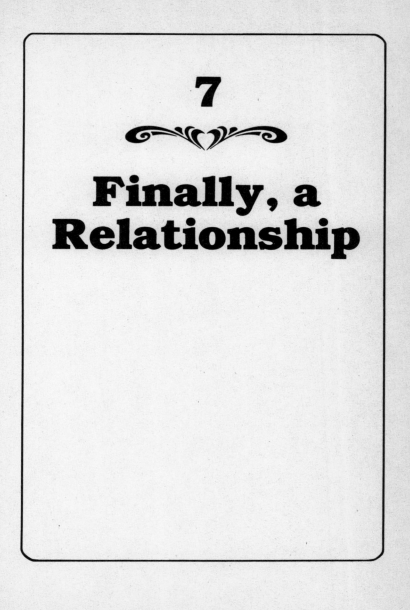

Finally, a Relationship

Remember when you kept saying you wanted to meet someone? Maybe you choked on the cliché "a meaningful relationship" but it comes down to the same thing. You wanted something of substance, someone special. You wanted to put your efforts where they would count, to be involved in a way that would go somewhere. It has.

You feel:

- Ecstatic. Beside yourself with love and appreciation. You cannot believe someone could make such a difference in your life. Or

- Uncertain. Swinging between affection and disinterest. You are sexually captivated, but you have serious reservations about lifestyle differences. Or, you've become dependent on his/her presence in your life; but you aren't certain you're in love. Or

- Anxious. You want this to work out, but it feels a little insecure to you. You tend to give in on things to avoid rocking the boat. You think: "I hope I don't mess this up. What does he/she see in me anyway? I'm afraid I'm going to get hurt." Or

- Content. This is nice. You don't know what it all means, but it's pleasant. You've come to care for someone. Only time will tell where it will lead. Or

- Nervous. Whoa! This is all going too fast. You can see down the road, and you're not sure you like where it is going. On the other hand, you sure

177

like the time you spend together. You'd miss it if
you called it quits. Or would you?

Often you'll be feeling some combination of all of these. No
wonder relationships are so complicated. Who could think
clearly through that kind of feeling mixture?

"Relationship" is the stage that most of us say we are
seeking when we begin a courtship. It is, in fact, a very nice
point at which to be. You have worked your way into something important without having to face the anxiety of something permanent.

The Spirit and the Structure

Your courtship has developed into a Relationship when you
have either the spirit of a Relationship or the structure of one.
Ideally you have the beginning of both.

The structure of a Relationship is simple: You are in a
Relationship when the two of you can assume you will be
together on some regular basis. Unlike Pursuit, when one of
you had to ask and the other to agree, in a Relationship you
take for granted that you will meet, whether it's every weekend or every night.

Like most of the differences between the stages of courtship, this different understanding between two people is more
of a gradual slide than an emphatic decision. Even in Seduction, some couples slip quite readily into the unspoken assumption that weekends are reserved for each other. By
contrast, some eight-month-old Relationships are formally
maintained by an invitation offered every Tuesday night for
the following Saturday.

The idea that you'll spend regular time together, especially
Saturday night, is such an ingrained social expectation that
it's easy to come to feel it after only two dates. Expecting
such constancy after only a few dates does not, of course,
mean the two of you have a Relationship. Rather, it's an
example of how expectations in romance can easily be premature. (One colleague tells me she always tries to interrupt

178

a female patient's rush of premature expectations by saying, "Don't buy the gown yet.")

There are quantitative and qualitative differences in the way your time is used when you develop the structure of a relationship. For one thing, you are likely to be spending *more time together*. True, by this definition of a regular and assumed schedule, you are in a Relationship even if it's limited to once-a-week dates. You are in it, but barely. Once a week is not enough time to reveal much of yourself or to get a clearer picture of your partner. If your Relationship has been stuck here for a few months, take some initiative to move it along or let it go.

You are probably spending not only more time, but more *unstructured time*. There's less need to plan your entertainment. You become more relaxed and include each other in more of your day-to-day real life. Saturday night dates start to include Sunday afternoon errands. Tuesday evening dinners make room for work brought home from the office. In the Relationship stage, you use your time to weave each other into the fabric of your ongoing life. During Pursuit, you are usually stepping aside from your life to make time for each other.

Finally, if one of you decides to disrupt the pattern of time you usually spend together, there now seems to be an obligation to explain. If you typically spend Sundays together and she makes plans to meet friends for brunch or he wants to go away for the weekend, you are expected to inform your partner. Actually, it goes beyond informing. For most people, it's not comfortable enough to say, "By the way, don't count on me this weekend." That kind of announcement is good enough for Pursuit, but a Relationship requires more explanation. Where are you going? With whom? Does it mean anything about us?

This change in the nature of your time together reflects the increasing *accountability* between you. Some of you welcome the need to check out your movements with someone who cares. For others, it's a distasteful burden that is resented and resisted. We'll discuss it at length in the next chapter.

Accountability reflects not only the changes in the way your romance is structured but in the way it is experienced.

Relationship means not simply a change in the structure of courtship but in its spirit.

The spirit of a Relationship is a developing sense of the two of you as a couple. You begin to *identify yourselves as a couple*, labeling your partner as "my girlfriend," "my boyfriend," "my partner," "my lover," my whatever we are calling them these days. You both think of yourselves as "going together," even if you haven't precisely defined where it is that you are going.

The spirit of a Relationship is the feeling of developing intimacy, love, and trust. You present more and more of yourself and your life to each other. You deepen your friendship. You begin to have a common history to which you can both refer.

The language of your conversation becomes much more personal, much less coded. The O.R. conversation, first introduced during The Switch, becomes a more frequent and more comfortable way of talking. You are each more willing to reveal your feelings for the other. This includes angry, anxious, or disappointed feelings as well as happy, loving ones. Your first big fight or petty spat is behind you. You are beginning to learn how to discuss problems. However, early in the Relationship stage, you don't have many to discuss. You are enjoying the honeymoon of the Plateau.

By the time you have reached the Plateau, certain significant events are likely to have occurred. These events are milestones on the path to commitment. They help clarify the status of your burgeoning relationship, and they further express its spirit.

- You've begun to meet each other's friends and family. They acknowledge the status of your courtship by automatically issuing invitations to you as a couple.

- You are openly expressing affection. You refer to each other by affectionate names. One or both of you has said, "I love you."

- You may make your first material purchase together. It could be small—a jointly owned record

180

album, plant, poster. It expresses "us" to both of you.

- You've tested your bond by spending an extended period of time together. Perhaps you took a vacation or a long weekend out of town. You've discovered you can continue to enjoy each other's company.

- You have begun to develop an exclusive sexual relationship. Neither of you is beginning courtship with anyone else. Maybe you've discussed this openly and agreed to be monogamous. Perhaps your exclusivity is unspoken, simply a sense you get from the amount of time you spend together.

- If either of you is especially eager for marriage, you will begin to sense a rising tide of expectation. It may come up in conversation, if only theoretically. Future children could figure prominently in your romantic fantasies. You may be living together or discussing the possibility. You are both testing the waters.

Your courtship will not necessarily include each of these milestones as a way to express the spirit of your developing Relationship. You can reach the Plateau with only some of these events behind you.

However, some of you have past or present Relationships that don't reflect much of the spirit described here at all. It is certainly possible to develop the structure of a Relationship (a regular pattern of dates that is assumed) without the accompanying spirit of that bond.

You may feel very close to a partner but reluctant to invest more time and obligation. Conversely, you may have fallen into a daily routine with someone, but the two of you are developing the emotional connections more slowly. A Relationship that progresses to marriage and intimacy needs both.

Happily Ever After: The Plateau

The Relationship stage unfolds in three overlapping phases: Plateau, Negotiation, Commitment.

Plateau is a fantasy time for both of you. All the uncertainties of early courtship are behind you. Most of the struggle to create a lasting bond is ahead of you. It's generally a delight.

Eventually, the world comes knocking. As you move closer to making a commitment to each other, you move closer to noticing the differences that make you hesitate. Negotiation begins as the reality of your differences sets in. It is the sometimes abrasive process of working out the kind of couple you are going to be, given the individuals you are.

Finally, Commitment is that phase in a relationship when a couple deals with all the questions of marriage.

The early months of a Relationship, which begin with Plateau, are especially enjoyable. You can strike a nice balance between your need to be close, part of a couple, and your need to be a freer, independent entity. A Relationship means you are emotionally involved, you are caring, loving, concerned. At the same time, you are not one hundred percent committed. You can get out. You can go back to your own place if you're angry. You can test yourself by flirting, insist on maintaining secret pockets of your life, experiment with getting angry or giving in. The Relationship stage can strike such a nice happy medium between having something important but nothing final that couples often linger interminably at this point of development.

You have both let go of much of the perfectionism of Pursuit. Your attention is likely to be directed toward the future of your Relationship, rather than toward a scrutiny of your partner. You are enjoying the emotional security of the Plateau.

Sexually, things are apt to be anywhere from fine to spectacular. You are less inhibited with each other, more open to exploration. Happily, you are still passionate, and your sexual interest and pleasure mask most of the other problems between you.

There are many points of view regarding how long the

Plateau does last and how long it should last. Some of you feel, if you've found the right person, the Plateau should last forever. It doesn't. But it can last a good long time. If you are still in school, separated by some distance, not divorced yet, or restrained by some similar life circumstances, your Plateau will be lengthened.

But this stage between The Switch and Negotiation can also be very brief. When your intimacy increases significantly, you are forced to become aware of and to deal with the differences between you. Living together is just such a circumstance. Contact on a daily basis pierces through the shell of fantasy you've constructed around your partner. More and more of the real person emerges. For better and for worse, you are hustled into Negotiation.

However long your Plateau lasts, one aspect of it is very important. It's during the Plateau that many people decide to marry. In the most romanticized view of marriage, the way you feel about your partner during the Plateau is the way you thought you were supposed to feel about someone you'd marry. You are growing comfortable with each other. Sex is still passionate and your illusions of extreme compatibility are still intact.

In some regards, society prepares you for marriage during the Plateau by warning you that the first year or two of marriage is the roughest. That's another way of saying that if you marry during the Plateau, you will still have Negotiation and Commitment ahead of you.

Negotiation and Commitment are easier for some of you to handle when you approach them as a married couple. You feel more secure with your partner. The stakes are higher and you believe you'll both try harder to work things out. Sometimes the legal and social bond of marriage does increase the likelihood that you will fight harder to resolve your differences and stay together.

For other couples, marriage during the Plateau has exactly the opposite effect, a rude awakening. You expected this lovely time to go on forever. When it doesn't, you find the change impossible to tolerate. You can't understand what happened. You explain, "Everything was wonderful until we got married," or "I never really knew her, I guess." The bond of marriage sometimes brings you too close together to

183

maintain the elasticity necessary to tolerate Negotiation. You feel scared and stifled when the conflicts emerge, instead of secure enough to work out differences.

Marrying during the Plateau, or, more impulsively, during Pursuit, is often a result of being "too attached to the outcome." You just want to get married; you'll worry about the kind of relationship it is later. Some couples marry during the Plateau in an effort to cut short the anxiety and pain of forming a relationship. Unfortunately, none of us gets to skip these difficulties entirely.

We need to go through all the stages of becoming a couple, positive and negative. Ideally we'd experience each of them to some degree before we decide to marry. If you marry during the Plateau, you run the risk of discovering that you've married someone with whom you cannot have a successful Negotiation. You can lock yourself into a life of disappointment and suffering. It hardly seems worth the risk, just to swap rings.

As traditional roles break down, it becomes more and more important for couples to spend some time in Negotiation before marriage. These days couples have more to negotiate.

Your grandparents probably married during the Plateau phase of their courtship. They were probably not living together, they were possibly not sleeping together. It's also unlikely that your grandmother had several lovers and chose your grandfather as the best of the lot. (If she did, she kept it to herself.) During the traditional marriage your grandparents made, both knew exactly what was expected. Wives cooked, cleaned, raised children, and performed their sexual duties. Husbands worked, took out the garbage, taught their sons to have strong handshakes, and cuddled their daughters until they got too old to cuddle. These couples were stable economic units with efficient divisions of labor. They were much less concerned with intimacy than we are. My grandmother referred to my grandfather by his last name ("Mr. Silverstein says . . .") through the fifty-five years of their marriage. She knew her role.

None of us knows our role anymore. It's an open question, resolved in courtship through the intricacies of Negotiation and the process of making a Commitment. When you two have begun to tackle the questions of what you'll mean to each other, what's expected of each other, why you disappoint each other, and how to make each other happy, you've begun to negotiate.

FINALLY, A RELATIONSHIP

Negotiation: The Intersection of Power, Love, and Real Life

Patrick and Susan are in love. They met on a blind date and have already decided to name their first child after the genius friend who thought to fix them up. On that very first date, Patrick told Susan that he wanted to marry her. Susan called her mother the next day to announce that she had "met the man."

Patrick and Susan immediately settled into a monogamous, routinized relationship. They got very close, very fast. It was easy to do. Susan simply put her life and her preferences aside to avoid any potential conflict with Patrick. He loves ice hockey and crosscountry skiing, generally sets up his life as an Outward Bound experience. Susan bought herself a down jacket and threw herself gamely into the outdoor world. She used to prefer to spend her leisure time reading junk novels and going on movie binges. These were pleasant diversions, but she did them alone. Now she has Patrick and everything has changed.

Susan turned herself inside out to maintain Patrick's interest. It worked. Patrick felt he had found the ideal "great girl." Naturally, when Susan started wanting to make less of an effort and to relax more, Patrick felt betrayed. He had never forced her into his activities, had he? They had simply been compatible. He had loved her open-minded attitude, enjoyed introducing her to his areas of expertise and having her as an eager pupil. Meanwhile, Susan realized that a few weekends on the ice was one thing, a lifetime on the ice was quite another. She began to ask for time off.

When the masks we don during Pursuit begin to be peeled back so we can be genuinely close, there is often as much disappointment generated as love.

186

♥ ♥ ♥

Maureen and Ted have been together for a year. They've begun to talk about getting married, though no formal plans have been made. But the direction of their conversations has had an effect on Maureen. She feels they are a much more solid couple. She believes they have a future. Her expectations begin to shift subtly.

When they were dating, Maureen never criticized Ted. She felt he was free to come and go as he pleased and to include her in his plans when he chose. After all, he didn't owe her anything. Lately her feelings are changing. A boyfriend is not just a date. A potential fiancé is even more important. Maureen began to feel that Ted should include her more. He could certainly spend every Friday night with his friends, but why couldn't he tell her where he went? She knows he has to travel on business, but can't he at least call her when he's away? And if he loved her, wouldn't he buy a small gift for her daughter's birthday? Kids are so sensitive to small gestures. Ted has one response to Maureen's criticisms: "I love you, but don't put rules on me."

As a relationship develops, expectations develop along with it. What may have been perfectly comfortable behavior during Pursuit no longer feels right for both of you. Your expectations probably won't develop at exactly the same time or in the same direction. Where there are differences, you will have to negotiate.

♥ ♥ ♥

Kaye and Bill have enjoyed a storybook love affair for six months. Their Pursuit took all of one date and if The Switch ever occurred, neither of them noticed. Bill is overwhelmed at his good fortune. He finds Kaye beautiful, sophisticated, and dynamic. Kaye is equally taken with Bill. She believes he is that rarest of males, one who actually listens when you talk to him. Last week they decided to live together, and they are immersed in apartment hunting. This joint project has highlighted differences between them of which they had been unaware.

Bill favors renting a small house, maybe with an option to buy. Neighborhood isn't important to him, but value for the

187

dollar is. Kaye sees them renting a larger apartment in the prestigious highrise in which she already lives. Bill's version of value is Kaye's version of tacky. Generally, Bill has been quite amenable to Kaye's preference. He has plenty of money and if she likes to spend it at nice restaurants, that's been fine with him. He draws the line at homes, however. He needs to be true to his own principles. Besides, everything else has gone Kaye's way; doesn't he deserve a little victory? A difference in values, a difference in priorities plus a challenge to the power balance—all likely elements for Negotiation.

♥   ♥   ♥

Each of these three couples is beginning to negotiate, to come to an agreement about the kind of relationship they will have. Each individual brings to the couple ideas about the "right" way to act, the "right" way to live, and the "right" way to love. During Negotiation, couples examine the differences in their beliefs and assumptions, and attempt to develop a commonly held set of operating principles.

Successful Pursuit is the delightful process of discovering the ways you mesh. Negotiation is the difficult process of coping with your differences.

More and more of the person has emerged from the fantasy ideal with whom you fell into courtship. It's rather like the fuzzy outlines of a Polaroid photograph becoming sharper and sharper as it fully develops. The clearer your picture, the more likely you are to be disconcerted by what you see. He is not as patient or as amenable as you had assumed. She is not so sweet or giving. He is not always the sharp businessman he appeared to be; she is not so consistently vivacious. She always knew that his alimony payments were high, but now she sees that he's in hock for life. He always knew that she loved her work, but now he is feeling neglected.

His children are no longer merely cute anecdotes. They are real-life limitations on his time and attention to her. Her obsession with fitness was initially a source of sexual delight. Now it's also an irritating source of lectures on his health habits.

You love each other. You are deeply involved. Lately, you are driving each other crazy. You have begun to negotiate.

This stage of struggle, ranging in intensity from mild annoyance to outright warfare, is the natural evolution of love. Evolution does not mean disintegration, though it may well feel like it to you at the moment.

Quite often during Negotiation it feels as if passion has disappeared to be replaced by irritation or a fragile peace. Needless to say these are very poor substitutes. You are likely to find the disappearance of passion a frustrating or frightening experience. Don't worry about it. It hasn't actually vanished, it's just submerged under the onslaught of Negotiation.

Passion will reappear eventually. So will love. When it does, you won't quite know where it came from or what you did to revive it. It will feel like a miracle. Actually, in a way it is. The miracle is that the spirit and the bond of a relationship may strengthen during the bad times. Negotiation is a necessary, difficult time that can deepen your mutual passion and love.

You've become a couple. Now you two are working out the details. The task of Negotiation is to decide what *kind* of couple you're going to be. It's not a conscious process, but it goes on nonetheless. The challenge of Negotiation is to handle the anger that comes up when you face conflict. You don't want to let the anger blow you apart. You don't want to swallow it and let it blow you up from the inside. Your challenge is to find the balance.

No matter how similar you two are, you won't get to avoid Negotiation. It is a cold hard fact of love.

Highly compatible couples with great similarities in family background and values may have an easier time than two lovers from wildly disparate worlds. Couples in which one or both people avoid conflict at all costs are likelier to have a quieter time than couples who have a taste for the dramatic. All of this will affect the style of your Negotiation—its frequency, intensity, and possibly decibel level. But you won't get to skip it entirely. Negotiation is unavoidable because, at a certain point in a developing relationship, a fundamental change occurs in the way the two of you see each other.

Negotiation begins when reality sets in. Reality has been likened to a cold shower. That should say it all. Reality impinges on the magic of love because:

- You get a more realistic picture of your partner.

- He or she gets a more realistic picture of you.

- Neither of you is entirely thrilled with what you see.

Falling in Love with Fantasy

The first reality that begins to set in is your dawning awareness of who your partner is. You've finally gotten close enough to see each other.

We begin every romance with an idea of our partner. As the courtship progresses we see more and more of the person himself. The gap between our idea and the actual person who emerges is the distance that must be traveled by Negotiation.

Up to this point, during Selection, Pursuit, and the Plateau, you may believe you have a clear picture of your partner. What you really have is a fantasy, a story you've told yourself about the person you've selected. What you've started with is your *projection*.

We all start courtship with a mix of projections and fantasies. We have nothing else to go on. The problem is, we're not usually smart enough to know it's a projection or a fantasy. We believe it's the truth.

The fantasy you create will be based on all the assumptions you make about your partner. We make assumptions about people all the time. You are blinded by lust and assume that any woman with a body like that will fascinate you forever. You believe that his silence indicates a deep thinker, that her career indicates a truly independent spirit. You figure that any man so highly regarded by his colleagues will always command your respect, any woman who can cook like that surely wants a child to care for.

Even if your emotions aren't running that high, you will still distort your picture of a partner. You simply don't have enough information to get a full reading. In the place of information you substitute your stereotypes, projections, beliefs about how men are or what women are like.

The difference between the fantasy person you fell in love

190

with and the real person you get is not always a disappointment. Some of us fall in love with someone we perceive as critical or tough. We are happy to discover a vulnerable heart behind the facade. Often a partner reveals a depth you never suspected or a strength you hadn't realized. Reality can be a delight as much as a disillusionment.

But, fantasy being what it is, you will probably tend to idealize your partner when you begin. She is charming, he is intriguing. You haven't had time to see the rest.

When we begin a courtship we cannot see our partners clearly because hope blinds us. We know what we want someone to be. Our own needs, longings, even love itself, make it hard to see the object of these feelings as much more than a dim outline for a while.

The while usually lasts eight or nine months. Yes, it can go much longer. Some of us won't start to look up from our fantasies for years. Yes, it can be a briefer period. Some of us are better at paying attention to reality from the onset of courtship.

Some courtships are less conducive to developing a real picture. The long-distance romance can linger in fantasy forever. Real life rarely intrudes. By contrast, when two experienced people with similar backgrounds, who are comfortable being themselves begin a courtship, each may get an accurate reading of the other early on.

Generally courtship fantasies and projections get tested only if you put in enough time. Given enough time with someone, you have more chance to learn his or her moods, sore spots, minor insanities. You discover what he eats, how often her hair is colored. Patterns of behavior emerge: Don't talk to him in the morning; she always cries the day before she gets her period; any conversation with her mother leaves her snappish for a good twenty minutes; any interaction with his ex-wife leaves him furious with all women for the rest of the night; she feels compelled to counsel her friends for hours on the phone; he insists on picking up the check for his.

Time together, which offers both variety and repetition, practically invites a more realistic picture to develop. It's only an invitation though. Lots of us, with plenty of opportunity, do not R.S.V.P. We cling to our fantasies because they are sweeter or safer. Spend time and force yourself to

191

notice. You may not love everything you see, but you will see more realistically. The strongest bonds are forged when you are able to love what is so, not just what you hope is so.

One other factor makes Negotiation likely at this point in the Relationship. When you get close to someone, he or she changes and so do you.

The Sea Change of Intimacy

Why is it that the whole world can experience you or your partner in one way, while in the privacy of your relationship both of you are something else? Why does a relationship that looks so inexplicable to the outside world often feel so comfortable to the people involved? This mysterious shift in behavior between public and private selves is the sea change of intimacy.

There are very few people with whom we establish close emotional bonds during our lifetime. Of the hundreds and thousands with whom you will have one sort of acquaintance or another through your life, probably only half a dozen or fewer will be intimate bonds. Connections of this kind might exist with your parents, your children, a uniquely close friend or two, and those romantic relationships that go the distance.

If you consider yourself in the context of these few relationships, one thing is clear. You are a different person to your loved ones than you are to the world in general. You may be a better person than the world knows you to be or a more difficult one. You may be a tough, no-nonsense employer, but a pussycat with your kids. You may be serenely self-confident to the world at large but reveal your uncertainties and insecurities to those few whom you trust.

The sea change of intimacy occurs in this way: When you have put in the time, the affection, and the emotional investment, you both break through the boundaries of your public self. You begin to show more and more of your intimate self.

The unrevealed self may be a part of you that you never examined very closely. It is the part of you developed in childhood. Our first and our most powerful relationship is with our parents. We all bring to a developing love relationship the style and beliefs of those primary bonds. This is not a conscious process. You don't decide to act as if your girlfriend is your mother or your boyfriend is your father. These are feelings and reactions bred deep within our psyches.

We learn to handle closeness, love, dependency, nurturing, anger, sexuality, acceptance, rejection, boundaries—all the facets of intimacy—first from our families. Conflicts between couples develop because each has a different set of emotional needs, fears, and expectations, learned in a different family. Here is an example of what can emerge:

After eight months, Lou and Marcy feel very much a couple. The Relationship that has developed between them is serious. Friends are starting to make wedding suggestions. Lately, Marcy has noticed a problem. Lou tends to tease her in public. He's apt to comment to a friend about her silly political opinion or her "motor mouthing." It's always done with an affectionate smile, but Marcy doesn't like it. She wants love, not criticism. It's starting to make her mad. She points it out to Lou when they are alone. He tells her she's too sensitive. She tells him that teasing is hostile; he tells her to cut out the analyzing. Each has difficulty understanding the other. Marcy wonders if Lou might not be as gentle as he first appeared. Lou finds Marcy insecure. They fight.

What's behind these differences? Lou's family expresses anger and affection in the same breath. They tease each other constantly. Dinner-table conversation is loaded with lightly veiled put-downs. When Lou's parents wanted to correct or criticize each other or one of the children, they tended to make a sarcastic remark in front of the family. Everyone laughed but the target of the criticism got the message. Lou was automatically using the same technique with Marcy that his mom and dad used with him.

Marcy was appalled. In her family, no one was permitted to say anything negative. It was a polite family, always sweet no matter how someone actually felt. Marcy was a good girl who "never gave her parents any trouble." Mom and Dad never raised their voices, at least in front of the kids. Any of the tensions of intimacy were swept under the carpet of denial.

It's easy to see why Lou and Marcy were at loggerheads. Lou was expressing his criticisms in the veiled, teasing way he learned at home. Marcy was hurt in an exaggerated fashion because her family intimacy training taught her that criticism is taboo.

When a couple is able to identify the roots of a current problem in their past experience, they are on their way to solving it. In this instance, Lou was able to see that Marcy was genuinely hurt and that there are better ways of conveying dissatisfaction than the public sarcasm his mom and dad used. Marcy was able to accept more expression of negative feelings than she had been taught to allow as a child. Both were able to move on together and create a relationship that built on the past but was more appropriate to the needs of the present.

It's difficult to see the conflicts in a current relationship as stemming from assumptions you learned in your family. It requires a degree of self-awareness and some dispassionate scrutiny of dearly held beliefs and behaviors. What gets in the way for all of us is the dead certainty that what we need, the way we do things, or what we believe is *right*.

Herb comes from a family where folks laugh, scream, yell, and generally emote all over the place when they are angry. Margarite's family goes dead silent for three days when there's a problem.

When Margarite and Herb fight, Herb screams and Margarite withdraws. Each experiences the other as "impossible to talk to." Who's right?

Ed had parents who interrogated him on his every movement. He resented the intrusions and spent his adolescence perfecting ways to dodge their scrutiny. Recently, when Ingrid makes a remark like "How was your day?" Ed reacts as if she were conducting the Spanish Inquisition. In Ingrid's home everyone happily reported their most minute activity; the whole family had hashed over every event, every decision. Ed rarely asks her anything. Doesn't he care? Ingrid asks Ed about everything. He wonders, doesn't she trust him? Who's right?

194

Don couldn't walk past his mom, even today, without getting at least an affectionate pat. Everyone was all over everyone else in his home, hugging, kissing, touching. His mom and dad still hold hands in the car. Don never questioned that physical display of affection. That's how love is shown.

When he shows his love to Gina in those ways, she winces. She doesn't feel comfortable with him clinging to her arm. It's not at all the kind of thing her dad would do. Her family loved each other, but they did not "paw" each other in public. It isn't dignified. Gina finds Don less attractive when he makes these gestures. He looks weak to her, unmanly. Don feels rebuffed more and more frequently. Gina appears cold to him and willfully distant. Who's right?

It's clear that no one is right or wrong in these situations. These partners learned different styles of intimacy. Unfortunately, when you are stuck in one of these intimacy differences, you think you're right. You are likely to believe that your assumptions, your needs are absolutely appropriate. Your partner starts to look misguided, undeveloped, uninformed, or dead wrong.

Thus the sea change of intimacy gives you a whole new view of your partner and, if you will look, of yourself. The new view emerges not only as a function of more information gathered through more time together, but because you are now behaving toward each other in new ways.

There probably will be significant differences between your version of intimacy and your partner's. Where these differences exist you need to find a patch of common ground, a DMZ. The process of finding such a meeting place is Negotiation.

Overcoming the Anger Taboo

Here's a general rule of thumb that capsulizes one of life's less pleasant truths: If you have not been angry with your partner, you have not been intimate. There is no intimacy without anger.

However natural an emotion anger may be, it is also natural to dread it. Few of us handle it well, most of us botch it up, and some of us are utterly defeated by it. If you or your partner has significant difficulty handling anger in courtship, you might notice the following kinds of patterns:

- The form of your relationship seems right, but something is missing in the spirit. You don't feel close or connected. You can't put your finger on why. Sometimes your partner seems a million miles away.

- You hesitate to bring up problems directly. It annoys you that he watches so much television, or that she doesn't seem to like your friends. You decide you'll worry about this "after you're married."

- You believe that if someone really loved you, he or she wouldn't be angry with you. You would be accepted as you are.

- Any discussion of a negative issue seems to get out of control. No matter how delicately you (or your partner) tries to raise a problem, it seems to provoke an explosion of rage. One of you ends up shouting, throwing, or threatening.

- You or your partner tends to withdraw from confrontations. You stop speaking for days, sulk, typically walk out of the room or the house during an argument.

- Either of you resorts to some form of physical abuse, however mild or unintentional.

Anger, and all of its bedfellows—frustration, annoyance, rage, hurt, irritation, betrayal—are an essential part of intimacy. It is the relationship that survives the experience of anger that has a shot at developing into love. Relationships that cannot tolerate the expression of anger cannot be close.

Of course, all of our fantasies of love are of acceptance, warmth, caring, excitement. Very few of us say, "I'll love

196

my mate very much and from time to time I will want to annihilate him.''

Intellectually, you may know sometimes you will be angry with your partner. Most of us realize that it's impossible to join lives without occasionally bumping up against each other. But the sort of anger we prepare ourselves to experience in a Relationship is the polite, rational variety. In this scenario, anger is an irritation that can be managed when two people with a ''good relationship'' sit down and discuss a problem in a civilized manner. The unpleasantness is resolved using ''good communication skills,'' and the couple advances one square on the intimacy board.

In fact, it does sometimes work in this fashion. The ability to express your thoughts and feelings and to have them received in a neutral environment *is* the hallmark of good communication. Conflict resolution is impossible without it.

More often though, anger is not so rationally dealt with. It is the bellow after an unintentional punch to a long-protected sore spot on the psyche. It scares the angry person and the target. It feels devastating. The source might seem a mystery (''Could his rage really be over the attention I paid to his cousin?''), the intensity awesome (''Yes, I was late again. But when she created the scene on the street, I was appalled.''). Finally, whatever first provoked the anger, its impact spreads way beyond the original issue.

A couple has to handle the initial event (''I'm mad because you said you'd call at six and I've been sitting by the phone all night.''). They have to weed through the defensiveness that comment provoked (''I got held up. Besides I said 'sometime around six.' I can't be reporting to you every hour.''). If it escalates, these two people, who are in a struggle to define accountability, will flood their relationship with accusations. (''You're so irresponsible/immature.'' ''Well, I can't stand how demanding you are. You never let me breathe.'')

The payoff to this confrontation could be a straightforward negotiation about accountability. Once the anger is expressed (''I don't like being kept waiting.'') and the conflict is established (''I don't like being obligated to anyone.''), these two people have opened the door to a discussion. ''How can we give you the sense of free will without keeping me dangling

197

like a fool?" "How much are you willing to have me depend on you?" Couples negotiate these kinds of issues all the time.

But it's scary. If you express your anger, you verbalize a conflict. Self-disclosure at this point carries a number of risks:

- You risk destroying the illusion that this relationship is perfect. Expressing anger punctures the myth that you and your honey have found perfection.

- You risk presenting yourself as demanding, difficult, dependent, jealous, or some other unattractive but human side of you.

- You risk rocking the boat. Maybe your partner will decide it's more trouble than it's worth.

With this self-disclosure, you risk your partner's rejection. And here you've been doing your best to be Miss Charming or Mr. Seductive Delight. You can get frozen between the conviction that you mustn't be a wimp and the fear that you'll reveal yourself as a monster.

The result is too often predictable. One or both persons bury feelings. In the interests of things "working out," you ignore your differences. Negotiations are stalled because you are afraid to identify problems. You are up against the anger taboo.

The anger taboo typically affects women more than men. Women have been raised to have more restrictions against aggressive behavior, and anger is an aggressive act. (To paraphrase feminist journalist Gloria Steinem: "A man is aggressive if he begins a war; a woman is aggressive if she puts you on hold.") Also, women often feel that they have the burden in a relationship to make things work. By this, she doesn't necessarily mean "work out to my advantage." She often means "work out well enough to keep him connected with me." Anger is a separation threat.

Ironically, many women who are sensitive to the need to assert their own feelings are able to do this with ease during Pursuit. In those first few months or so, women can be very verbal and direct about annoyances. They often pride themselves on "not letting a man walk all over me," on independence and self-esteem. The sense of autonomy that supports this attitude is often eroded as she develops a sense of becoming part of a couple.

Even if it's a risky business, the expression of anger is necessary in a Relationship because:

- It's a normal human emotion, and you need to test whether your relationship can tolerate it.

- It highlights differences so that couples can deal with them directly.

- You need to learn to adjust to each other's styles of expressing negative emotion.

You can minimize the risk of expressing anger if you learn to feel comfortable with Negotiation. Successful negotiation can take the taboo out of anger.

A Guide to Negotiation

According to Roger Fisher and William Ury of the Harvard Negotiation Project, authors of *Getting to Yes*, "Negotiation is a process of communicating back and forth for the purpose of reaching a joint decision." According to Tina, forty-three, a divorced veteran of several courtships, "Negotiation is when you go from the compliments to the issues."

Whichever definition you subscribe to, when you negotiate you are embarking on a communication process. Your ultimate aim is not to punish, ventilate, prove yourself, or dominate, though these feelings and goals may all be a part of the process. Ultimately, your aim is to *resolve*.

The first step toward resolving an issue is to identify it. This means that you will have to overcome the anger taboo enough to express your concerns. It does not have to mean that you explode, rant, sulk, pout, withdraw, or throw something in order to get your message across. All you have to do is take the risk of confronting the issue and expressing your feelings directly. You need to say, "I want to talk about . . . I'm upset about . . . I get angry when you . . . I don't like . . ."

Next, you must prepare yourself for the likely response. It probably won't be perfect. It's scary for your partner (or for you, if you are on the receiving end) to deal with anger. Anger poses a separation threat. It sounds like an attack, however gently you phrase it. For most of us, the automatic response to a threat or an attack is defense. When you are defending yourself, you are not interested in compromise or content. You are interested in self-preservation.

This cycle of attack/defend can be a major stuckpoint of Negotiation. It can look like this example:

He was late.

She says nothing, sulks, withdraws, makes sarcastic remarks. She uses whatever signals she has in her repertoire to telegraph anger without actually risking the expression of anger. She wants to see if he notices and/or cares enough to inquire. Eventually, he does.

He: What's wrong?
She: Nothing.

This kind of interchange will put off all but those who know how to handle the sulkers or mopers who have to be cajoled into expressing themselves.

He: Oh, come on, honey. I can see you're upset about something.

He continues in this vein until he either gives up in angry frustration (now both of them are withdrawn) or she expresses herself.

She (accusing or hurt): You were late. You know that I hate that.

You just do it because you like me to be the one who's waiting.

You need it for your ego.

He has been attacked. It's the rare person under attack who will acknowledge whatever elements of truth are in it immediately. Instead he either:

- Counterattacks: "*My* ego. What about your constant need to have me compliment you all the time? Talk about egos!"

200

- Defends: "Hey, I can't keep to an exact schedule. It was important."

Either way, this couple is involved in a dead-end discussion of an issue. She may escalate her anger in order to get him to pay attention to it. He may escalate his anger in order to get her to back off.

The first task of Negotiation is to work out a system of expressing anger in a safe way that gets past the automatic defenses of the recipient of that anger. The assumption is that you will be willing to risk anger and that you will also be willing to tailor the way in which you express it—all in the interests of working toward a mutually satisfactory resolution of the problem. It presumes that you are not venting anger just to push your partner around. It presumes your pique is not a hidden love test. It presumes you aren't angry with your girlfriend because your boss was angry with you. All of these causes for anger will sometimes be true for both of you, but they have little to do with resolving an issue.

There are a variety of techniques a couple can call on to make it safer to express anger. You must learn the best time, place, and style for negative communication.

Timing is crucial for some of you. I cannot discuss an issue with my husband in the morning. He hears my smallest complaints as the Raid on Entebbe if they are voiced before noon. I can't always abide by this consideration because I'm impatient and it's hard for me to control my feelings. But if an issue is important, I can usually hang on until the time is riper for a sympathetic hearing.

Some of you will have partners who cannot tolerate conflict over a meal or as soon as they get home from the office. Some women try to voice an upset feeling during a playoff game, and some men attempt serious Negotiation while their partners are coping with a crying child. It's foolish to expect that your feelings will get anything but the shortest shrift under these circumstances.

Couples counselors suggest that if you and your partner have difficulty discussing issues at a natural time—when they arise—you may consider designating a specific period. You could declare a time-out on, say, Tuesday evening. This is your moment for an O.R. conversation. You establish a rule

201

that each of you is to be given a complete hearing for your grievances, with no rebuttal, no defense, permitted. Your only goal is to be heard and understood.

In an interview with columnist Darrell Sifford, the well-known psychiatrist O. Spurgeon English revealed one of the secrets of his own marriage of more than fifty years. He and his wife have this agreement: If either of them speaks their "magic word," the other must agree to listen without interruption and wait a full three minutes before replying. English is describing his marital technique for raising a negative issue without simultaneously raising the defensive hackles. If you'd like some information on other couples' Negotiation strategies, refer to *The Intimate Enemy* by psychologist George Bach.

Place is another consideration when you choose to confront an issue. Bed is a bad place, and so is calling your partner at the office to let him (or her) know he's in trouble. As the two of you work out a system, you will come to identify the settings that are most effective.

The third factor in successfully labeling and working through an issue is the style in which you express your anger. As we discussed earlier, you will initially express your anger as you learned to do within your family. If they yelled, you'll yell. If Mom shouted but Dad withdrew to the basement, you might unconsciously seek to re-create that pattern in your own courtship. The two of you have to learn each other's native tongue for anger. You may each have to adjust your style in order to make it easier for your partner to receive you.

When you've identified the time, place, and style of expression most likely to be easily received, the two of you can begin to negotiate your conflict of needs. You may not be able to identify that conflict initially. Instead it will probably appear that you are righteously angry because you've been hurt or misused by some "wrongness" on your partner's part. His unreliability bothers you. She doesn't help to clean your apartment like a good girlfriend should. She won't tell you how she spends her free time. He won't make plans more than two days in advance.

Your next step is to try to elevate the conflict from the specific issue to the underlying problem. She won't clean, or

202

he won't plan? The struggle is over the different expectations you each bring to the role of girlfriend or boyfriend. If you stop discussing cleaning and planning and start discussing the differences in your expectations, you are on your way to successful Negotiation.

Fisher and Ury describe the first step in successful conflict resolution as "separating the people from the problem." This is the negotiating specialists' version of *Don't take it personally*. It means you need to distinguish your feelings of hurt, disappointment, offended pride, and anxiety from the underlying problem, which is a clash of expectations. Too often we get stuck focusing on and easing our upset feelings without ever addressing the issue.

The greatest enemy to separating the person from the problem is *blame*. ("I'm angry because you refuse to plan. You refuse to plan because you are a selfish adolescent who . . ." "I'm angry because you won't help me clean. You won't clean because you're a spoiled princess who . . .") Blaming someone else can give you a wonderfully self-righteous feeling, but it cannot help you to negotiate.

When you are absorbed with placing the blame you leave yourself open to a whole gamut of potential distortions and miscommunications. Blame sets you up to be a mind reader ("You treat me this way because you have no respect for women.") It makes the blamer helpless to improve things ("I won't be happy unless *you* stop . . .") It makes the object of the blame as defensive as possible. He or she must tune you out, prove you wrong, in order to protect himself.

Most of us slip into blame because it feels right. Rightness doesn't matter, as Ury and Fisher point out. Blame won't work in Negotiation, even if it's justified. It's easy to miss your own tendency to blame. You are probably blaming when:

- You say "you" instead of "I." For example, "You were mean," or "You broke your word," instead of "I feel hurt," "I expected something else." You cannot be wrong if you are describing your own experience, but you are on shaky ground when you describe someone else's.

203

- You cannot articulate your partner's point of view. Instead, you fall back on the bad/mad theory. In that approach you account for your partner's behavior by saying that he or she is either bad ("He's always totally selfish."), or mad ("She gets irrational.") If you are relying on the bad/mad hypothesis you aren't listening, you are blaming.

- You feel helpless. The situation seems entirely out of your hands because you are not the cause of the problem. Once again, instead of identifying a conflict, you've decided someone is to blame.

Once the problem is identified as separate from personal feelings, there are three more steps to a successful outcome, according to Ury and Fisher. The intent of each step is the same: to help you and your partner focus on feasible, creative ways to negotiate differences and combat the tendency in all of us to lock into rigid judgmental positions that make resolution impossible. You'll find the details of their strategies in *Getting to Yes*.

There's one last important point. The object of successful Negotiation in courtship is not winning, it is compromise. If you win and your partner loses, you lose. If you need to prove you are right, you are not seeking successful Negotiation in courtship. You are seeking victory.

When you have a difference in any of the arenas of conflict, neither of you is right—you are different. You need to seek an adjustment that will accommodate the difference.

Arenas of Conflict

Negotiation in courtship is a subtle version of the power struggles that married couples drag with them like a piece of toilet paper stuck to the marital shoe. The theme remains the same: What do we do about our differences? The psychological issue is the same: I didn't expect this relationship to cost me so much. Am I losing more than I gain?

The feelings aroused in Negotiation during courtship are likely to be less intense than when the same conflicts re-emerge after marriage. Your awareness of the deep differences between you dawns slowly. These are new quarrels, and they don't carry with them the weight of frustration, exhaustion, or bitterness that years of go-rounds on the same topic can generate. The content of battles during courtship tends to be more trivial than during marriage because the two of you do not yet share major life responsibilities. A disagreement over whether taxicabs are a frivolous waste or a necessary self-indulgence will echo the same themes of power, money, and social class as a later battle over buying a house. But taxis are a lot easier to give in on.

You may feel mild disapproval during courtship if your partner is routinely chaotic about paperwork and detail. When you are sharing a joint tax return, mild disapproval can become rage.

Your partner's long-standing commitment to Sundays with the family can be a trial or an irritation. You may or may not be interested in challenging this plan now. But four or five years of routine Sunday dinners is an unacceptable bore.

All these factors may constitute a subtle undercurrent rather than a tidal wave of conflict. The undercurrent is there. If you could bring yourself to pay attention to it, you could probably define a more satisfying Relationship for yourself. It's hard to pay attention to, though, because at this point your eyes are likely to be focused on the goal. One or both of you is hoping that things will "work out."

You will find endless possibilities for working things out. During Negotiation, the topics you can find to fight about are as numerous as there are couples in love. However, the general themes of these battles can be grouped in several major areas. These are the arenas of conflict. They include:

- Money
- Sex
- Accountability
- Expectations
- Personal flaws
- Family and friends

205

Each of these issues is discussed separately to give you the clearest picture of the threads of Negotiation. Keep in mind that these threads are usually bundled into one lumpy knot. It's the knot that sends you screaming to your friends, cursing your beloved in particular, and the opposite sex in general.

The toughest part of the knot is that at its center is the struggle for power. The bottom line of every Negotiation is this: How are we going to run this show—your way or mine? All Negotiations ask, at least in part, who is going to give in to whom? What kind of couple are we—your kind or mine? To the extent that you are engaged in a power struggle, you will each be less interested in finding a comfortable compromise than you are in winning. If you do get stuck in a power struggle, and we all do sometimes, following the rules for successful resolution can help you come unstuck.

Money

Money is one of the hallowed battlegrounds of the married couple. Unmarried couples usually get to skip most of the battle because, with the exception of some couples who are living together, few courting couples take the step of pooling their money. Each person remains the sole authority on the question of how much to spend on what. A partner might hint, pressure, or cajole, but because the money isn't shared there is no true negotiation possible.

What conflict does exist in courtship over money occurs mostly around the question of who pays for what. Generally the question is dealt with early in Pursuit. It is a tricky question because the rules on money and courtship are currently fuzzy. Instead of direct Negotiation, dating couples rely on a vague formula described by Peter Applebome of *The New York Times*. It includes:

- Who did the asking

- The degree to which people accept traditional sex roles

- Who has the most money

As a couple develops an ongoing relationship, they may need

206

to adjust their arrangement. They may assume large financial burdens, like vacations, that necessitate direct discussion of how to divide the expenses. They may begin to make joint purchases, like gifts to mutual friends, which can open up the arena of financial negotiation. They may begin to save for a common goal—a wedding, a house—that is a first step toward pooling money.

None of these common projects really strikes the emotional nerve that negotiating over how to spend our money stirs. In a sense, this is unfortunate because newly forming couples don't have the opportunity to test themselves on this tough issue. In another sense it's a welcome reprieve. You and your beloved have a chance to practice negotiating on less sensitive issues first. These will help to prepare you for the interesting conversation you will have when your partner wants to invest the wedding present money in an incredible stock tip and you want to buy a sailboat.

Sex

Sex is another great arena of conflict in marriage that rarely troubles a thriving courtship. For one thing, whatever sexual problems you might have are masked by the newness of your passion.

Eventually a couple may discover that he only needs to make love every month, while she prefers every week. During courtship they may both be interested every day. He actually prefers the morning, she prefers the night. During courtship, any time might strike either of them as a good time. How often, when, in what position, for how long—all these are likely to become more negotiable as the freshness of your passion fades.

When you are aware of sexual problems early in courtship, you may be tempted to terminate the relationship rather than negotiate. It's hard for a dating couple or a new relationship to handle the strains of sexual incompatibility, impotence, premature ejaculation, the inability to achieve an orgasm— that whole litany of sexual malfunctions to which we are all sometimes prey. If the problem resolves itself quickly, a relationship can continue to form. If it lingers, a couple can get stuck. New couples don't have the history or language to negotiate their sexual problems freely together. Sexual difficulties are rarely resolved by symbolic communication. You need to get right down to the mechanical nitty-gritty to make progress. Sex therapy can be very helpful to couples in this area, but new couples often resist the intimate involvement implied by joint therapy. It feels like too much too soon. For all these reasons, rather than negotiate sexual conflict, courting couples often either deny the problem or break up over it.

The one exception in the sexual arena that many couples must negotiate is the question of monogamy. Strictly speaking, monogamy is not a negotiable issue. If you believe in it strongly, this belief will form the bedrock of your relationship. It rarely works to compromise this value or to seek a middle ground. In the best of all cases, if you feel strongly about a monogamous relationship, so will the partner you've chosen. Conversely, if you believe strongly in a sexually open arrangement, hopefully you will find partners who share your beliefs.

What is necessary for many couples to negotiate is the timing of the commitment to monogamy. Sexual exclusivity is a step on the road to Commitment. It's unlikely that both of you will want to take this step at exactly the same time. There is a difference between simply not sleeping with someone new and making an agreement to be sexually exclusive. Either you or your partner may actually have been monogamous for months, if only because it's too risky or time consuming to juggle lovers. However, you've still reserved the right to be sexually free. You enjoy the luxurious psychological room of knowing that you could make love to an interesting stranger if the spirit moved you.

Agreeing aloud to be sexually exclusive removes this sense of potential. It also deepens the bond between you and your partner. This is the trade-off that many of us will negotiate.

Like every Negotiation about commitment, your questions about monogamy are likely to be "When should I expect it?" "How long should I wait for it?" "If I don't get it, what should I do?" The answers are individual, but the general guidelines are universal:

208

- Don't expect instant monogamy simply because any degree of freedom for your partner threatens you. Try to control your own rush into a monogamous affair. Quite often this is less an expression of love for your partner than of a desire for security on your part. Remember, your attachment to the outcome of courtship can make you race through some of the necessary unfolding of feelings. It's not to your benefit in the long run.

- The commitment to monogamy is appropriate when the bond between the two of you has deepened into a significant relationship. If you've reached this emotional point, you may have to wait for your partner to catch up. Wait as long as you possibly can while you still feel good about yourself. Don't wait one minute past this point.

- When you feel uncomfortable, you will need to raise the question, air your feelings, and listen to your partner's. It's a good time to remember courtship's cardinal rule: *Don't take it personally.* A partner who is hesitating over monogamy is not necessarily hesitating over you. It's just as likely that he or she is hesitating over Commitment itself.

- If, over time, discussion, and more time, the agreement to be monogamous is not forthcoming, you have a decision to make. How important is this value to you? Could you live without it? Could you close your eyes to small transgressions?

If your self-examination makes it clear that you cannot give up your belief in monogamy, you will have to leave.

Love is based on trust. If monogamy is one of your necessary building-blocks for trust, as it is for most of us, there can be no substitutions.

Accountability

Accountability is the hallmark of childhood and the bane of adolescence. Having survived these two, accountability becomes a negotiating point of courtship.

Accountability refers to the degree to which you need to report, explain, or predict your actions now that you are part of a couple.

Accountability may mean:

- Accurate and complete reporting of the time you spend apart

- Communicating immediately and directly any change of plans

- Responding openly to direct, intimate questioning

- Planning your time in conjunction with someone else's requirements.

Accountability exactly hits the sore spot between freedom and attachment, between autonomy and dependence. It's the eternal ouch between these two conflicting needs of our souls.

You've come across these conflicting human needs many times in this book, because they represent the core costs and rewards of intimacy. Courtship, the process by which you become deeply and securely attached, is the path to the rewards of intimacy. If you successfully complete a courtship and marry, you deliver into your life companionship, security, love, and the intense joy of being known, understood, and accepted.

The price is your freedom.

When lovers negotiate accountability, they are negotiating one of the costs of love. Accountability is a struggle to the degree that the two of you vary in your comfort with it. If you are both comfortable with, even delighted by, an anchor for your movements, it's not likely to be a problem. Many of us are more soothed than threatened by limits.

It becomes a problem when one of you resents or resists limits while the other only feels secure to the degree that limits exist. There is no "right" amount of accountability, no correct limitation to freedom toward which you should strive. Your goal in Negotiation is to come to an agreeable level of limits with which you can both be comfortable. One of you may have to surrender the prerogatives of freedom and spontaneity in order to allay the anxieties of a partner. One of you may have to sacrifice the reassurance of being constantly consulted in order to soothe the trapped feelings of a partner. You will be able to reach a middle ground if you are able to focus squarely on the problem, separate it from your personal feelings, acknowledge your different needs, and negotiate a compromise.

Expectations

Since courtship is a social ritual, it offers carefully prescribed social roles that we are asked to assume. Last year you were you, but this year you are someone's boyfriend or girlfriend. One of the chief problems of courtship is the difference between your personal interpretation of the role and your partner's expectation of how you'll play the role. The difference between his/her expectation and your interpretation is an arena of constant Negotiation.

Valerie felt that Walt, as her boyfriend, should have made a special effort on her birthday. She wouldn't have minded a terrific fuss—a surprise party or a romantic gesture. She'd never insist on that; it would be expecting too much. But it really got to her when he did *nothing*! She couldn't believe it.

Walt noticed that she was angry. He was genuinely perplexed. Valerie knows he'd made lunch reservations at the best restaurant in town. He's sorry that a crisis at work forced him to cancel. She knows they're going to go next week. Walt feels awful for having hurt Valerie but he feels rather put upon too. Birthdays in his family are low-key affairs. At most he sends a card. What's Valerie's problem?

There is no end to the list of potential events or issues about which you and your partner might have different expectations. Birthdays, vacations, Christmas, New Year's Eve, Valentine's Day, Mother's Day, Super Bowl Sunday, your anniversary, are all fertile ground for a clash of expectations. Time, money, decision making, leisure, sex, and chores (if

211

you even half-live together) are all possible points of contention depending on how expectations differ.

Everywhere your expectations differ you will have the opportunity to negotiate a compromise. You will be handed the opportunity, but quite often you won't take advantage of it.

Instead, you may ignore the disappointment or anger that your unfulfilled expectations cause. You pretend it didn't bother you. You discharge your feelings by complaining to a friend. It's safer than complaining to your partner. Or, you sulk, pout, withdraw, get sarcastic—anything to signal anger without actually talking about it.

Some of you focus all your energy on becoming the ideal boyfriend or girlfriend. You get a keen sense of what's expected of you and do your best to turn into it. You only feel the pain of failing to live up to your partner's expectations. You don't take your own seriously. You are more likely to say, "We'll work that out after we're married," than to express your feelings.

A clash of expectations is a legitimate arena of Negotiation. It's crucial that the two of you develop a negotiation style for discussing these differences. The expectations attached to the roles of "husband" and "wife" are even more elaborate and more likely to stir conflict.

The "Personal Flaw"

Many couples negotiate intimacy and distance in a different arena. They establish an "I love you, but . . ." bond and have a power struggle, or a commitment battle, over some personal habit that is annoying, offensive, or unacceptable.

Hal hates Marlene's smoking. He says he'd live with her, marry her, but he cannot commit himself to a lifetime of smoke-filled rooms. Yes, she was smoking when they met. But it bothers him more now that they are involved. Marlene is willing to abide by a series of complex rules that involve smoking outside, by an open window, etc. They all miss the point. Hal wants a nonsmoker, and besides:

- His friends agree that he's right.
- Everything he reads agrees with him.

212

- If she loved him, she'd give it up!

Donna finally let Mark know that she wishes he'd take off 25 pounds. It embarrasses her to introduce him around. She never saw herself with a fat man, doesn't respect that part of him. Besides, it's a sign of poor self-esteem. She has taken to watching what he eats. Every morsel of dessert on his fork is reflected in disapproval on her face. Mark has resorted to eating maniacally on the nights they are apart so that he can escape disapproval when they are together. He knows it's crazy, but he can't seem to stop. The more she presses, the more he resists. Donna is convinced she's being reasonable. She wants Mark, she wants a thinner man, and besides:

- All her friends agree with her.
- Everything she reads validates her point of view.
- If he really loved her he'd lose weight!

The "flaw" can include perpetual lateness, chronic sloppiness, perceived cheapness, childish jokes or behavior, poor table manners. You and your sweetheart may even invent one all your own over which to negotiate.

The battle over the personal "flaw" is usually a pure power struggle. The critic wants to redesign the partner to his or her own tastes and specifications. All the arguments about the "rightness" of the critic's preferences are a justification for the naked impulse to control.

The partner who is the object of criticism enters into the game with equal vigor. He or she struggles for power by defining an area of personal autonomy and refusing to give in. Ironically, this expression of any individual's right not to conform or to be controlled can backfire. It can lead you to hold on to a habit or behavior that is self-defeating or dangerous, just to establish your right to do so.

The only way out of this power struggle is to stop all attempts at Negotiation. The critic may be "right," but he has to back off anyway. Responsibility for a personal flaw is in the hands of the person who has the problem. She (or he) is the only one who has the choice of changing.

The critic has a choice also. The critic can learn to live

213

with the flaw, or leave. That decision is usually difficult enough to require all the energy that was once directed toward your partner.

Family and Friends

A couple draws a circle around itself in order to define "us." One of the side effects of this necessary circle is that everyone who falls outside is automatically labeled "them." Some of those who've become "them" are people with whom you used to be "us."

Your family must make this kind of transition. Your family of friends must make a similar adjustment. Each one of these people must be moved aside to some degree in order to make room for the new person in your life. Each one experiences some sense of loss. Eventually, so do you.

You and your partner will negotiate the boundaries of your circle. These boundaries must be solid enough to give the two of you a firm sense of being each other's primary person, They must also be fluid enough to include the bonds of love, loyalty, and support each of you has with significant others. Most probably the two of you will disagree about precisely where to draw your boundaries. Where you differ, you will have to negotiate.

Your goal is to get your family and friends out of your courtship, but to keep them in your life. The precarious balance you achieve will need to be acceptable to your new partner, to your old support system, and to yourself. Achieving this balance can be a process of endless negotiation. To keep your social network out of your courtship:

Don't introduce a new partner too soon, or with too much fanfare. You will attract endless commentary ("Should I be planning the shower?" "Is she still around?") which can only increase your anxiety and upset your courtship.

Give yourself the opportunity to explore your own feelings before you solicit the thoughts and feelings of the people who influence you the most. Naturally you'd enjoy hearing the sound of applause when you bring home your new lover. Quite often what you get instead is a big Bronx cheer. After all, your family and friends have their own projections about

214

who is right for you, what you should require in a partner, whom they'd prefer to bring into the social circle. Don't please them, please yourself.

Don't allow family and friends to judge the structure of your relationship. If you encourage it, your social group will have opinions not just on who your partner should be but on how your relationship should be run. You can inadvertently encourage these judgments by reviewing each step of your courtship with them. When you depend heavily on the advice and guidance of your friends, don't be surprised if they are offended when you refuse to follow it.

Work hard to keep your family out of your internal monologue. Their views of you, beginning in your childhood, can become powerful self-fulfilling prophecies.

For example, Diane's mother has always been desperate for Diane to marry, but doubtful that she'd ever be able to. Mom has disapproved of the way her daughter "handles" men from as far back as Diane can remember. ("You'll never get one to marry you." "You don't know how to make him want you." "You don't know how to make him happy.") At any difficult point in courtship, Diane tends to fall apart. She is consumed with an anxious dread. She gets stuck on the thought "Here I go again. I'll always ruin things."

Through psychotherapy, Diane was able to recognize her thoughts as the automatic expectations she had absorbed from her mom. Diane's own internal monologue was programmed by her mother's image of her.

In order to counteract any negative self-image that might have been generated by a critical parent, you'll need to closely examine your own internal courtship monologue. If it reflects old negative family images of you rather than what you've worked to become, you will need to edit it. Even loving families can be a negative influence. To keep them out of your courtship, you need to keep them out of your head.

Though it's important to keep your loved ones out of your courtship, it's equally important to keep them in your life while you are developing a relationship. You need to balance

215

the requirements of time, attention, obligation, and loyalty between your old ties and your new one.

You do this not simply because they need to feel loved and cared for. So do you. Your support system is your safety net. It keeps you balanced, satisfies some of your dependency needs so you don't overwhelm your partner, helps you to preserve your independent identity when love threatens to engulf you. Losing touch with your family and friends is losing touch with yourself.

Try to strike a balance between including your new love with your old friends and spending time with old friends on your own. Never including your new lover is rigidly compartmentalizing your life. Always insisting on including your "other half" is denying your friends access to you. Having him or her around changes things. That's nice sometimes but it's a burden on a regular basis.

Use symbolic gestures. Send cards, gifts, cut out an article, remember birthdays. Be there in whatever way you can. Your family and friends need the evidence that you still care.

Don't pass on criticism of your partner. Quite often, in order to lend support to a point we're negotiating, we're apt to refer to the private comment of a friend. "Rosalind thinks you're immature too." "Bill said he'd never put up with your sloppiness." Long after your negotiation is satisfactorily resolved, these remarks linger in the memory.

Don't criticize your partner's friends or family. Oh, you will be tempted, just as they are tempted to criticize you. Resist. There's no reason why you and your lover should have the same taste in people just because you have a taste for each other. Unless you are being seriously consulted as to your opinion, don't offer it.

If you or your partner has a child you have a special problem. It is right and appropriate that we separate from our nuclear family and invest time and attention in a new person. Even if it hurts your parents or siblings, even if your

216

friends complain of your neglect, everyone understands that this separation is in the natural course of events.

It is not in the natural course of events for you to separate from your child. Your child separates from you, when he or she is ready, usually with a fair amount of anger and ambivalence. Your unfolding courtship is a direct threat to your child. Developing a relationship with your partner's child is equally sensitive. This is the one instance in which family cannot be excluded from the courtship. You and your partner may require professional support to work out the complications. You will certainly require unending patience and an insane sense of humor.

None of these suggestions is easy to follow, especially if you are wildly in love and have only the dimmest appreciation that there continues to be an outside world. Eventually, however, you and your mate will have to take your places in that outside world. The two of you will have to decide what your relationship to that world is going to be. You will have to set boundaries and to test them. All this requires successful and ongoing Negotiation.

How Much Is Too Much?

Many of the conflicts in these arenas—money, sex, accountability, expectations, personal "flaws," family, and friends can be negotiated to a successful resolution. Some will be permanent thorns in your love. You will learn to live with them, continue to battle forever to change them, or end your courtship because of them.

There is one final key to successful Negotiation in courtship: your attitude. If you are seeking to develop love, you need to know that it thrives in an atmosphere of uncritical acceptance. In the best of all worlds, love would be limitless.

Every time you notice a difference between what you wanted in a partner and what you've got, ask yourself this question: Can I live with it? Then, bend over backward in the direction of living with it.

Yes, a lot of changing has to be done in order to develop

an intimate bond. But most of us put our efforts into changing our partners. The smart place to put your energy is in changing yourself.

If your partner needs a high level of accountability and you need a great deal of freedom, don't put your energy into changing your partner. Change yourself. Ask yourself first, Can I give in on this? Can I give up my need for the sake of his or her happiness? Then give and give and give. Give with love, give for the sake of love, give in the interests of your own happiness. Give because changing yourself represents your own personal growth and because it's the vehicle for your own satisfaction. Give because love is accepting someone, not changing someone.

In order to be giving when you love, you have to let go of the critical, judgmental part of yourself. In the interview with columnist Darrell Sifford mentioned earlier, psychiatrist O. Spurgeon English precisely identified this problem.

> Young people—and some not so young—desire too much and have too little to give. They are looking for fulfillment and know too little about how to fulfill. Instead of using a gentle way to patiently help the growth of their mate, they resort to the shortcut or lazy way of getting what they would like by nagging and criticizing. The human psyche in this latter part of the 20th century isn't strong enough or mature enough to take, much less use, the comments of a mate who believes that he or she is speaking for the good of the other.

What worries you about this advice? You are afraid of being steamrollered. You are afraid of doing all the giving, of being exploited as a result. You've been encouraged to take your anger seriously, to stand up for your individual needs, to assert yourself. It might seem that you are being asked to let go of all this, in the interest of love.

Both of you need to let go of a lot of it. Pick your issues carefully. Once an issue has been aired, do your best to see if it's one you could possibly give in on. You won't be able to accept and live with all of the differences between you and your partner. Some will drive you mad. But you should be able to let go of some. The question is, How much is too much?

In the real world, love is not limitless, nor should it be. We need to place limits on our willingness to give in order to protect ourselves.

There are only a few situations that seem to automatically require that you go beyond the boundaries of healthy compromise in order to maintain the relationship. These include trying to negotiate a relationship with:

- Anyone who physically abuses you
- An unrecovered addict, whether the addiction is to drugs or alcohol
- A compulsive gambler
- A pathological liar, con man, sociopath
- Anyone who subjects you to mental abuse by their constant criticism and depreciation of your personal worth

Beyond these five behavioral extremes, only you can make the judgment as to whether you've reached the limits of your ability to love. You probably won't find this very comforting. Most of us look for some objective standard when we are confronted with the need to compromise a cherished belief or desire. We ask, "Don't I have the *right* to expect . . ." (That a man will support me? That a woman will want children? That he'll do his share of the housework? That she'll be home with me on the weekends?)

It's the obvious question, but it's not a productive one. You have the right to *expect* anything you want. What you expect and what life has to offer are quite often separate realities. The useful question is, "If I live with what I've got in this Relationship, what will it cost me?"

If all it costs you is an unfulfilled set of expectations, you can probably work that out. After all, which would you rather build a life around—a firmly cherished set of expectations or a dearly loved, real live person?

If, on the other hand, you discover that the cost of the relationship is your self-respect, you have reached the limits

219

of love. Each of us requires something different in order to feel good about ourselves. One man needs to be head of the household, while another needs to be half of a working partnership. One woman needs to be an independent achiever, while another wants to be loved enough to merit financial support.

You can compromise on how you always thought things should be or would be. You cannot compromise on what you need to feel good about yourself. Of course, it helps if your sense of self is not so shaky that your partner must be perfect in order for you to feel okay. In general, the better you feel about yourself, the fewer limits you will place on your ability to love.

The more positive your self-image, the more people you will be able to love. Your requirements will be fewer, because you aren't so needy. The better you feel about yourself, the more often you'll be able to invoke the magic words of Negotiation: "I'm sorry." "I apologize." "I was wrong."

FINALLY, A RELATIONSHIP

Commitment, Aargh

There is just no way around it: Commitment during courtship is symbolized by the decision to marry. This is a truth that has felled strong men and reduced normally functioning women to a blithering frenzy.

It makes no difference whether the question "Will you marry me?" has been put to you point-blank, or whether it's just been in the air for months. Once the question has been raised, the jig is up. There are only two answers: yes or no. "Maybe," "later," "someday" and "let's not talk about it now" are not answers. They are delaying tactics. There is an answer yet to come.

While most of courtship is a sea of change, a constantly shifting flow of attachment and distance, marriage is a black-and-white choice. You can be sort of living together, kind of going together, or semiserious. But you are either married or you are not. You either do it or you don't. There's no place to hide. That's what can make it so scary, but also what makes it so interesting.

The question "Will you marry me?" may be black-and-white, but the answer is frequently delivered in a thousand shades of gray. "Not yet . . . I'm not ready . . . it's not you, it's me . . . You know the financial pressure I'm under . . . It's some sort of block I have, I'm working on it . . . I'm scared to marry because my parents were so unhappy . . . divorce ruined my childhood . . . Why ruin a great Relationship?!"

However jaded or sophisticated we have become as a society, the act of marriage has a powerful meaning for all of us. It means things like "in sickness and in health," "for richer, for poorer," and " 'til death do us part." You can't get much more forever than that.

221

Paradoxically, in a society with a 50-percent divorce rate marriage continues to be viewed as a permanent state. The ease with which divorce is possible is not seen as a reassuringly available exit. Instead, it is a threat to our happiness and stability. As with most threats to our well-being, we deny the possibility of divorce as best we can. Even Zsa Zsa Gabor on her way to wedding number eight was quoted as saying, "This time, dahlink, it's forever."

If you think of it beforehand, you are likely to be quite troubled by the implications of marriage. Frankly, when people used to talk to me about Commitment, I would get an image of some lunatic asylum where they sent married people. I could not fathom giving my life over to a stranger, and I probably didn't think that anyone would want me.

On the other hand, some people appear quite capable of not thinking the notion through at all. They appear to be the opposite of scared. They are nonchalant. Some men and women talk about wanting a "committed relationship" as if it were a consumer product and they need to know the best place to shop. ("Where do I go to meet someone? I'd like to have a committed relationship.")

Most of us are in the middle, eager to find someone we can love enough to form a partnership, anxious about the sacrifices that partnership will require.

What you are hoping is that you'll be so besotted with love that it will overwhelm any anxieties you may have about commitment. You are hoping you will know it's right, and your beloved will know exactly the same thing about you at the same time. The two of you can then stage a magical engagement moment, followed by living happily ever after.

If your own courtship is not exactly a replica of this fantasy, don't be concerned. Many aren't.

Realities of the Decision

The reality of deciding to get married very often involves anxiety, disappointment, external pressure, and a thousand other unattractive elements you were hoping to have nothing to do with. Love, sex, passion, and dependency get mixed

222

in a bundle with independence, obligation, social expectations, and plain old fear. Deciding to marry is a process of carefully and repeatedly weighing your bundle. If the load feels too heavy, you'll try to kind of shift it around on your psychological back until it's more comfortable.

Does getting married really have to be such an ordeal? No. As with every other phase of courtship we've discussed, some couples glide right through and others are thrown into a convulsion. This chapter focuses on the potential upheaval of commitment. What is a crisis for some couples is the natural next step for others.

Laurie, thirty-five and three times married, describes her latest and best marriage this way: "There was no proposal. We had each left someone else to be together. When we got disentangled it was more like, 'Well, what do we do now?' It was very casual, no prolonged conversation. It didn't make me nervous. It was just the next step. I couldn't imagine myself not married. That's just the way I set up my life."

Libby and Frank felt they recognized each other instantly. Frank says, "We'd both been hurt by divorce, and we'd both been knocked around by the singles scene. Two weeks after we met, I felt more comfortable with Libby than I had with my ex-wife after two years. Anyway, Libby and I and her kids were like an instant family. Marriage seemed a natural evolution."

Jose and Francie had a seven-year courtship, but it started when Francie was only fourteen. She says, "Jose was my only boyfriend, practically my only date. I was sure I'd marry him when I was still in junior high. I thought then that twenty-one was a perfect time to marry so we made a pact. When I turned twenty-one, we carried it out."

Other couples responded to a push. It made the step easier.

"We wanted to buy a house. Finally I said, 'Well, a house is just as big a commitment as marriage. So we might as well.' "

"This sounds crazy for a woman of twenty-eight, but we wanted to be able to sleep together when we visited our parents. Marriage was the only way."

"I was constantly on the road commuting between his college and mine. I was thinking of transferring to where he was, but my dad said, 'Forget it. I'm not putting you two any closer to each other!' I called Kenny and said, 'My dad's giving me all kinds of trouble about transferring. What should we do?' He said, 'I think we ought to get married.' It was really a matter of logistics."

For many of you, it won't be this easy. You will feel the full force of ambivalence as you work through the question of commitment.

"We'd been a couple on and off for years. She was always the one to break up with me, and I guess it made me feel insecure about her. Anyway, this time she wanted to get married and all of a sudden I had a thousand doubts. I just kept thinking, 'Could I really never sleep with another woman for the rest of my life?' Of course, I told her what I was worried about and she got furious. Oh, God, lots of tears. Finally, she gave me an ultimatum. Marry me or else! You know, I think I just needed to hear her say it. Before that moment she always had one foot out the door."

"I was so young, twenty-one. I got engaged because I felt I should. It was just the next thing to do. But the first day I got my engagement ring, I had it lying on the dining room table. It needed to go to the jeweler to be fitted. Anyway, I cleared off the table and looked at the ring, and I confused it with the tab of a soda can. I threw it away. Two hours later, I found it at the bottom of the trash. Do you think I was trying to tell myself something?"

"Lee was upstairs playing with my five-year-old son. My son asked him, 'Are you going to marry my mom?' He said, 'I don't know. Let's go ask her.' Lee came into the kitchen and said, 'I think it's time we got married.' All I could think of was 'why?' He started going on about insurance policies and then he added 'Incidentally, your son asked me to ask you.' When you're a single mom and your son picks out a man, that's a pretty powerful persuasion. Besides, when Lee moved in and I was nervous about it, he said, 'Trust me, it'll be OK.' I did and it was. I decided to trust him again. I said yes. I cried my eyes out at the wedding and my son held my hand the whole time.''

The Watershed Moment

The entire ritual of courtship is a gradual process of easing you into Commitment. Courtship tries to set it up so that Commitment sneaks up on you.

As you move from Seduction through The Switch to the Plateau and beyond, you are trading a part of your autonomy for attachment. You've given away greater and greater chunks of your life, rewriting the label on your time from ''mine'' to ''ours.'' It's the beginning of Commitment.

If your O.R. conversations have been working well, you've exposed the private, normally guarded, parts of yourself. If these parts have been received with sympathy and under-standing, you've created a unique connection with your partner. That connection is the beginning of the Commitment stage.

You have probably also, at least in a limited way, ''for-saken all others.'' You have been testing monogamy during courtship. Either eventually or immediately, you and your partner have stopped seeing other people. You don't begin new romances or follow up on flirtations that have potential. Probably the two of you have discussed the matter and agreed to be sexually exclusive. You may have your doubts or the occasional pang of lust for someone else. But, either tenta-tively or passionately, you've taken the step to become sex-ually committed.

Besides all the communicating and negotiating you have been doing together, you've probably been doing some pri-vate thinking on your own. For many of you, there is a mo-ment or series of moments in which you have a private

225

conversation with yourself; this dialogue constitutes the real beginning of your commitment to your partner. It's the moment when you first take him seriously, or first allow yourself to admit what she's come to mean to you. It reflects a major shift in the way you label the relationship and what you expect from it. This moment is a watershed in the entire courtship. Here's how some men and women recall it:

"I remember exactly. I was driving along Route 40 on my way home, and I suddenly had the thought, 'This is it. I'm going to marry this man.' I felt it right in my stomach—a rush of adrenaline, panic and excitement all at once. I don't know what suddenly triggered the thought but once I had it, there was no going back."

"We had just visited friends in the hospital who had their first child. Afterwards, we took a walk along the river and I suddenly had the flash, 'This could be the man I have a child with.' Then I thought, 'No, no, not him. I'm not that sure, don't be silly,' but I couldn't put it out of my head."

"It was the one time in my life that I made a completely selfish decision. I was walking out on a pregnant wife to go to Anita. When I left with a bag in each hand, I thought, 'Well, there's no turning back now. She's it!' "

"I knew the moment I walked into her house. I took one look at the kid and the dog and the comfortable mess of books and I knew I wasn't leaving."

"One day Norman and I played tennis. My ex and I used to play a lot and it was always a nightmare. He'd be all over the court and I'd be backed up into one little corner. I'd be sulking and he'd be yelling if I missed a shot. I hated it. When Norman and I played it was just—tennis. It was so nice to have fun and be cared about. I began to love him for making me feel good."

One might think that with the major issues of accountability, fidelity, and self-disclosure behind you and this much of

226

a bond between you, the question of marriage would not be such a traumatic one. Often it's not.

But often it is. When it is, it can be an awful, unhappy power struggle or the miserable sense of a gun at one's head. It can feel like the despairing certainty that this has all been a mistake or simply a wild, undeniable impulse to stay young and free.

This chapter makes one essential point: If Commitment is a crisis in your romance, it doesn't necessarily mean that your romance was wrong. You can have the absolutely right romance, feel deep love, and still find the Commitment stage paralyzing.

The opposite is true too. Just because the two of you have no doubts and your families are rooting you on does not necessarily mean that you've chosen "right." Poorly matched, ill-suited, and immature couples can find it as easy to leap into marriage as two people who've learned to love and accept each other.

The crisis of Commitment is not necessarily a reflection of your true feelings about your partner. It is at least as likely to be a reflection of your true feelings about marriage itself. If you don't have at least some mixed feelings about marriage, you haven't allowed yourself to appreciate its realities.

This perspective runs directly counter to the folk wisdom about marriage. One thirty-one-year-old physician explained his hesitations this way: "My family keeps telling me if I have any doubts, don't do it! Well, I do have doubts, and I can't imagine how they're going to disappear."

Many of you are operating under this pressure. You really feel you should be sure. Instead of feeling certain, what you feel is some measure of threat. "Half of everything I have will be hers. You have to be pretty damn sure to risk that!" "Once you marry a man, he expects all kinds of things of you that he'd never dream of asking a girlfriend for. Suddenly you're doing the cooking and you're responsible for calling his sister. I don't know if I want to take on all that."

The point of this chapter is that you have to be sure, and it helps to have your doubts too. The feelings that come up at this moment in courtship have as much to do with feelings about marriage as feelings about your lover. The sorting-out process can be agony. Don't let it upset you. Romeo and

Juliet would have agonized, too, if they had dated for a year or so.

Getting Married Versus Being Married

Most often at this point in the courtship ritual it is the woman who is pressing matters forward and the man who is frozen in his tracks.

Whether you are pressing for commitment or running from it, you are likely to make a mistake in your thinking. You are seeing marriage as an endpoint, rather than an opportunity to begin.

Both men and women react to marriage as if it were a static event. One may view marriage as a giant long-awaited Christmas present, while the other dreads a booby prize. But both are thinking along the lines of a final outcome—marriage.

Commitment and marriage are far from static events. They are both dynamic processes. They change. They get better and they get worse, and sometimes they get better and worse in the same week. You don't get a marriage when you get married. What you get is the opportunity to create a marriage.

One person may worry: What if I get married and it turns out to be a mistake? The misunderstanding is that marriage does not "turn out" to be a mistake. It's not a movie with a built-in finish. If your marriage is a mistake, it's because you let it develop that way. You are not a passive victim. You are in the active role of creating a new family. How well or poorly you do that task depends on you, not on "it."

One person may fantasize: If only we can get married, I'll worry about the rest later. The ceremony becomes the goal. In fact, beginning immediately after the ceremony you are thrown into the challenge of creating a marriage. Getting married is only the entry point. Being married is an ongoing effort.

The same distinction is true of Commitment. During courtship, the most you are being asked to commit to is to *get*

228

married. Later on, sometimes years later, you will make the decision to *be* married. The *commitment to be married* is at the heart of every successful marriage. It is the bottom line. All the other qualities that are necessary to resolve differences—good communication, respect, shared values, sexual satisfaction—are secondary. The basic decision is to be married. Period. That's it. We're married. We aren't leaving. We either work out those problems or battle over them forever, but we're staying together. We'll do whatever we have to do. We're *married*.

It's the rare, exceptional couple who can make this kind of commitment during courtship. For most couples it comes a few years into marriage. Larry, thirty-six, describes it this way:

"I didn't make a decision to be married until the tough times came a year or so down the line. Up to that point it was mostly a great physical relationship and lots of fun. Eventually, we started having a conflict about how I was handling money. She disapproved. I hated having to change. That's when I took myself aside and asked, 'Hey, are you really serious about this marriage?' I guess she must have done the same thing, because that's when we became a marriage."

Fran describes a similar deepening of commitment. "For four years we were kids playing house. All of a sudden he wanted to go back to school. It meant all kinds of upheaval for us—no money, having to move. I had to ask myself, 'Is this what I want? Should someone else effect my life so much?' That's when it hit me. I'm married."

No one is asking you to be able to make the decision to be utterly and permanently married when you take the courtship step of getting married. You are only committing to give yourself the opportunity to try. You are inviting yourself and your partner to begin to create a life together.

The proper question to ask yourself now, or at any point in courtship, is "Do I want this romance to continue, to move forward? Or am I willing to let it decay?"

Not Sure, Not Ready, Not Interested: The Fear of Commitment

When the question of marriage sneaks or screeches into a courtship, you may feel you have reached the limits of the maxim we began with: *Don't take it personally*. It's impossible to be impersonal about the decision to marry. You never have the opportunity to work out your feelings about marriage in the abstract. She is choosing him. He is choosing her. Or not.

Ironically, as purely personal as the decision to marry is, the maxim, *Don't take it personally*, is never more true than at this moment in courtship. The obstacles to Commitment are powerful, and they existed long before you two met.

Fear of Commitment is the last face of the fear of intimacy to emerge during courtship. You two may have struggled with its closely related cousin, the fear of entrapment, much earlier in your courtship. The theme's the same for both: "Oh, God, What am I getting into!"

The focus tends to be different. Early in courtship, especially during The Switch, fears are likely to be focused on the person you've picked. That's where all the perfectionism we discussed comes into play. You or your partner gets stuck on those idiotic but powerful thoughts like, "I could never stand a man who is such a poor tipper," "She's terrific but her thick ankles turn me off." Over and over you go, raking the object of your affections to bits, until you've found a flaw you can fix on. The flaw allays your fears of the trap because it keeps you from going forward.

Fear of commitment reflects the different anxieties that come up when a courtship has progressed much closer to marriage. Instead of focusing entirely on your partner, fear of commitment tends to focus on the institution of marriage itself. "What if I wake up in five years and I don't feel the same way?" "How could I promise to never sleep with anyone else forever??" "Is this true love or just an accident of timing? I don't want to end up married to someone by accident!"

Fear of commitment is a complex phenomenon. Yours or your partner's may include any of the following themes.

The Fear of Losing Control

The fear of commitment is the fear of losing control of your life. Suddenly the autonomy of being single looks attractive. One man, facing the new experience of living with a woman after fifteen years as a solo operator, went through his list of concerns: "Will we have our own rooms? What if I want to read late at night? Will she insist that I come home for dinner every night? I'm pretty messy. I keep everything. I bet she'll make me straighten up all my piles of papers. She'd better not. . . ."

My own husband startled me in the middle of our courtship when he started to complain, "I've always had an idea that I'd like to keep a carp in the bathtub. Now that you're living here, I'll never be able to." He was quite serious. I always consider it one of my proudest moments that I did not burst out laughing. I was able to manage, "Darling, if you want to keep a carp in our only bathtub, I'm sure it's perfectly OK with me. I love to bathe with fish." He never carried out his threat, though he did keep a worm farm in the basement for some months during one fishing season. I considered it a test and gave every worm a name. That seemed to reassure him.

When you are a single adult, you may be lonelier than you'd like or less satisfied, but you are also supremely powerful. To the extent that one can ever control life, you can control yours. Some of us have to struggle to give up that control, even when we are trading it for love.

The Anxiety of Taking Action

A couple may have made it through each of the previous four stages of courtship on a cloud of lust and joy. Now the question of marriage has come up. It's a very difficult question to just slide right past. You have to actually do something. Doing is a very effective antidote for dreaming.

It's not that often that we are called upon to take an active role in steering our lives. Mostly it unfolds in front of us, guided by parents, teachers, bosses, circumstances, luck, opportunity. Most of us take a relatively passive stance in our own lives. We end up with work we feel we "fell into." We make our friends by proximity. We do what's expected of us.

For most of us, the big decisions in life feel less like decisions than inevitabilities. Did you decide to go to college, or did it seem the natural thing to do? Did you decide to divorce, or was it your inevitable reaction to outside events? Did you choose to be a lawyer, take over your father's business, become a parent, or did it simply come to pass as the most logical next step?

Marriage was certainly a logical next step for most of the members of previous generations. In chapter 1 we talked about how much harder it is now to complete a courtship. Marriage is no longer a necessary next step. Now you and your sweetheart get to decide.

The sheer novelty of having to make a major life decision is part of what throws us into a panic. We are accustomed to following life's path willy-nilly. We talk about wishing for change, but it requires massive human effort to effect it. Now change, in the form of marriage, is being held out as a possibility. How do you feel? Frozen.

Buyer's Remorse

In some cases, marriage is not experienced as a decision—it's simply the next logical step. Remember, courtship has a life of its own. It pushes *you* forward as much as you push your courtship forward.

Oddly enough, if this is the case, you too are likely to be frozen into inaction. You could be suffering from that strange phenomenon known as buyer's remorse. Quite often in real estate transactions, once house-hunters make an offer, they may be overwhelmed with second thoughts. The price is too high, the roof looks leaky, the kitchen's too small. Sometimes regrets are so strong that nothing will make a buyer comfortable except backing out of the deal.

Lovers can suffer equally from buyer's remorse. When marriage is merely an inevitable next step, you might feel as if you've made a thoughtless deal. You don't actually remember *deciding* to marry. Things just seemed to work out that way. Now you have second thoughts: He is too weak. She's too critical. You never really liked his children, her friends. Buyer's remorse can make it very difficult to feel good about Commitment.

232

The Paralysis of the Permanent

Marriage is a major redirection of your life. It crosses that vast psychological chasm between temporary and permanent. Commitment is the bridge, if you'll both cross it.

Some of our best, freest moments in life come when we are experiencing the temporary. Temporary is the feeling that allows a woman to smile at every strange man when she's on vacation, though she is a stone face at the bar near her office. Temporary is what allows the Italian man to live with his Jewish girlfriend though he would feel claustrophobic if she were Italian.

Temporary is not a period of time but a state of mind. Some couples are in "temporary" relationships for four and five years. There is always the thought, in the back of the mind, "This isn't serious. It'll last as long as medical school, as long as I'm getting my business off the ground, as long as it lasts." It's clear what serious means. It means permanent.

A major element in the fear of commitment is the awesome, inhibited feeling we get when we are confronted with the concept of permanency.

Permanent, above all else, is something we associate with growing up. Temporary is the wonderful, playful attitude of the adolescent. Permanent is what the adults do.

"I'm too young to die." None of the men or women I've worked with on the fear of commitment has ever said these words to me. But somehow I often hear them, lingering, unsaid, at the end of the conversation. I hear them when one patient after another says, "I love her, but I'm not ready to take the step." "Shouldn't I feel ecstatic? All I feel is depression." "All of a sudden it's so serious. I feel like I'm with my father, not my boyfriend." "He was talking insurance benefits and mortgage points. I wanted to run out and get high." "I think we have a great relationship. I love her a lot and no one will ever love me more. But she mentions marriage and I feel a trap closing around me. I don't want to stop seeing her, but half of me is shouting 'get me out of here.' "

The agreement to marry is a death. It marks the end of one of the hallmarks of youth: the sense of limitless possibilities.

To be young is to be all potential. Depending of course on

233

social class and situation, to be young is to feel an endless stretch of time and opportunity ahead of you. The process of becoming an adult is the process of choosing among all those possibilities and creating a life.

Marriage is one of the key choices. It is one of the events in our society that marks you as an adult. Yes, you can be an adult without being married. And yes, plenty of people marry without having done much growing up. Still the psychological meaning of Commitment holds true. It means letting go of your youthful fantasy that anything could occur.

The Social Realities of Marriage

The current social realities of marriage also contribute to the fear of Commitment. The frequency of divorce is no comfort to the man or woman panicked by the decision to marry. A near-fifty-percent divorce rate may seem to you to communicate one thing: Almost half the people who make this decision make the wrong one. The punishment for a wrong decision appears steep. You get months or years of unhappiness, followed by an agonizing separation that results in financial chaos, emotional havoc, and a lifetime of divided kids and patchwork families. It's enough to give you pause.

There are other social realities that may contribute to problems with Commitment. Prime among these may be your resistance to the social roles of marriage. The truth is that "husband" and "wife" can come with a heavy burden of obligation and expectation that "girlfriend" or "boyfriend" do not carry. You are probably not sure what the trappings will evolve into for the two of you. But, like an animal in the forest, you sense danger and you want to run.

It's an uphill battle to resist the stereotyped duties that society has assigned to "husband" and "wife." A couple can carve out their own understanding of these roles, but they have to be on top of the issues all the time to avoid resentment and disappointment.

He senses that once he makes this Commitment he'll be obligated to share his paycheck. It's not that he minds, exactly. But he resists the sense of obligation. He has an idea that "husband" might mean no spontaneous late-night drinking sessions with the guys. Even if he hasn't been out

234

with the guys in two years, he's uncomfortable with the idea that he can't anymore. He has a mental image of "husband." A husband has slightly thinning hair, a complacent pot belly, and a gently harassed look that comes from saying "Yes, dear" over and over. It's not the way he sees himself.

She senses that once she makes this Commitment, she'll suddenly be obligated to keep a refrigerator stocked. Actually she likes the idea of having a reason to have food around. But she cringes at the prospect of a required weekly visit to the supermarket. She has an idea that "wife" might mean being responsible for matching sheets and never again spending a whole week's salary on a great dress. She has a mental image of "wife." She's a woman standing in front of a pile of someone else's dirty underwear. This is not exactly her desired self-image.

Your Own Life Experience

There are, of course, any number of individual experiences that may contribute to your or your partner's fear of commitment. A bad first marriage, a bitter divorce battle, the divorce of your own parents, the nondivorce of your own parents, a particularly intrusive mother, an especially critical father, an inability to separate from your nuclear family, depression, a particular high personal value placed on adventure and change, an especially acute need for sexual variety—all these and more can be individual factors that make you or your lover especially averse to Commitment.

Whether you are responding to the pain of your past, or some unique facet of your personality that calls out for freedom and variety, you are always responding to some extent to the underlying bases of fear of commitment which we've discussed. You hesitate to give up control over your life. You are anxious about choosing, because you risk failure. You are uncomfortable with the idea of permanent, because temporary is so much easier. You resist the feeling of growing up, because youth has so many possibilities. And you are uncomfortable becoming a "husband" or "wife" because, in your mental image, they aren't much fun.

So here you are. You've been going together for two years

235

and you feel, by and large, that you're happy together. You certainly feel attached to her and actually you couldn't imagine your life without her. However, this does not mean you are ready to marry her. Or anyone else. And lately it seems to be on her mind all the time. She's always making remarks, sometimes she's crying over it. She's mad at you more than usual, and you know at the bottom of it is this thing about marriage. You've been trying not to think of it but now the pressure's on. Well, you're certainly not going to allow yourself to be pressured into anything.

Still, something will have to be done. You're not sure what you feel. On the one hand, you figure you love her and she's great to be with, plus she really seems to love you. On the other hand, *you are perfectly happy with things exactly as they are*. The two of you are together as often as you want to be. You're comfortable. Who needs to stir all that up with weddings and guest lists and family meetings? Why does it have to change? Why can't I stay my own man and have her too? Fear of commitment.

Coping with a Partner's Fear of Commitment

You cannot ''get'' a man or a woman to make a commitment. Commitment is an internal act. The ability to make a commitment is something we grow up to. It's a developmental point, a willingness to be an adult. It is the ability to choose, to direct one's life. It happens inside.

However, you will need a coping strategy to survive this difficult time. Your beloved's apprehension will probably be agony for you. When someone you want very much says he or she is not sure, not ready, or not interested, your happiness is threatened. A normally stable and cheerful person may be transformed into an anxious, clinging maniac. Or, you might become a sniper, lying in wait to get your digs in. You are angry, or hurt, or frantic, depending on which is your customary response to a threat. Most of us are all three.

It's a situation in which, while you have not precisely been rejected (yet), your partner's response could not be characterized as wildly enthusiastic. You might feel that you are on probation. How do you react? Here is a typical scenario:

First, you will probably spend some time hating yourself. "Why aren't I good enough for him, for her?" You may feel boring, dumb, poor, a loser, whichever is your sensitive spot.

You will probably also spend some time hating your partner. Why does he/she have to be so immature, indecisive, or plain mean? You rip your partner's character apart while you are ripping your own to shreds, looking for an outlet for your awful feelings of rejection.

At some point you may begin to ruminate. You will wonder, "How long should I allow this to go on? Should I leave? *Could* I leave? I don't want to deliver any ultimatums, but I don't want to be a fool either. Should I try to make him/her jealous? I don't want to date other people but maybe I have to. Will we ever work this out? Does this mean I'm not loved?"

Meanwhile, your relationship might come to focus on your partner's "problem." Possibly you'll become involved in endless O.R. conversations about it. Some people seek psychotherapy as a couple or for their partners in the hope that a doctor can "straighten him or her out." The partner goes to therapy to figure out if it's you or marriage that is so appalling and impossible. This can be quite unnerving. You will be craving reports, casually querying, "How's it going?" as if your happiness didn't depend on the answer.

Initially, you strive for calm and sympathetic understanding. Eventually, you feel more hurt and rejected. Something must be done.

The dilemma facing you as the loving partner of a reluctant mate is this: How can you exercise control over a situation that seems to be out of your hands? You've been placed in that most passive of positions: awaiting a verdict. If you try to influence the verdict, your partner may complain that you are pushy, pressuring, or nagging. You naturally worry that if you push it will backfire.

On the other hand, if you don't push, who will? You are hoping that your partner will have some sort of spontaneous remission. One day he or she will make the decision, announce it joyfully, and the ordeal will be over. With this in

237

mind, when your partner pleads for "more time," you are initially inclined to give it.

For some couples, more time is enough. Change is a matter of a cautious toe in the water for some of us. It could be that he or she needs to turn the idea over and over, gnaw at it, ease into it. If this is the case, you'll find conversations that once began "if we're married" turning into "when we're married." There will be lots of idle inquiries such as "Where would we live if we did such a thing" or "Would a wedding have to be such an enormous, complicated event?"

If your relationship is gradually moving in this direction, you don't have a problem. Your partner is working out the fear of Commitment on his or her own. The pace of this work might irritate you. If you curb your impatience, you'll probably get what you want in the end.

The rest of this section is for those of you who are now, or might be in the future, stuck. You're in love, involved—and going nowhere.

You have come close to the limits of your patience. You have no more time to give. You want action. If it can't be a yes to marriage, you'd at least appreciate a definite no. You are tired of hanging. What do you do?

Something! Eventually you can only handle this situation by shifting from a passive to an active role. You may not be able to control your partner's decision but you can control your own life. You've been placing your future in someone else's hands. He's not doing a great job with it. *Take it back*.

The following are examples of taking control. In each case one person was pushing a courtship toward marriage. Each used a different coping style for working it out with a loving but reluctant partner. "Loving" is used judiciously. When you are struggling with a partner's fears of commitment, nothing feels very loving.

There are three options:

- Don't take no for an answer.

- Convince, don't insist.

- Give an ultimatum.

238

Don't Take No for an Answer

Barry, thirty-five, was divorced for three years when he met Joan. Barry has two preadolescent daughters who live with his ex-wife. Until Joan came along, they were the only women in Barry's life.

Joan, thirty-two, has never been married. She's a successful securities analyst, but lately she finds her career a lot less rewarding than she had hoped.

Barry and Joan have been a couple for eighteen months. Barry is surprised to find himself in love. He swore after his divorce that he'd never risk love again. Joan is more comfortable. So far as she can see, she and Barry are meant to be together. Even his daughters, who were little monsters initially, have eased up lately. They seem to accept Joan as an inevitability. As the eldest daughter told Joan, "We figured we could have done worse." Joan interpreted this as encouragement—and proposed.

Barry turned her down flat. He was not opposed to marriage in principle. Someday, when it felt right, but this was just not the time. Time, he was fixated on time. It was too soon. His kids couldn't handle it. For that matter, he couldn't handle it. He needed more time, more experience. He needed a sense of freedom. Maybe he should have dated more after his divorce. Maybe he should date more now. Maybe he should do anything other than marry Joan.

Most women would be flattened by this kind of rejection. Joan never even blinked. She did not intend to take no for an answer.

She told him "Darling, it's perfectly reasonable for you to want more time and more freedom. Believe me, if I had it to give, you would be the very first person I'd give it to. But I don't. It's not a situation I could handle. I'd crumble. So sorry, but that alternative won't work."

She also empathized with his doubts. She told him she knew how disconcerting it was to find himself in love when he had not intended to let this happen. She could understand that he'd be happier if he'd dated frantically and felt he'd fully sampled the market. Joan let Barry know that she didn't take any of his reservations personally. Her message was:

"Of course you're going to marry me, and of course initially you'll hate the idea. You'll get over it."

Finally, Joan encouraged Barry to be cautious in his reaction. She pointed out that he was unlikely ever to meet her match. She told him that she was undoubtedly the finest, most loving, and most interesting woman who would ever love him. If he really wanted her to leave she would, but she thought he'd probably want to reconsider.

He did. Joan started working very long hours and he got a taste of life without her. He found he missed her. Joan never wavered from her original position that if he pulled back, she pulled out. Period. Joan was that emphatic not because his request was unreasonable, but because she wasn't able to satisfy it. You can only give what you have to give. She also never wavered from the attitude that he'd be foolish to lose her. Eventually, he saw it her way. They were married in a ceremony that he now describes as "the happiest moment of my life." Joan has restrained every impulse to say "I told you so."

It took some time and tolerance on Joan's part to see her courtship through this difficult period. No one can tell you how much time to give or how much ambivalence to tolerate. In general, a person who won't take no for an answer is operating on a short schedule—certainly weeks or months as opposed to years. The strategy of insisting on the outcome you desire is a bold one. It would scare most of us who are afraid of pushing too hard or in some way forcing our partners into marriage. Besides, you may feel that a marriage you insist on is not an expression of love. Love must be given freely. Refusing to take no for an answer can be seen as an attempt to force love and commitment.

Joan didn't see it that way. She separated Barry's love for her (which she felt was strong) from his ability to make a commitment (which she felt was weak). Then she set about shoring up a weakness in her partner by lending him the strength of her certainty. Notice that she did not increase his anxiety with an ultimatum. Instead she weighed in on one side of his ambivalence with her absolute conviction of what was right for them. To carry out this strategy required a good deal of self-esteem and confidence on Joan's part. She needed to feel good enough about herself to know that she was of-

240

fering Barry a good deal. And she needed to remember not to take his rejection personally.

Convince, Don't Insist

Chloe also took control by taking a stand. She was less insistent, less confrontational than Joan in the last example. But Chloe argued, defended, and in every other way pressed her case. She felt that her future was too precious to sit back and await his decision. In order to convince, you must be a person who is not stuck with the feeling that anything you have to ask for is not worth having. Instead, Chloe felt that anything worth having is worth fighting for.

Chloe, forty-two, and John, forty-six, had each been married once before. When they met, Chloe had been separated for a year and a half, John for a scant two months. Neither was "ready" for marriage, though Chloe was closer to being ready for a relationship. John, escaping an unhappy, guilt-ridden marriage, was mostly ready to go wild.

Therefore, they progressed slowly through the courtship ritual, with several Switches involving John's forays into the singles world. He always came back and Chloe always welcomed him, though with increasingly acerbic comments.

By the end of their second year together, they had made it to a Plateau. Neither was dating anyone else, both thought of themselves as a firm couple. But John was reluctant to become more entrenched. Each maintained a separate home. He frequently took a separate vacation, if only to assert his right to do so.

Finally, Chloe was clear about what she wanted. She says, "I was tired of being a bag lady. I was tired of being half-time at home, half-time at his place, carting my clean underwear in my purse. I wanted to be married."

John didn't. He was also quite clear about it. He said, "I love you, but I can't stand the thought of being enveloped. I can't breathe. I want my time and my life to be my own. I want to be with you when I want to and not because I have to. I've been married and I know what happens. It takes over your life. I don't want it and I won't do it."

Chloe did not fall apart. She says, "I knew my man. I knew what I hated about him and what I loved. I set out to

241

reassure him, not to force him. I explained, 'Well, when I'm feeling secure you can have all the freedom you want. I only get crazy and clinging because I'm afraid you're going to reject me.' '' Chole knew that John feared a woman who would be emotionally dependent on him, constantly claiming his care and attention. His fears came from his experiences with his ex-wife and his mother. She believed that she was able to be different, to handle her own needs and her own emotions. But she wanted to do it inside a marriage. She needed Commitment.

Their struggle lasted two and a half years. It was quite overt. Chloe used to say to John, ''I wonder if my patience will outlast your ambivalence.'' Her approach was positive and subtle. ''I never wanted to say, 'Marry me or else.' I was scared to do it and it felt wrong. Instead I said, 'If you never want to get married, I understand and I respect your right to make that decision. But I do want to remarry someday. If you've definitely decided that you don't, I guess we can't be together. It's sad.' I felt that took the focus off of his rejecting me and put it where it belonged—on John's feelings about marriage. We were both more comfortable with that. I was always saying I can prove to you that marriage doesn't have to be the burden you think, if you'll give me a chance.''

Eventually, John and Chloe agreed to buy a house together that could accommodate her kids and his computer all in one place. When they found the house, John said, ''I guess we ought to be married.''

Chloe says, ''I really convinced him to do it. To get married. Now he says, 'Thank you, darling. I'm so happy.' And why shouldn't he be? I take good care of him. I know what my man needs and I see that he gets it. After all, he finally gave me what I needed.''

The Ultimatum

The classic take-control approach to a Relationship bogged down on the road to marriage is the ultimatum. One partner says, ''Marry me or I'm leaving.''

It's a tough-minded, high-risk approach. If you say it, you'd better mean it, and you'd better be prepared to leave.

Ultimatums are scary moves for both partners because they exert maximum pressure on a very sore spot. An ultimatum is not recommended for a first or even a second alternative. But when you've run out of "more time" to give, when you've done as much convincing or insisting as you can, when your patience is at an end, you must decide to accept the limitations of your romance forever—or put an end to your agony. The ultimatum is the court of last resort in court-ship.

The battle over Commitment is a necessary part of many courtships. If you remember not to take it personally, it won't do much damage for a while.

Eventually it is too personal, too unpleasant, too much of a rejection to tolerate. Anyone who longs for Commitment and gets a "maybe" feels rejected. Nothing could be worse than living with the constant drip, drip, drip of rejection. It eats at your self-esteem, makes you doubt your sex appeal. You worry that you are boring or unattractive. Eventually, your anxiety makes you pushy, unsexy, and clinging. Get yourself out of it. You need to breathe the air of love and approval again. You've forgotten what it feels like.

How long is too long to stay in the situation? When should you give your ultimatum?

It's time for an ultimatum when:

- You can't stop thinking about marriage. You've become obsessed.

- You are anxious and upset or angry a lot because your relationship is not going anywhere.

- You have many critical thoughts about yourself. You feel you aren't good enough.

- You are embarrassed by your own behavior. You've become insecure, you need constant atten-tion and reassurances that he/she cares.

- The relationship has become a constant battle over marriage. You can't seem to find anything else to talk about. Every dumb fight over which movie to see is really a fight about marriage.

What follows are several examples of ultimatums. Each was delivered in a slightly different style and at a different moment in courtship. No one can tell you the right time to deliver an ultimatum. The timing depends on the intersection of your readiness and your patience. An ultimatum is not a manipulative strategy. An ultimatum is not to be issued for effect, just to "see what will happen." It's not meant to push your partner around or to demonstrate your power over him or her. An ultimatum is a style of resolution. It is a last resort to get you both out of a painful struggle that you've been unable to resolve by more pleasant means.

The Deadline Date

An ultimatum can take a variety of forms. Most common is an artificial deadline, where one partner says to the other, in effect, "You have until X-date to make up your mind. If you can't make a decision by then, I'm moving on."

Doug, thirty-four, and Jenny, twenty-eight, resolved their Commitment crisis in this way. After a year or so of dating, Jenny began to inquire about their future. She started low-key, expressing her need to plan her life. Jenny's inquiries were gradual—no dramatic scenes or tearful attacks, just a clear communication of her feelings. A few months later, after the holidays, she became more specific. She told Doug that she needed a Commitment by June. Jenny didn't threaten. She was very matter-of-fact. Six more months was all the time she had to give.

Doug didn't doubt that he loved Jenny. In fact, he was amazed that he had come to terms with the "flaws" that were troubling him so six months earlier. Now he could accept her quietness, though he'd always envisioned a livelier woman. He was no longer critical of her sense of humor; it was "just her and I love her."

He loved her, and he did not want to get married. At all. Oh, maybe someday, but that was far in the future, not now. What tormented him most was the idea of forever. How could anyone agree to anything for the rest of his life? What if it's a mistake?

By April, Doug's anxieties increased. He suddenly realized that the summer was approaching and with it his deadline.

He believed Jenny was serious about her ultimatum. She was very nice about it, but very firm.

In May, Doug realized it was decision time. By this time, through therapy, he had come to the following realizations:

- There are no guaranteed successes in marriage. It's always going to be a risk.

- He was not prepared to leave Jenny and start all over with someone else, only to end up where he is right now. In effect, the decision to marry was already made, once he knew that he couldn't put her out of his life.

- Marriage does not "turn out" to be a success or a failure. Doug and Jenny will create a marriage, build it, work on it. The outcome is not as out of control and mysterious as it seems to him.

In mid-May Doug and Jenny became engaged. Doug found a surprising feeling of pride and excitement. He got so much support from friends and colleagues. Even the wedding plans failed to dismay him.

Doug has thanked Jenny for her clear, firm decisiveness about their relationship. Without a deadline date, he felt he could have floundered forever. He describes Jenny's deadline as "putting a frame around my fears so I could look at them."

The Gentle Kick

Not all ultimatums involve a precise deadline. Some can be framed more realistically: "You have as much time as I can give. After that, bye-bye." It's honest, it's loving, and it's taking control.

In the four years since they'd met, Diane and Tony had fallen into a familiar pattern. They'd get together, become lovers, and Tony would pull a Switch. He always felt Diane was wonderful, but "too nice" and "not exciting enough." They would stay apart for months or, in one case, a full year. Then they'd reunite for another go-round.

Eventually, as Tony passed his thirtieth birthday, he began

245

to take Diane more seriously. He moved in with her, still doubting but willing to try.

After just a few months together, Tony started to feel some urgency for marriage. Living with Diane taught him to appreciate the specialness of their bond, a feeling he'd never been able to achieve with any of the "exciting" women he'd dated. He was ready for a Commitment. At precisely that moment, Diane decided that she was not.

Tony crumbled. Diane was the one person in his life whose love he was sure of. Suddenly, all he was hearing about was her doubts. Worst of all, her doubts were all sexual. Could she be faithful? Had she experienced enough other men? She had spent so many years waiting around for Tony that she hadn't enjoyed life as she should. Now she felt time running out and she couldn't handle it. Diane wasn't asking Tony to move out, but she was not about to get married!

After several months of depression on his part, guilt on her part, unending discussions of the "problems," Tony pulled himself together. He delivered the following speech: "Darling, I understand you are upset and not ready. I just need to let you know that I don't know how much rejection I can handle. I know you're not doing this to hurt me, but it hurts anyway. When I can't take the hurt any more, I'll have to leave you. I'm prepared to do so, but I think I can last another few weeks."

The effect of this obviously sincere and calmly delivered ultimatum was immediate. Diane was forced to get a grip on her own anxiety and do some self-examination. She had been so caught up in her own feelings, she hadn't appreciated Tony's pain.

When she took a hard look at her behavior, Diane saw that two factors stood as obstacles to her willingness to marry. First, a lot of her ambivalence was unconscious anger at Tony for all the times that his uncertainty had made her feel rejected and unloved. Now that he was willing to make a Commitment, she felt secure enough to express some of that anger.

Second, during most of their relationship, Tony was dealing with his fears of intimacy for both of them. As long as he was so reluctant, she didn't have to confront her own fears. As soon as Tony got past his fears, Diane was suddenly confronted with her own. She was unprepared to handle these fears because her relationship with Tony kept her from experiencing them consciously. If you are never threatened with Commitment, how can you discover that it scares you?

Tony's ultimatum brought these issues to the surface. It gave Diane an opportunity to understand her emotional reactions and to work past them. By getting past her own anger and anxiety, Diane was able to get on with a life with Tony.

The Ultimatum as a First Resort

In this example, the ultimatum was both a first and last resort. Cory, thirty-five, had experienced too many relationships that got hung up at the almost-but-not-quite-committed stage. She wasn't willing to risk that agony of indecision again. Besides, experience had taught her a valuable perspective. There are many men with whom she could hope to have a successful relationship, something she would never have believed at age twenty.

If you believe there are many opportunities, you are free to call the question of a possible future relatively easily. If you believe that your current partner is a one and only, you become dependent on his or her whim. You can't risk an ultimatum, as a first or a last resort.

On one of Cory and Glen's earliest dates, in the typical relationships/life/love conversation that often precedes sexual intimacy, Glen mentioned that he believed a man knew in six months whether he wanted to marry a woman. Cory said nothing, just stored the conversation away.

On their sixth-month anniversary, Cory invited Glen to dinner. Over dinner she reminded him of his comment and said, "So, what's it going to be?" Glen hemmed and fumbled and let it be known that he hadn't meant to be taken so literally. He was certainly not ready to make a Commitment. Cory wrapped his dessert in a doggie bag and told him not to bother calling until he was ready.

Two nerve-wracking weeks later, Glen showed up at her door with a ring. Cory says she was thrilled, ecstatic, but she insists she would never have allowed herself to call him. Her attitude was "There are too many men I could love, who would love me back. I don't need to waste my time with one who doesn't."

247

Glen always laughs when they tell the story of how they got engaged. He says, "Cory still puts her foot down from time to time. Sometimes I step on it and sometimes I step back. But she always saves us a lot of time."

Each of the stories I've relayed had endings that created the opportunity for a happy beginning of marriage. A happy beginning is a possible outcome of an ultimatum.

There is another obvious outcome of an ultimatum which is usually less happy, at least for the person pushing for marriage. She gets a "no" answer, and she has to leave.

A "no" answer most often comes in the form of no answer at all. It's the exceptional man (or woman, if the roles in this Commitment struggle are reversed) who will say firmly and clearly, "I've decided not to marry you." It's too painful and too risky. He doesn't necessarily want to end the relationship, he just doesn't want to marry . . . her . . . now . . . or maybe ever . . . he's not sure . . . and he needs more time.

If the person who issued the ultimatum stands by it and separates, it's sad but positive. This is a person who was able to get on with life. This woman or man faced a bitter truth and lived to tell the tale.

There is only one outcome to an ultimatum that is negative all around. It's the ultimatum that is ignored by both people. The deadline date comes, passes, and both of you pretend that you forgot it. But nothing is resolved between you, so a new ultimatum is eventually delivered. And ignored.

Often she will halfway carry out her threat to leave. She breaks it off, is lonely, he calls, they're back together. It's nice for a while. Then she wants marriage, he has the same doubts he's always had, and she leaves again. Some couples repeat this cycle for a decade. Each uses the relationship to avoid the risk of new ones. Each runs back to the relationship as pseudosecurity when they suffer rebuffs and defeats in the outside world. Neither knows how to get unstuck.

Don't issue an ultimatum until you are able to mean it. If you are stuck in a relationship that you know won't get you what you want but that you can't bring yourself to end, go for help.

This is not a book about destructive, dead-end courtships

that can endure for years and break your spirit in the process. If you need to learn more about such relationships, you might want to read Stanton Peele's *Love and Addiction* or Robin Norwood's *Women Who Love Too Much*. You might want to consider psychotherapy.

Whatever you do, get help. You are no longer in courtship. You're in trouble.

Coping with Your Own Fear of Commitment

Marriage is a social institution. It's only sensible to hesitate any time you are about to be institutionalized. If you don't have any hesitations about making a Commitment, you are either (*a*) so ready that you're overripe or (*b*) so in love that you cannot focus.

Perhaps you've blended so closely that you can barely see your partner. All you notice are the ways she matches your hopes. It's like making a Commitment to live with yourself forever. It's a temporary delusion, but it definitely makes "Will you marry me?" easier.

Fear of Commitment does not refer to reasonable hesitations, flashes of anxiety, or prewedding cold feet. All of these are mild, nonproblem varieties of the fear. They express uncertainly about Commitment, but they don't get in your way.

If you have a larger problem with this issue, it's sometimes tough to identify. You may have a suspicion, as Doug did when he entered psychotherapy questioning his pattern of anxiety in relationships. Your lover may have told you, point-blank, that you seem to have problems with the idea of marriage. Your friends may have hinted that your romantic problems have more to do with you than anyone else.

The biggest obstacle to becoming aware of your fear of Commitment is subscribing to the myth of the right person. If you buy this myth whole hog you never have to examine yourself at all. You can dismiss all your fears and doubts by deciding that this person must not be the one.

You may have a problem with Commitment if:

- You have a pattern of serial monogamy. You get into longterm relationships but, for one reason or another, they end short of marriage. A variation on this is serial marriage—one short-lived marriage after another. For some the wedding ceremony is a way of saying good-bye.

- You have a conscious negative attitude about marriage. You've told everyone that you are not the marrying kind, or you'll never do it again, or you've learned your lesson.

- You hear yourself make lots of negative jokes about marriage.

- You've gotten stuck in a dead-end relationship with someone you know you'd never marry, but somehow you can't get out.

- You are faced with the possibility of marriage, and you show physical symptoms. Stomach pains, headaches, uncomfortable anxious flutters can be examples of expressed fear through your body.

- You've set up your life so that you can't marry. You wouldn't consider losing your alimony; you live with aging parents and you couldn't think of leaving; your work keeps you on the road 300 days a year and you have no time to create a marriage; you've never gotten around to getting a divorce though you've been separated for several years.

- Every time a relationship gets close and solid, you do something to mess it up. Suddenly, you have an affair, or sulk around her family, or start acting obnoxious, or go on a surprise trip—whatever is guaranteed to frustrate, irritate, or drive away a partner.

- You are comfortable with the notion of the right person. You explain your own doubts and anxieties as a reflection on your partner, rather than on yourself.

Any or all of these signs might alert you to your own fears

of Commitment. Awareness is the first step toward change. For some, it's sufficient to effect change. Just knowing the obstacle is *inside* you and not the effect of the wrong partner is a big step. Now you can work on it.

The work involves thinking through your reservations and reevaluating your goals. You've been saying you want to get married someday. Could it be that your feelings are more mixed about that goal?

You will need to reflect on your own development as it relates to each of the underlying themes of fear of Commitment. How are you handling your aging? Are you more comfortable thinking of yourself as a kid than as a grown-up? Does marriage interfere with your preferred self-image?

How comfortable are you being responsible for your own major decisions? Do you feel you've ever made one before? What were the results? Are you hoping to be pressured into taking this step so that, if it fails, you will have someone to blame?

Does your fear of failure make this permanent step feel too risky to you? Some of us cannot permit ourselves to risk failure, any more than people frozen in the Selection phase can permit themselves to risk rejection. Rather than fail, you don't risk. Rather than risk, you seek the certainty of perfection. You find there is no perfection and no marriage without risk. You are paralyzed.

Are you shying away from the increased obligation that Commitment brings? One man explained, "I love Marion and I have no intention of leaving her. But I'm not ready to be legally obligated to her kids. They are more than I want to be responsible for."

Linda explained her long and highly rational aversion to marriage this way: "I loved Mark, but for a long time living with him suited me fine. My resistance to marriage was mostly because he has a huge family and I don't. When we lived together, I felt I could choose what I'd participate in with his family. Now that we're married, I feel obligated."

Hopefully, your answers to these questions will point you in a direction. They will suggest an area where you may need to do more thinking, more self-examination, or more work. They may also help you to understand some of your reservations about your lover. It's hard to know how to proceed

251

on the question of Commitment without a clear understanding of what's making you hesitate.

These are complicated thoughts and feelings. Their origins will have something to do with your family and childhood, something to do with your life experience, and something to do with the way you've been influenced by our culture as a whole. If the problem is severe, the anxiety overwhelming, it will take more than a good conversation with yourself to sort it out. Here's where a psychotherapist can help. It's a problem very amenable to psychotherapy, and I'd encourage you to give it a try.

Marriage without Commitment

Unhappily, many marriages take place without even the beginning of a Commitment to be married. These are couples who experience stormy early years, frequent separations, and a whole lot of drama. One or both people hasn't gotten the idea yet that they are married. Period. It's a constant testing process, always working out the question: Am I willing to be married? Is this a permanent condition?

Again, some degree of this kind of testing is normal and necessary. Remember, the Commitment to *get* married is as far as you can go in courtship. The decision to *be* married, with all its limitations, obligations, and disappointments, can usually only be made fully during a marriage.

Degree is the crux of the matter. If you have worked through your feelings about marriage enough, if you are ready, if you are grown-up enough and separated from your own family enough, you are able to begin a marriage with the necessary conditions to make a Commitment. Unfortunately, lots of people aren't.

What happens? Well, in the best of cases couples hang together, grow up together, and come to their Commitment long after they are married.

In the unhappy cases, two people engage in romantic warfare until one or both limp away exhausted and confused. Usually, they say, "I don't know what happened. Once we got married, everything fell apart." Sometimes, in the heat

252

of battle, one accuses the other. "I never wanted to get married. You forced me into it." It's a convenient shift of responsibility and it hurts.

Beginning marriage without deep Commitment is reasonable. It's too soon. Marriage without any sense of Commitment is frightening. You are locked into a day-to-day relationship that shapes your entire life, without the feeling that you've chosen these limits or that you know what you traded your freedom for.

Commitment without Marriage

In our society, heterosexual couples express their Commitment to each other by marrying. They become a legal, economic, and social unit—a family. If you and your partner aren't able to accomplish this, it says something about your Commitment. Perhaps one or both of you needs to keep a psychological door open for a fast getaway.

The exceptions are few, primarily legal snaggles. Sometimes, an ex-spouse makes divorce such an impossibility that you and your partner are legally unable to wed. Sometimes children and estates are involved to the degree that responsibility for a child's financial well-being makes a commitment to a partner inappropriate. Often people with such legal or financial barriers to marriage have a craving for a ceremony of Commitment. Sometimes they stage such a ceremony, affirming their relationship before family and friends. It may not be legal, but it is certainly loving.

Besides these few exceptions, most couples must deal with the question of marriage. It's a question which rocks the boat in any relationship. Some long-established couples prefer to avoid the whole thing because they cannot tolerate the rocking.

These couples typically stay together by burying conflict instead of resolving it. Burying means ignoring conflict because it feels unresolvable and because it's too painful to address. A certain amount of burying is necessary to any long-lived love. But too much and you are walking on eggshells with each other, unable to develop as a couple.

253

Buried conflicts often derive from powerful reservations about your partner. You disapprove of her family, can't see yourself formally associated with it. At heart, you dislike his children though you could never tell him so. Or, she is not all you'd hoped for sexually. You continue to be monogamous, but marriage implies that this is all you can expect forever. It's a disappointment you don't want to face. Or perhaps he is not a professional success. It bothers you, but as long as you aren't his wife you don't have to deal with it.

Somehow, it's possible to go on day to day ignoring these issues and feeling relatively comfortable. You are able to stay in the status quo, but you are not able to move ahead comfortably. In order to ignore your reservations, you must ignore the possibility of marriage.

What you are really doing is holding back on your Commitment. You may both be telling yourselves, "We don't need to marry." What you are actually signaling is that one or both of you would be relieved if you didn't.

On Being Engaged

There is one final scene left to play in the social drama of courtship: being engaged. Your engagement officially begins when you call your mother (or your brother, cousin, best friend, mother surrogate) to say "Guess what? We're getting married." It ends when you say "I do."

Prior to the moment when you make the fateful announcement, you are both likely to be sane, rational, and fairly well functioning people. Almost immediately after you tell the world you are engaged, all this changes.

You automatically assume a role for which you have no preparation: bride-to-be or fiancé. If you are planning any kind of wedding, this role requires that you function as chief executive ("The guests will be transported from the church to the reception as follows. . . ."); social arbiter ("If we invite Harold and Grace, we can't ignore Marilyn and George. . . ."); skilled mediator ("Your mother wants the men in formal wear, and my father refuses to wear a monkey suit, and your brother refuses for political reasons to wear a tie, but my sister is holding out for a long dress, so I figured that if I call all of them and threaten to elope . . ."); seasoned diplomat ("We loved the clock you gave us, Aunt Ethel. Imagine a clock disguised as the stomach of a pig. So clever . . ."); tactful friend ("Since Susan has a bit of a weight problem, why don't we put all the bridesmaids in matching pink tent dresses. I think it could be very original. . . .").

With so many people to please and so many details to decide, a wedding provides endless opportunity for conflict. Conflict is never a delight. But it might be less of an ordeal if you understand its function in your development as a couple.

You and your partner are forming a new family. Your wedding is the send-off party and the first joint activity of your two newly extended families. How could you expect it to be easy?

Just as many of you envisioned love as a matter of meeting the right person and then sliding rapturously toward Commitment you also expected your engagement to be a period of unmixed excitement and pleasure. You will know you are one of these people if you hear yourself protesting, with varying degrees of outrage, "But it's my wedding, Mother. I want to do it my way."

It's not just your wedding. It's a wedding in your family. You are the bride or the groom. You certainly have the starring role. But the supporting players are equally involved. That's as it should be. Courtship is a social ritual. Marriage is a social symbol. Everyone in your immediate social world will have feelings about it. Everyone wants your wedding to be beautiful, to be perfect. It's just that they all will have vastly different ideas about what constitutes perfection.

Though the content of your conflicts will be wedding details, the theme is family power and family loyalty. Each of your original families has to let go a bit for you and your partner to form a strong enough bond to create a new family. As happy as they may be about your choice, your family is still a bit threatened by it. They will test your loyalty to their values and their style by arguing vehemently for white invitations as opposed to beige. His mother tells him that her mother's choice of baked ham is inappropriate. Her mother tells her that his mother's turquoise dress is going to clash. Each is reestablishing a primary family loyalty.

Within your own family, the conflicts over your wedding will echo all the issues of separation and autonomy that you've been working on for years. Ostensibly the bride and her mother are arguing over centerpieces; below the surface is their age old power struggle.

All this is especially true of first weddings. When you've been married and divorced or widowed, your family usually acknowledges your status as an adult. Your second wedding is therefore less of an expression of your family's values than of your own.

Besides the power struggle between families, and the one you may have within your own family, the two of you will undoubtedly have something of a power struggle with each other.

Weddings mean decisions. Decisions mean power. And power often means a contest of wills. Many men believe they will handle these potential conflicts by distancing themselves utterly from the decision making. Sensing their lack of power, they choose to make the wedding her event. "Just tell me where to show up." This attitude often hurts her feelings. She wants him to care. It's their wedding, not just hers.

Some men shock themselves by discovering that they do care, very much, about some aspects of the wedding. A wedding is after all a social event. Men are capable of being every bit as socially self-conscious as women. The very man who declared himself completely uninterested in the wedding nonsense of women is surprised to discover that he cares where his boss is seated; that he can't be married without every cousin invited; and that he refuses to be married without approving the brand of champagne.

Some of you will choose to avoid these conflicts by eliminating this courtship step entirely. You will elope. Your engagement consists of a drive to a chapel with only the briefest of residency requirements or a phone call to two friends asking them to meet you at City Hall. It's certainly one way to do it. It avoids the family conflict and escalating tension that usually accompany an engagement. It also eliminates something very special.

The great specialness of a wedding is reflected in the way

other people regard the occasion. There are few moments in your life when everyone who cares for you will make a Herculean effort to be there for you. For most people there are only two occasions when people will take trains, planes, buses, rearrange their lives to publicly acknowledge your importance to them: your wedding and your funeral. If you do choose to endure the tension and conflict of preparing a wedding, you will receive a huge payoff: Everyone you love will be together under one roof, and they will all be wonderful to you at the same time. You will not simply affirm your love for your new mate. You will experience the love of all the people who matter to you. It makes the endless negotiation of being engaged worth it.

Your relationship has been tested by reality. Your love has been strengthened by the resolution of conflict. You've found each other, pursued each other, fought with each other, and, finally, made a public Commitment to each other. You have gone all the way.

8

Going All
the Way

To be single is to live life on an edge. To be married is to live life in a niche. It is not a trade-off. Married is better.

Married is not better for everyone or at every stage of life. But for most of us, through most of adulthood, the niche has it all over the edge.

The edge you teeter on when you are single is the edge of possibility and of discouragement. Socially, you are constantly looking, testing, measuring. When you meet someone who is available, the edge inside you sharpens. You experience tension, anxiety, uncertainty. Your possibilities seem so limited. When you are confronted with one, it's hard for you to enjoy it. You are too worried about blowing it.

The niche in which married people dwell is carved out by Commitment. Commitment deliberately rules out other possibilities. Your energy and attention are invested in one project—the creation of your marriage. If your project is going well, its byproduct will be contentment and peace of mind.

It's certainly a value judgment to rank life in the niche of Commitment over life on the edge of possibility. You may not agree. If the edge still seems exciting to you, if the concept of a comfortable niche strikes you as a deadly bore or a psychological death, you will not appreciate marriage. If, on the other hand, you feel that a niche would be a wonderful relief, a letting go of adolescent frenzy, a step forward into the substance of your life, then you are ready.

If you are ready, maybe you feel like I'm rubbing it in. Perhaps you've been trying to get yourself married for years. If you are a single woman who has read every discouraging statistic, it may make you angry to be urged toward a goal that you've been assured is probably impossible. If you are a single male, it's irritating to hear that you have every op-

261

portunity to marry. Your experience tells you that, no matter how hard you try, the right woman never seems to want you.

But it's certainly *not* impossible. Your thinking has been getting in your way. You've had trouble with courtship because you believed these myths:

- The myth of the right person
- The myth of romantic love
- The myth of knowing
- The myth of marriage as an endpoint

The Myth of the Right Person

Courtship is the process of developing a powerful bond with another person. It is not the strike of lightning, followed by the exchange of roses, followed by the pledging of vows that you have been eagerly anticipating.

There is no one right person. There is only your ability to give and receive love. Some people are more right for you, only because they are easier for you to love and more likely to love you in return. If you have the capacity to love, you have the capacity to love many. If your capacity for loving is restricted ("I could never love a man who is shorter than I am." "I could never love a woman who had no career."), your opportunities for going all the way are equally restricted. You are entitled to limit yourself in whatever ways you choose. But it helps to understand that these restrictions are limitations in your own ability to love. They are not clues for identifying your right person.

The Myth of Romantic Love

Dave, struggling with the decision to propose: "I guess what worries me is that I feel different than I thought I would. There were so many women that I flipped out over. I never really flipped out over Donna. She was just so crazy about me and so good to me and I was just sort of in it. . . ."

The myth of romantic love—across a crowded room . . . fireworks, passion . . . a sense of knowing, an instant connection . . . an overwhelming physical arousal . . . a magically easy and endlessly sweet physical satisfaction.

Does it happen? Oh, yes. Is it true love? Not necessarily. Do you need to have this kind of experience in order to make the right marriage? Definitely not!

If you subscribe to the myth of romantic love, you are likely to cut short many, many courtships. If the chimes don't peal, you're out of there. If you look across the crowded room and what you see is a gold chain or white socks, you won't look twice. If two dates don't "turn you on," there won't be a third.

Even worse, the myth of romantic love leaves you feeling permanently cheated, or terminally uncertain, even when you've formed a meaningful attachment. Like Dave, you are perpetually wondering if you ever really loved your partner. You agonize, "Maybe I've talked myself into it." "Maybe this is just an accident of timing." "Maybe I just want to get married."

You've ignored some realities of marriage. The ability to "talk yourself into it" is a necessary ingredient in making a Commitment. Accidents of timing are really expressions of readiness. And wanting to be married is the essential ingredient in making a successful marriage.

The myth of romantic love has buried your understanding of these realities. You are praying for instant passion because it's easier than eventual decision making. Easier isn't always better.

Again, it is not the intensity of love with which you begin a courtship that counts. It's what you are experiencing at the end that matters to your future.

The Myth of Knowing

Some of us agonize so much over our romances because we can't seem to achieve that inner sense of knowing. We've been forcefed a myth.

The truth about knowing seems to be this: Some of you

will "know," perhaps instantly, often eventually, that your choice to marry your partner is absolutely right. This inner knowing will ease your courtship immeasurably, especially if the two of you both know the same thing. It's better to know when it's right because it makes your decision miles and miles easier.

But some people will never know in this way. Maybe you aren't capable of this kind of knowing, because your fears of intimacy interfere. Sometimes you fall in love with a man or woman who is so different from your picture of the right person that you cannot reconcile these discrepancies enough to know. Sometimes you think you know, but your family and friends don't see it your way and that erodes your inner certainty. Whatever the cause, it is not always possible to achieve that internal sense of knowing. If you can't, what does it mean about your choice?

Probably not much. People who are sure and people who aren't still equally confront the task of creating a marriage. That is always a risk, and there is always the opportunity for failure. Knowing cannot protect you from difficulty or divorce.

If you can't achieve the sense of knowing, it is not the same as having grave, unconfronted doubts. We've discussed doubts many times in this book, always operating on the same principle: Some doubt is necessary because of your conflicting needs for the warmth of attachment and the freedom of separation. Some doubt is inevitable because you are choosing to begin a risky venture. Some doubt is rooted in the fact that you are unsure of yourself and your real needs. And some doubt is stirred out of the difference between the way you always thought love and courtship would be and the way you've discovered it is.

Some doubt is not grave doubt. Only you can distinguish the difference. You can do this best by looking inside yourself, reexamining your motivations for courtship, understanding who your partner is to you, and what kind of couple you've become so far. These are tough questions and they will require some effort on your part. You don't have to hamper your effort by becoming confused by the myth of knowing. Don't get sucked into believing that if you don't know, your doubts must be grave. Sometimes that's true. But some-

264

times you won't be certain it's right because you are an adult and your appreciation of reality is strong. It's possible to know too much to have certainty. Having a realistic appreciation for marriage can do serious damage to your ability to "know" in advance how it's going to turn out.

The Myth of Marriage as an Endpoint

Marriage is not a product, it's a kit. You don't buy it, you build it.

When you are single, you are encouraged to look at marriage as a product rather than as a process. We speak of "getting married" as if we were getting a car or a home computer.

Naturally, when you slip into this way of thinking, you are subject to any of the concerns that accompany a major purchase. You worry about whether you are getting a good deal, making the right choice. You need to make sure you've done enough comparison shopping. Some of you, just at the moment of finalizing your purchase, will feel the need to rush out and test a few competitive brands, just to be sure. You worry about whether you are getting your money's worth, and whether other people will be impressed with your selection.

It's a lot of energy spent unproductively. No matter how well you choose, no matter how much you "know," it's not all decided on the day you say "I do."

Marriage as a process is scary, but it gives you more control over your future. The risk is heightened because you have to acknowledge that, no matter how perfect your choice, you still have to learn to create a marriage with your partner. The best choice does not guarantee the best marriage. The control you achieve is the sense that if you want your marriage to be great, you can help to make it so. Your happiness does not rest entirely on your choice of partner. It rests mainly on what you and your partner create after you've chosen each other.

That's the good news. Like the relief of appreciating that much of courtship's pain is impersonal, marriage's joys are subject to your own influence. To the degree that you are adult enough to accept the limitations of marriage, secure enough to allow a degree of freedom in your marriage, energetic enough to create a life outside your marriage, and loving enough to accept the realities of marriage, you can create a good marriage.

If you can tolerate self-awareness, criticism, and personal failure, you can create a good marriage. If you can move beyond the myths of your childhood and accept the realities of adulthood, you can create a good marriage. If you are willing to love what *is* instead of what should be, you can be happy in a marriage. And if you will take the risk of exposing your feelings, communicating your uncertainties, and sharing control of your life, you'll have a real marriage.

The Payoff of Work

I have not intended to make courtship sound grim or marriage sound difficult. The best laughs you'll ever have come from one or the other. There's no denying it though, they are both a lot of work.

It would be quite natural for you to wonder if all the work involved was worth the effort. You've managed to develop a satisfying life on your own. You have your friends, your work, a home. You have enough money in the bank to see you through, enough leisure to travel, sail, or read everything in sight. You are relatively secure, usually happy.

Perhaps it's taken you quite some time to achieve this serenity. Your memory of past forays into relationships is not happy. You've sacrificed weeks of your life hoping your phone call would be returned. You've fought the feeling that you aren't good enough, inflicted by someone who should have been grateful for thirty seconds of your time.

Maybe you have married. If you are single again, chances are you've survived an ordeal of some kind in the interim. You are only too willing to see the difficulties of marriage. You were defeated by them.

Whether you have successfully structured a life as a single person or painstakingly reconstructed a life after divorce, you are likely to wonder, What's so great about all the compro-

266

mise, strategy, and self-improvement necessary to make it through courtship? What do you get afterwards but the opportunity to do more of the same?

Every great endeavor in life raises these same questions. Is it worth it to struggle for independence, for identity? They are both a good deal of trouble to achieve. Why should we bother to deepen our relationships with truthful confrontation when polite lies make the surface so much more pleasant? Is there any purpose to developing a sense of ethics when dishonesty is so well paying? Why do the hard things in life?

We take on these tasks not so much for what they bring us in the outside world but for what they bring to our spirits, to our inner selves. The measure of whether any of these endeavors was worth the effort is not success in the material world, but success in the inner world. It is measured by the degree to which we have expanded our capacity as human beings to love others and ourselves, to accept responsibility for our lives, to give something back as adults instead of merely receiving like children.

Courtship and marriage are opportunities for the same kind of inner development. It's not enough to push yourself through them because it's expected of you, because you want a family, because you are tired of being alone. The best reasons to take the step forward from courtship to marriage are the opportunities you give yourself to move on psychologically.

The Opportunity to Take a Risk

When you structure your romantic life around the long wait for the perfect person, you are trying to avoid the risks of love. In general, avoiding all risks is a pretty flat life strategy.

Every time you screen someone out during Selection, you are taking the safe bet. The courtship will never develop and you'll never risk knowing you were wrong.

Every time you give up your attempts at Seduction because you don't want to risk more rejection, you are taking the safe bet. At least if you cease your Pursuit, you are protected against embarrassment. You have your pride. It's a poor substitute for love, but it's safer.

Every time you turn off during a Switch, you have the

option of sticking it out or starting over with someone new. Starting over is safe—you've been there before. Sticking it out is the risk. Stick it out long enough and you could end up married. Negotiation requires that you risk anger, marriage requires that you risk Commitment. In the end, the realities of courtship are worth the bother because they give you the opportunity to take a psychological risk.

The Opportunity to Get on Higher Ground

It's a fair bet that if you are doing the same thing romantically at forty that you were doing at twenty-two, something went wrong in the meantime. Life does not have to be a constant process of repeating yourself.

There is no challenge in falling in love with someone who suits your ideal picture. But you get an incredible internal stretch when you struggle to love someone who is all too human. That's higher ground.

It's kid stuff to be sexually aroused for a year or so by a perfectly erotic body. It's a mental growth spurt when you can stay faithful to and interested in a body that time has begun to irreparably alter. That's higher ground.

It is always the child's way to lose interest in the old toy and be drawn to the shiny new one. The child says it's the toy's fault, but we know it's a reflection of the child's attention span. It's a grown-up who can pick a partner and stick with that choice despite the countless shiny new possibilities in the path. That's higher ground.

The best reason to go all the way in a courtship is that it opens you to the possibility of a future instead of constantly reliving different versions of your past. The future is your higher ground.

Someone to Love

All this sounds perfectly reasonable—and it makes you mad. You think marriage is terrific. You'd be more than happy to take the risk and do the necessary developing if only you had the opportunity. You feel like you don't. You can't seem to find someone to love. It isn't fair.

268

If you are unable to find someone to love, ask yourself one question: How loving am I?

If you are loving, you'll begin a great many courtships, understanding that Selection is not the time to be picky. You'll get picky later on, when you have something important to be picky about. The stricter your requirements for Selection, the more restricted you are willing to be in your capacity for love.

The more loving you are, the more you are willing to be a giver. Giving does not always mean accommodating. Sometimes what you have to give is the benefit of your anger. Being a giver means not evaluating your partner like a business deal. It means not counting everything you get and insisting that you come out on top.

Giving and loving are inextricably linked.

If you are having trouble finding someone with whom to begin or complete a courtship, I'd suggest you check yourself for an error in your orientation. You are probably making the mistake of looking to receive love from a proper source rather than to give it with a generous spirit.

You are screening the world to determine who might be worthy of your love. You decide that not very many other people are, a decision you refer to as "having high standards." When you do encounter someone who might inspire your love, you send a desperate message: *Please love me back! Please think I'm enough!* You have forgotten that it is better to give than to receive.

This is such a fundamental, universal error in thinking that I can promise you one thing. If you focus on increasing the number of men or women to whom you are willing to offer love, you will eventually find a grateful receiver.

When you do, keep in mind each of the principles of courtship that we've reviewed.

First, don't take it personally, especially in the early stages of romance. Remember that his doubts or her hesitation are built into courtship itself. They are not indictments of your personal worth.

Push yourself to risk rejection. Don't let your fear of the pain it can cause stand in your way. Find your own system for reducing that pain. Give yourself as many opportunities to love and be loved as you can.

Fight the impulse to let the anxiety built into courtship turn you into a clingy, pushy wimp. That wimp lives in all of us. He or she is not the product of some neurotic outbreak in your psychological undergrowth. Give that wimp a talking to when he shows his face. Remember who you are and what you are worth. You don't have to run away from courtship or cling to it desperately, just because it occasionally brings your wimp to the surface.

Come to understand how your own fears of intimacy typically express themselves. You can reduce your obstacles to Commitment if they are front and center in your consciousness. Learn to pay attention to your romantic patterns. You'll get better at them.

Keep in mind that love is something you build, not something you find. Courtship is the process by which you develop love while you simultaneously handle your fears of it. You need its moments of distance as much as you need the process of attachment.

You don't need to have a perfect courtship. You don't need to have a perfect partner and you certainly don't need to be perfect yourself.

You will need to:

- Take a risk, confront a fear
- Love a real person instead of a fantasy, and
- Be good to yourself in the process.

If you are able to do all three, you are guaranteed a fine romance.

Bibliography

BOOKS

Bach, G., and R. Deutsch. *Pairing*. New York: Avon, 1970.

Bach, G., and P. Wyden. *The Intimate Enemy*. New York: Avon, 1981.

Barbach, L. *For Each Other*. New York: New American Library, 1982.

———. *For Yourself: The Fulfillment of Female Sexuality*. Garden City: Doubleday, 1975.

Branden, N. *The Psychology of Romantic Love*. Los Angeles: Tarcher, 1980.

Brothers, J. *What Every Woman Ought to know about Love and Marriage*. New York: Ballantine, 1985.

Brown, H. G. *Sex and the Single Girl*. New York: Pocket Books, 1963.

Brush, S. *Men: An Owner's Manual*. New York: Simon and Schuster, 1984.

Cassell, C. *Swept Away*. New York: Bantam, 1985.

Colgrove, M., H. Bloomfield, and P. McWilliams. *How to Survive the Loss of a Love*. New York: Bantam, 1977.

Cowan, C., and M. Kinder. *Smart Women, Foolish Choices*. New York: Potter, 1985.

Dowling, C. *The Cinderella Complex*. New York: Pocket Books, 1981.

Ehrenreich, B. *The Hearts of Men*. Garden City: Anchor Press, 1983.

Erikson, E. *Childhood and Society*. New York: Norton, 1963.

Fezler, W. *Breaking Free*. New York: Acropolis, 1985.

Fisher R. and W. Ury. *Getting to Yes*. New York: Penguin Books, 1981.

Friday, N. *Jealousy*. New York: William Morrow, 1985.

271

Fromm, E. *The Art of Loving*. New York: Perennial Library, 1956.

Goldstine, D., K. Larner, S. Zuckerman, and H. Goldstine. *The Dance-Away Lover*. New York: Ballantine, 1977.

Grice, J. *How to Find Romance after Forty*. New York: Evans, 1985.

Hamel, M. *Sex Etiquette*. New York: Delacorte, 1984.

Huxley, L. *You Are Not the Target*. Los Angeles: Tarcher, 1986.

Johnson, R. "Stirring the Oatmeal," from *Challenge of the Heart*, edited by John Welwood. Boston: Shambhala, 1985.

Kiley, D. *The Peter Pan Syndrome*. New York: Avon, 1984.

Kübler-Ross, E. *Questions and Answers on Death and Dying*. New York: Macmillan, 1974.

Levinson, D. *The Seasons of a Man's Life*. New York: Knopf, 1978.

Morgenstern, M., and G. Kettlehack. *A Return to Romance*. New York: Ballantine, 1986.

Norwood, Robin. *Women Who Love Too Much*. Los Angeles: Tarcher, 1985.

Paul, J., and M. Paul. *Do I Have to Give Up Me to Be Loved by You?* Minneapolis: Compcare, 1983.

Peck, M. S. *The Road Less Traveled*. New York: Touchstone, 1980.

Peele, S., and A. Brodsky. *Love and Addiction*. New York: Signet, 1976.

Perls, F., R. Hefferline, and P. Goodman. *Gestalt Therapy*. New York: Dell, 1951.

Perper, T. *Sex Signals: The Biology of Love*. Philadelphia: ISI Press, 1985.

Piaget, J. *Construction of Reality in the Child*. New York: Ballantine, 1986.

Pietropinto, A., and J. Simenauer. *Beyond the Male Myth*. New York: Signet, 1977.

Remoff, H. *Sexual Choice*. New York: Dutton, 1985.

Rubin, L. *Intimate Strangers*. New York: Harper, 1983.

Rubin, T. I. *One to One*. New York: Viking, 1983.

———. *The Angry Book*. New York: Macmillan, 1969.

Sheehy, Gail. *Passages*. New York: Bantam, 1977.

Sills, J. *How to Stop Looking for Someone Perfect and Find Someone to Love*. New York: St. Martin's Press, 1984.

Simenauer, J., and D. Carroll. *Singles: The New Americans*. New York: Signet, 1982.

Stein, R. "Coupling/Uncoupling," from *Challenge of the Heart*, edited by John Welwood. Boston: Shambhala, 1985.

Welwood, J., ed. *Challenge of the Heart*. Boston: Shambhala, 1985.

Zimbardo, P. Z., *Shyness*. New York: Berkeley, 1977.

ARTICLES

Applebome, P. "Dating Game and the Check: Who Pays?" *The New York Times*, January 27, 1986, 15.

Baxter, L. A., and W. W. Wilmot. "Secret Tests: Social Strategies for Acquiring Information about the State of the Relationship." *Human Communications Research* 11, no. 2 (1984): 171–201.

Black, H., and V. B. Angelis. "Interpersonal Attraction: An Empirical Investigation of Platonic and Romantic Love." *Psychological Reports* 34 (1974): 1243–1246.

Booth, A., D. B. Brinkerhoff, and L. K. White. "The Impact of Parental Divorce on Courtship." *Journal of Marriage and the Family* (February 1984): 85–93.

Collins, J. K., J. R. Kennedy, and R. D. Francis. "Expectations of How Behavior Should Ensue During the Courtship Process." *Journal of Marriage and the Family* (May 1976): 373–377.

Cozby, P. "Self–Disclosure: A Literature Review." *Psychological Bulletin* 79, no. 2 (1973): 73–91.

Daigneault, Lorraine. "Testing Love." *Self* (April 1986): 141–143.

Dulleg, G. "Relationships: Marriage Versus Living Together." *The New York Times*, February 14, 1983: 136.

Givens, D. "Romancing the New American Man." *Harper's Bazaar* (November 1984): 102–110.

Givens, D. "The Nonverbal Basis of Attraction: Flirtation, Courtship, and Seduction." *Psychiatry* 41 (1978): 346–359.

DeMaris, A., and G. R. Leslie. "Cohabitation with the Future Spouse: Its Influence upon Marital Satisfaction and Communication." *Journal of Marriage and the Family* (February 1984): 77.

Goldman. "Demography of the Marriage Market in the U.S." *Population Index* 50, no. 1 (1984): 5–25.

Hill, C. T., Z. Rubin, and L. A. Peplau. "Breakups Before Marriage: The End of 103 Affairs." *Journal of Social Issues* 32, no. 1 (1976): 147–168.

Jason, L. A., A. Reichler, and W. Rucker. "Characteristics of Significant Dating Relationships: Male Versus Female Initiators, Idealized Versus Actual Settings." *The Journal of Psychology* 109 (1981): 185–190.

Kephart, W. "Some Correlates of Romantic Love." *Journal Of Marriage and the Family* (August 1967): 470–474.

Klagsbrun, F. "Staying Married—Is It Worth It?" *New Woman* (August 1985): 43–48.

Laner, M. R. "Competition in Courtship." *Family Relations* 35 (1986): 275–279.

Larzelere, R. E., and T. L. Huston. "The Dyadic Trust Scale: Toward Understanding Interpersonal Trust in Close Relationships." *Journal of Marriage and the Family* (August 1980): 595–604.

Lesses, S. R., and B. R. Easser. "The Marital Life of the Hysterical Woman." *Medical Aspects of Human Sexuality* 3, no. 5 (1969): 27–37.

Lester, M. "Making Music Together: A Sociological Formulation of Intimate Encounters Between Males and Females." Presented to the American Sociological Association Meetings, (August 1979).

Lloyd, S. A., R. M. Cate, and J. M. Henton. "Predicting Premarital Relationship Stability: A Methodological Refinement." *Journal of Marriage and the Family* (February 1984): 71–75.

Lustig, B. "The Agony of Getting Dressed for a Date." *Glamour* (October 1985): 290.

Morrisroe, P. "Forever Single." *New York* (August 20, 1984): 24–31.

Murstein, B. I. "Mate Selection in the 1970's." *Journal of Marriage and the Family* (November 1980): 777–792.

Murstein, B. I. "Person Perception and Courtship Progress among Premarital Couples." *Journal of Marriage and the Family* (November 1972): 621–626.

Rubenstein, Carin. "The Modern Art of Courtly Love." *Psychology Today* (July 1983): 43–49.

Rubin, Z., C. T. Hill, L. A. Peplau, and C. Dunkel-Schetter. "Self-Disclosure in Dating Couples: Sex Roles and the Ethic of Openness." *Journal of Marriage and the Family* (May 1980): 305–317.

Rubin, Z. "Lovers and Other Strangers: The Development of Intimacy in Encounters and Relationships." *American Scientists* 62 (1974): 182–190.

Rubin, Z. "Measurement of Romantic Love." *Journal of Personality and Social Psychology* 16 (1970): 265–273.

Sanoff, A., and M. Galligan. "Sex, with Care." *U.S. News & World Report* (June 2, 1986): 53–57.

Sifford, D. "How to Build a Happy Marriage." *The Philadelphia Inquirer*, May 11, 1986.

Snyder, M., and J. A. Simpson. "Self-Monitoring and Dating Relationships." *Journal of Personality and Social Psychology* (December 1984): 1281–1291.

Stambul, H. B. "Stages of Courtship: The Development of Premarital Relationships." *Dissertation Abstracts* (May 1976): Vol. 36, 5872.

Trotter, R. "The Three Faces of Love." *Psychology Today* (September 1986). 46–54

Waggoner, G. "Take Her Out to a Ball Game." *Esquire* (January 1985): 26.

Walster, E., G. W. Walster, J. Piliavin, and L. Schmidt. "Playing Hard to Get: Understanding an Elusive Phenomenon." *Journal of Personality and Social Psychology* 26, no. 1 (1973): 113–121.

West, V. "The Politics of Courtship." *Working Woman* (March 1982): 83–85.

Index

279

ABOUT THE AUTHOR

Judith Sills, Ph.D., is a clinical psychologist and the author of two other books, *How to Stop Looking for Someone Perfect and Find Someone to Love* and *Excess Baggage.* For the last decade she has appeared regularly on such national television shows as "Donahue," the "Oprah Winfrey Show," "Sally Jessy Raphael," and "NBC News." She lives in Philadelphia with her husband and daughter.